Language Assessment
for Classroom Teachers

Published in this series
Oxford Handbooks for Language Teachers

Language Assessment
for Classroom Teachers

Lyle Bachman and Barbara Damböck

OXFORD
UNIVERSITY PRESS

Great Clarendon Street, Oxford, OX2 6DP, United Kingdom

Oxford University Press is a department of the University of Oxford.
It furthers the University's objective of excellence in research, scholarship,
and education by publishing worldwide. Oxford is a registered trade
mark of Oxford University Press in the UK and in certain other countries

© Oxford University Press 2017

The moral rights of the author have been asserted

First published in 2017

2021

10 9 8 7 6 5 4 3 2

ISBN: 978 0 19 421839 9

Printed in China

This book is printed on paper from certified and well-managed sources

ACKNOWLEDGMENTS

*The authors and publisher are grateful to those who have given permission to
reproduce the following extracts and adaptations of copyright material:* p.14
adapted from Table 1.1 from p.12 of *Statistical Analyses for Language
Assessment* by Lyle Bachman, Cambridge University Press, 2004, reproduced
by permission; pp.17, 20, 31, 32, 89, and 112 adapted figures reproduced
by permission of Oxford University Press, from *Language Assessment in
Practice* by Lyle Bachman and Adrian Palmer © Oxford University Press
2010; p.18 adapted figure from 'How can we link teaching with assessment
when teaching English to young learners?' by Annie Hughes, presented at
the 'Learning and Assessment at Primary Schools' Conference, Cambridge,
2009, reproduced by permission of Annie Hughes; p.154 table from p.58
of *Common European Framework of Reference for Languages, Learning, Teaching,
Assessment*, Corporate Author Council of Europe © Cambridge University
Press 2001, reproduced by permission; pp.188 and 191 adapted extracts
reproduced by permission of Oxford University Press, from *Headway*
4E Upper Intermediate SB/WB by Headway Soars © Oxford University
Press 2014; pp.207 and 210 extracts reproduced by permission of Oxford
University Press, from *Engage* 2E Level 3 Teacher's Book by Christina
De la Mare, Alicia Artusi, Gregory Manin and Lewis Lansford © Oxford
University Press 2012; pp.217 and 220 extracts reproduced by permission
of Oxford University Press, from *Insight* Elementary Teacher's Book by Jayne
Wildman © Oxford University Press 2013; p.261 adapted extract reproduced
by permission of Oxford University Press, from *Engage* 2E Level 3 SB &
WB by Alicia Artusi and Gregory Manin © Oxford University Press 2012;
p.264 adapted extract reproduced by permission of Oxford University Press,
from *Engage* 2E Level 3 Teacher's Resource Multi-ROM © Oxford University
Press 2012.

CONTENTS

ACKNOWLEDGMENTS

As this book emerged from an idea into what you have in your hands, we have benefited from the input, advice, and help of many individuals. We would like to thank the following:

The authors of *Language Assessment in Practice: Developing Language Assessments and Justifying their Use in the Real World* for providing the general conceptual framework that we have adapted and extended to the specific setting of classroom-based language assessment.

Colleagues who provided feedback on various chapters and versions of the book as it evolved: Nathan Carr, Gu Xiangdong, He Lianzhen, Lorena Llosa, Gary Ockey, Adrian Palmer, Yasuyo Sawaki and her students, Masaki Eguchi, Kana Matsumura, Tatsuro Tahara, and Takumi Uchihara.

Colleagues who tried out parts of the book with their classes in language assessment: Nathan Carr (TESOL Program, Department of Modern Languages and Literatures, California State University, Fullerton, USA), Gu Xiangdong (English Department, College of Foreign Languages and Cultures, Chongqing University, Chongqing, China (Student leader: Yu Zhong)), He Lianzhen (School of International Studies, Zhejiang University, Hangzhou, China), Gary Ockey (Department of English, Iowa State University, USA), and Yasuyo Sawaki (Department of English Language and Literature, School of Education, Waseda University, Tokyo, Japan)

The participants of our many workshops around the world, where we presented the AUA-based approach to classroom-based language assessment. The comments, questions, and suggestions of the participants in these workshops have been critical in helping us understand the needs and "real worlds" of classroom language teachers, and in shaping our approach to classroom-based language assessment.

Alex Birtles and Antoinette Meehan of Oxford University Press for believing in our vision for showing classroom language teachers a new way to assess their students, Antoinette for guiding our manuscript through the editorial and production process, and Helen Wendholt and Danielle King for their editing of the final manuscript.

Several anonymous reviewers who provided constructive comments and suggestions on our original proposal.

PART I: INTRODUCTION

In Part I, we introduce the book and provide an overview of classroom-based assessment. In Chapter 1, we discuss the origin of our approach, our reasons for writing this book, our intended audience, and what is in the book. In Chapter 2, we discuss the role of assessment in instruction, introducing some concepts relevant to classroom-based assessment, and provide an overview of the process of using classroom-based assessments.

1

A NEW APPROACH TO CLASSROOM-BASED LANGUAGE ASSESSMENTS

When you think about assessing your students, what questions do you ask yourself? When and how often should I assess my students? What aspects of my students' language ability should I assess? What kinds of assessment tasks or items should I use and how many should I include in the assessment? How will I score my students' responses? How many points should the assessment be worth? How will I make sure that the results of my assessment are consistent and provide meaningful information about my students' language ability?

These are some of the questions that teachers often ask about classroom assessment. Each of these questions reflects a reasonable concern that you will need to address when you plan to assess your students. However, they also relate to very different assessment issues. While these issues are different, they are not independent of each other, but are interconnected. In order to answer the question about what kinds of assessment tasks to use, you need to know what aspects of your students' language ability you want to assess. Likewise, in order to know when or how often to assess your students, you need to know what you will do with the information you obtain from the assessment. The answers to individual questions like these will not provide an integrated approach to assessing your students. Furthermore, they will not enable you to develop assessments that you can justify to your students, their parents/guardians, school officials, or others who might be interested in the results of the assessment. But most importantly, they will not enable you to develop assessments that you yourself feel confident about.

In this book, you will discover what we believe is an entirely new way of looking at the way you assess your students. In this approach, you begin by first asking yourself what beneficial consequences you want to help bring about by using an assessment. For example, "How will using an assessment help me improve my teaching?" or "How will this help my students learn better?" This approach will then lead you through a process of linking these intended beneficial consequences with *what* (areas of language ability) and *how* (kinds of assessment tasks) you will assess. By following this process, you will be able to develop and use classroom assessments that are clearly linked to and support your classroom instruction. That is, these assessments will provide information that will help guide both your instructional activities and your students' learning.

Where does our approach come from?

Our approach to classroom-based language assessment is based on current theory and practice. In the past 25 years or so, the field of language assessment has undergone dramatic and exciting developments, in the way language assessment is conceptualized and in the way language assessments are developed and used. Language assessment is no longer viewed primarily as a technical activity of obtaining test scores and analyzing these statistically. Rather, it is now viewed much more broadly as a socioculturally embedded process. Specific language assessments are seen not simply as measurement instruments, but rather as activities that ideally reflect the values of the culture in which they take place and also help realize those values in the purposes they serve. Regarding the development and use of language assessments, rather than focusing mainly on the abilities to be assessed and the kinds of assessments to be used, there is a much greater concern for the consequences that using assessments have for the individuals and institutions who will be affected by the *use* of the assessment. Finally, the field has also broadened from a relatively narrow focus on tests that are used to make major decisions about large numbers of test takers, to include classroom-based assessment, which can provide information to help teachers improve their teaching and students improve their learning. These developments are summarized in Table 1.1.

	Before	**Now**
Language assessment	Viewed primarily as a technical activity of obtaining test scores and analyzing these statistically	Viewed broadly as a socioculturally embedded process
Language assessments	Seen as measurement instruments	Seen as activities that reflect the values of the culture and help realize these
Language assessment as a field	Narrow focus on tests used to make major decisions about large numbers of test takers	Broadened focus including classroom-based assessment that provides information to improve learning and teaching

Table 1.1   Developments in language assessment

The work of Bachman (1990) and Bachman and Palmer (1996, 2010) has both contributed to and drawn upon these developments. Our approach to classroom-based assessment is based on the general approach to language assessment described by Bachman and Palmer (2010) in their book, *Language assessment in practice: Developing language assessments and justifying their use in the real world.* Bachman and Palmer's approach to language assessment is being used by test developers to guide the development and use of high-stakes, large-scale language assessments. More relevant to this book, their approach is also being used extensively in teacher preparation courses (e.g. Diploma, Certificate, Master's degree, Ph.D.), and has been used around the world for many in-service training courses and workshops in language assessment for classroom teachers.

Many of the concepts, terms, and ideas we discuss throughout this book come from Bachman and Palmer's *Language assessment in practice* book. However, since this is not a scholarly, academic volume, rather than citing Bachman and Palmer wherever we draw on their work, we offer a general acknowldgement here.

Why did we write this book?

We have had extensive experience working with language teachers in both pre-service and in-service training programs. For over 30 years, Lyle taught university-level courses, both undergraduate and post-graduate, in language testing in the USA, and has also conducted workshops for classroom teachers around the world. Barbara was a classroom language teacher in both elementary and secondary schools for 20 years, and was a teacher-trainer for eight years in Germany. For the past five years, we have been conducting workshops for classroom teachers together.

In our experience of observing classroom language teachers and in working with them over the years, we have become familiar with their needs, in terms of classroom assessment, their knowledge and beliefs about classroom assessment, and their anxieties and concerns about their ability to assess their students. We have learned that what most language teachers know and believe about language assessment is generally based on their own experience, rather than on specific education or training in language assessment. We have also learned that those who have had specific training in language assessment have typically taken courses or workshops that focused on principles and techniques that have been developed primarily for large-scale tests and that may not be entirely relevant to classroom-based assessment. Such courses often focus on general principles of language testing, such as reliability, validity, and authenticity, and techniques in *what* and *how* to test: what areas of language ability to test, what kinds of test items to write, how to score students' responses to these items, and how to analyze these scores statistically.

Based on our experience, we realized that we needed to develop a different approach to language assessment that would be relevant to the needs of classroom teachers. This approach is focused on developing and using language assessments that will help improve instruction and learning, and that will empower teachers to more effectively and confidently assess their students' language ability. In developing this approach, we have extended and adapted the general approach of Bachman and Palmer (2010) and applied it to classroom-based language assessment.

As we used this approach in our teacher-training workshops, we found that teachers found it intuitively understandable and that they could see its relevance to their needs and concerns about their own classroom assessments. Our own thinking about how the approach can be most effectively used in classroom-based language assessments also evolved from one workshop to the next. The positive reception of our approach by classroom teachers and our refinement of the approach led us to believe that we wanted to share this approach with a wider audience. The most obvious way to achieve this would be to write a book, and this is what you now have in your hands.

The writing of this book has also been an evolutionary process. We revised our original proposal to Oxford University Press on the basis of comments and suggestions from their editors and a group of anonymous reviewers. We also wanted to get feedback from a wider audience than these reviewers. We thus decided to ask a number of language assessment specialists we know, who teach pre-service courses for classroom teachers, to try out the chapters of the book with their students. We were extremely fortunate that everyone we asked was happy to do this, and the feedback we received from them was invaluable. (We have included a list of these individuals in the *Acknowledgments*.)

Who is this book for?

If you are a classroom language teacher and want to learn how to better assess your students, we wrote this book specifically for you. We have included many examples and activities that we believe make the book appropriate for self-instruction. This book is for classroom language teachers:

- at any kind of school, public or private, at any level, from pre-school to elementary, to secondary, to university, to adult education, or in a language school or program
- in different countries, whose students come from many different cultural and linguistic backgrounds
- who may be using very different approaches (methods, syllabuses, textbooks) to teach language.

If you are a student or a teacher in a teacher preparation course or in-service training program, this book is also for you. Based on the feedback we have received, we believe that this book is appropriate for students and teachers in:

- Certificate or Diploma courses in language teaching
- Master's degree programs in applied linguistics, language teaching, and language assessment
- in-service training programs.

What is in this book?

This book includes several different features aimed at engaging you in different ways. These include:

Discussions of concepts and procedures

In the discussions, we introduce and explain new material. Much of the material is interrelated and cumulative, so we relate new material to material that has already been introduced. This cyclical discussion leads to some repetition of concepts, but we feel that this is helpful for reinforcing the knowledge you are accumulating as you work through the book.

Definitions of terminology

We have defined terminology throughout the book that we believe you will find useful to understand and remember. So that they are easy to recognize, the terms are in bold and indicated with an arrow bullet point, as in the following example:

➤ A **language use task** is an activity that requires individuals to use language to achieve a particular goal or objective.

These terms are also listed alphabetically in the *Glossary* at the back of the book.

Illustrative examples

Most chapters include examples that illustrate the particular points covered in the discussions. These examples are parts of the fully developed *Examples* that are provided in Part IV.

Activities

Most chapters include activities that we hope will enable you to reinforce your learning of the concepts presented in the discussions. The purpose of these activities is not to test your understanding, but rather to lead you to reflect on and arrive at possible answers to the specific issues raised in the discussion. Example answers to these activities are provided in Appendix 3 and in the *Examples* in Part IV.

Examples

In addition to these features, Part IV of the book provides fully specified examples of language assessment tasks. These examples illustrate assessment tasks of all four language use activities (listening, speaking, reading, writing) for different age groups (young learners, teens, adults) and different levels of ability (beginning, intermediate, advanced). These examples provide templates for classroom-based assessments that you can easily follow for developing your own assessments. They also provide practical examples of assessment tasks that can be replicated for your own classroom assessment situations. These examples can be adapted for other language-use activities, age groups, or levels of ability. (Further examples can be found on the companion website at: www.oup.com/elt/teacher/lact)

Other features

- Appendix 1: a checklist that provides a quick reference for the steps in our approach to classroom-based language assessment
- Appendix 2: a summary of the parts of an assessment task template
- Appendix 3: answers to the activities in Chapters 2 and 3
- Suggestions for further reading

What will you learn from this book?

We believe that, by using our approach, you will acquire the knowledge and skills you need in order to develop and use classroom-based language assessments. Using this approach will empower you to improve your use of classroom assessments, and give you the confidence you need to justify your assessments to your students, their parents/guardians, school officials, and others who might be interested in or want to use the results of your assessments.

Happy reading and happy assessing!

References

Bachman, L. F. (1990). *Fundamental considerations in language testing.* Oxford: Oxford University Press.

Bachman, L. F., & Palmer, A. S. (1996). *Language testing in practice: Designing and developing useful language tests.* Oxford: Oxford University Press.

Bachman, L. F., & Palmer, A. (2010). *Language assessment in practice: Developing language assessments and justifying their use in the real world.* Oxford: Oxford University Press.

2 USING CLASSROOM-BASED LANGUAGE ASSESSMENTS

In this chapter, we discuss a number of concepts and issues that we believe teachers need to be familiar with in order to understand the role and use of assessment in the language classroom. Specifically, we discuss language teaching and the role of language assessment in language teaching, including two different modes of classroom-based assessment. We then discuss the decisions that are made on the basis of classroom-based assessments. Next, we discuss the process of using classroom-based language assessments. We then discuss the roles of test developers and test users in the process of using language assessments. Finally, we discuss practicality and what we need to consider in order to assure that our assessments will be practical to use.

Language teaching and classroom-based language assessment

If you want to understand classroom-based language assessment, you need to think about it in the context of the language classroom. In other words, you need to think about how language assessment functions as part of the language teaching process. You can do this by asking the following questions:

- What is language teaching? Why do I teach?
- What is language assessment? Why do I assess?
- What are the similarities and differences between language teaching and language assessment?

Language teaching

In the language classroom, when you teach you engage your students in language use tasks, or tasks that require them to use language. The purpose of these language teaching/learning tasks is to help your students learn the language you are teaching. That is, you engage your students in language teaching/learning tasks in order to help them improve their language ability.

➤ A **language use task** is an activity that requires individuals to use language to achieve a particular goal or objective.

➤ **Language teaching** is the process of engaging students in language use tasks for the purpose of improving their language ability.

➤ A **language teaching/learning task** is a language use task in which teachers and students engage for the purpose of improving students' language ability.

The primary purpose of language teaching and of language teaching/learning tasks is to improve students' language learning. However, these tasks can also serve a number of additional purposes, for example, enhancing learners' cognitive, emotional, and social development, motivating students, or helping them to develop positive attitudes toward the language and culture they are studying.

Language assessment

In the language classroom, when you assess you also present your students with tasks that require them to use language. However, the purpose of these language *assessment* tasks is to collect information about your students' language ability – what and how much they have learned.

➤ A **language assessment task** is a language use task whose purpose is to collect samples of students' language performance. (Note that language testers often use the term "item" with essentially the same meaning as what we call an assessment task.)

➤ The term **language assessment** is used in two ways. In the singular ("a language assessment"), it refers to a collection of many different individual language assessment tasks or items. As a general term ("language assessment"), it refers to the process of collecting samples of students' language performance.

➤ A **classroom-based language assessment** is a language assessment that is developed and/or used by one or more teachers in the classroom.

Note that language testers use different terms, such as "assessment", "measurement", and "test" to refer to what is essentially the same activity – collecting information. Some language testers make a clear distinction between assessments and tests. However, for our purposes, we will use the terms "assessment" and "test" more or less interchangeably.

It is important to think of language assessment as a process. This is because giving a language assessment to students is the first step in a larger process of using the results of an assessment to arrive at interpretations about students' language ability, and to make decisions in order to help bring about beneficial consequences for students, teachers, the school, and perhaps other individuals and institutions.

Similarities and differences between language teaching and language assessment

Both teaching and assessment are processes or activities in which teachers and students participate. In both teaching and assessment, teachers present their students with tasks that require them to use language. The main difference between teaching and assessment is in their purpose. Teaching is aimed at promoting learning, while assessment is aimed at collecting information. The similarities and differences between teaching and assessment are summarized in Table 2.1.

	Teaching	**Assessment**
Participants	• Teachers and students	• Teachers and students
Task requirement	• Teachers present learning tasks to students • Students engage in tasks that require them to use language	• Teachers present assessment tasks to students • Students engage in tasks that require them to use language
Purpose of tasks	• Promote or facilitate learning • Enhance learners' linguistic, cognitive, emotional, and social development	• Collect samples of students' performance

Table 2.1   Similarities and differences between teaching and assessment

Although language teaching and language assessment are intended to serve different purposes, they inform each other. Language teaching informs classroom-based language assessment in two very important ways. First, the way you define the areas of language ability you want to assess will be based on the content or learning objectives of the language instruction – the syllabus, the teaching materials, and the teaching tasks in which you engage your students. Second, the kinds of assessment tasks you use will generally be based on the kinds of teaching/learning tasks you use in the classroom. Assessment can also inform teaching. The information you obtain from assessments can help you make specific changes in the way you teach and also in the specific areas of content you may need to review or emphasize.

Decisions made on the basis of classroom-based assessments

The information that you obtain from language assessments about your students' language ability is used to make decisions. You, as a teacher, use this information to make decisions that you believe will help you improve your teaching and help your students improve their learning. You also use the results of classroom-based assessments to assign grades or marks to your students. In many countries around the world, these grades or marks are also used by others to make decisions about students.

Decisions you need to make in the classroom

In the classroom, you are constantly making decisions as part of your teaching. You make decisions about what materials you will use, what learning tasks to present to your students, when to review material with the class, and when to move on to the next lesson. Sometimes, you may decide to change the materials or teaching tasks you use, or you may decide to give feedback to your students to help them direct their own learning. You may need to place students into groups or levels in the language class, or decide which students will pass to the next level or course.

The information you collect about your students' language ability through assessment can help you make these decisions. For example, if you give your students a short quiz at the end of a lesson and find that most of them have not mastered the learning objectives, you may decide that you need to present the material again, or you may decide that you need to change the ways you have presented the material, or change the learning tasks that you have given to your students. If you need to decide which students will pass the course or progress to the next level or grade, you will most likely use a number of assessments throughout the course of instruction to identify those who have mastered the learning objectives of the course. However, you might also use each of these assessments to give feedback to your students.

Purpose of the decision

All of the decisions that you, as a teacher, make on the basis of classroom-based assessments can be described according to their purpose. Two terms are useful to help you think about and remember the different purposes of the decisions you make.

➢ **Formative decisions** are decisions that lead to activities that are intended to improve instruction and learning. They can:

- o involve making changes in teaching and learning tasks, in the teaching materials, or in the teaching syllabus
- o involve providing feedback to students
- o involve placing students into different levels to facilitate instruction and learning
- o be made *before*, *during* or *after* the processes of teaching and learning.

➢ **Summative decisions** are decisions that are aimed at two purposes:

- o Advancement: making sure that students who advance to the next level or course are prepared to benefit from instruction at the next level, and that students who do not advance will benefit from receiving additional instruction at the same level.
- o Certification: making sure that students who are certified to be at a certain level of language ability have actually achieved the appropriate level of language ability specified in the certification.

Summative decisions:

- involve classifying students into groups; these groups may consist of, for example, students who advance or do not advance or students who are certified and those who are not
- are made *after* the processes of teaching and learning.

Note that both formative and summative decisions may be made *after* the process of teaching and learning. For example, you might give your students a test *after* completing a unit of instruction. You could use the results of the test to provide feedback to your students or to make changes in your teaching (formative decisions). You could also use the results of this test as one part of the grade or mark for the entire course to make pass/not pass decisions (summative decisions). The differences between formative and summative decisions are summarized in Table 2.2.

Formative decisions	Summative decisions
Aimed at improving instruction and learning.	Aimed at assuring that students will benefit from instruction at the appropriate level, or that students are certified on the basis of mastery.
Involve making changes in teaching and/or learning tasks, in the teaching materials, or in the teaching syllabus.	Involve classifying students into groups.
Can be made *before, during,* or *after* the processes of teaching and learning.	Are made *after* the processes of teaching and learning.

Table 2.2 *Differences between formative and summative decisions*

Activity 2.1

Which of the following decisions are formative, and which are summative? Put a check (✓) in the appropriate box in the second or third column in the following table. When will the decisions be made – before, during, or after the process of teaching and learning? For each decision, write *before, during,* or *after* in the fourth column. (The first answer is given.)

Decision	Formative	Summative	When made?
1 Changing teaching (e.g. materials, tasks)	✓		During or after
2 Making changes in approaches to, or strategies of, learning			
3 Placing learners into appropriate groups or levels in a language program	✓		
4 Deciding which students pass to the next grade in school		✓	

5 Deciding which students will move to the next level in a language course	✓		
6 Deciding what areas to focus on in studying	✓		
7 Deciding whether or not to move to the next unit of instruction			
8 Certifying students' levels of language ability			
9 Deciding what areas to focus on in teaching			
10 Deciding on supplemental materials for teaching			
11 Deciding which students will not pass the course			

Photocopiable © Oxford University Press

(Answers to this activity are provided on page 272.)

Relative importance of decisions

The results of your classroom-based assessments may also be used by others to make decisions about your students. You generally assign grades or marks to indicate your students' achievement at the end of a course of instruction, which might range from a single unit to a longer grading period covering a week, a month, a term, or an entire year. These grades are generally based on a number of different classroom-based assessments that you give to your students during the course of instruction. The grades you give your students—particularly at the end of a school year—may be used, for example, by universities as part of their admissions decisions, or by employers to help them make employment decisions.

All of the decisions that are made, both by teachers and by others, on the basis of classroom-based assessments can be described according to their relative importance. The decisions that are made on the basis of classroom-based assessments are not all equally important for stakeholders.

➢ **Stakeholders** are people, language programs or courses, or institutions that may be affected by, or benefit from, the use of the assessment. Stakeholders will always include ourselves, as teachers, and our students, as the test takers. In addition, for any particular assessment, the stakeholders may include our fellow teachers, school administrators, parents/guardians, employers, government officials, and the general public.

Some decisions have very important consequences for stakeholders. For example, the decision about what qualifications students will have when they leave school will affect their lives in a major way. It may determine, at least in part, which students are admitted to secondary school or university, or which ones find the jobs they want. It may also affect you, other teachers in the school, and the school itself, as well as the students' parents/guardians. Other decisions are not so important. For example, deciding to give feedback to a student that he needs to spend more time on his pronunciation is not likely to affect his life in a major way.

Three terms are used to describe the importance of the decisions you make. These terms are useful to help talk about the relative importance of the decisions you make on the basis of your assessments.

➤ **Low-stakes decisions** are minor decisions. If we make the wrong decision, the costs for stakeholders are very low, and the mistake is easy to correct. Deciding to provide feedback to students on their performance on a classroom quiz and changing our teaching tasks are examples of very low-stakes decisions.

➤ **High-stakes decisions** are major, life-affecting decisions. If we make the wrong decision, the cost is very high for stakeholders, and the mistake is very difficult to correct. Deciding which students will pass or not pass a course, which students will be awarded qualifications when they leave school, or which students will be admitted to university are examples of very high-stakes decisions.

The importance of the decisions we make is relative, ranging from low- to high-stakes. Many decisions, such as the examples given above, are very low-stakes or very high-stakes. However, many of the decisions that we make on the basis of classroom-based assessments are neither very high- nor very low-stakes, which is where the third term comes into play; medium-stakes decisions.

➤ **Medium-stakes decisions** are neither very high nor very low-stakes. Placing students into different ability levels in a language program and deciding which students will move to the next level in a course are examples of medium-stakes decisions.

You need to know how important the decisions you make are because this will affect the amount of time and effort you put into developing the assessment. The more important the decisions are, the more time and effort you need to put into developing the assessment. Most of the decisions that you make in the classroom are relatively low-stakes, while some are medium-stakes. In some cases, however, classroom-based assessments are used to make high-stakes decisions. These features of decisions are summarized in Figure 2.1. The wavy line indicates that the differences between low- and medium-stakes and between medium- and high-stakes decisions are not always clear-cut.

Low stakes	Medium stakes	High stakes
• *Minor* decision • Decision errors *easy* to correct • *Low* costs of making wrong decision		• *Major*, life-affecting decision • Decision errors *difficult* to correct • *High* costs of making wrong decision

Figure 2.1 *Relative importance of decisions (adapted from Bachman, Statistical Analyses for Language Assessment, Cambridge University Press, p. 12.)*

Activity 2.2	Which of the decisions in the following table are low-, medium-, or high-stakes? Put a check (✓) in the appropriate box in the second, third, or fourth column. (The first answer is given.)

Decision	Low-stakes	Medium-stakes	High-stakes
1 Changing teaching (e.g. materials, tasks)	✓		
2 Making changes in approaches to or strategies of learning			
3 Placing learners into appropriate groups or levels in a language program			
4 Deciding which students pass to the next grade in school			
5 Deciding which students will move to the next level in a language course			
6 Deciding what areas to focus on in studying			
7 Deciding which students to admit to a university			
8 Deciding whether or not to move to the next unit of instruction			
9 Deciding which students need to take additional instruction focusing on specific learning objectives			
10 Deciding what qualifications students will have when they finish school			
11 Certifying students' level of language ability in order for them to get a job			
12 Deciding what areas to focus on in teaching			
13 Deciding on supplemental materials for teaching			
14 Deciding which students will not pass the course			

Photocopiable © Oxford University Press

(Answers to this activity are provided on page 273.)

Modes of classroom-based assessments

Classroom-based assessments can be done in many different ways. In the language classroom, we assess our students continuously, making instantaneous, almost automatic decisions as we teach. For example, we might ask a question and call on a student to answer. Then, depending on how the student responds, we might decide to correct the answer, give a brief explanation to the class, ask another student to answer the same question, or move on and ask another question. We might even decide to change the lesson plan if we see that the students have not understood or have forgotten something that we need in order to continue the lesson.

There are also times in the language classroom when we need to assess our students solely for the purpose of collecting information about their learning progress. For example, at the beginning of a new unit of instruction we might inform our students that there will be a short test at the end. Then, at the end of a lesson, we might tell our students to put away their books, take out a piece of paper and a pencil, and then give them instructions for the test.

These two examples illustrate two different modes of classroom-based assessment, both of which are important to teaching, but which function very differently. Two terms can be used to describe the different modes of classroom-based assessment. These terms are useful to help think about and remember the different modes of assessment.

➢ The **implicit mode** of classroom-based assessment is:

   o instantaneous
   o continuous and cyclical
   o a part of classroom teaching
   o used mostly for formative decisions, but can also be used for summative decisions.

In this mode, students are largely unaware that assessment is taking place. (This mode of assessment is sometimes referred to as "dynamic assessment" or "informal assessment".)

➢ The **explicit mode** of classroom-based assessment is:

   o continuous and cyclical
   o a separate activity from teaching
   o used mostly for summative decisions, but can also be used for formative decisions.

In this mode, both the teacher and the students know this activity is an assessment. (This mode of assessment is sometimes referred to as "formal assessment.")

The similarities and differences between implicit and explicit modes of assessment are summarized in Table 2.3. In our experience over the years in working with classroom teachers, we have found that teachers are generally quite able to use implicit assessment as part of their teaching. Indeed, most experienced teachers do this almost intuitively, without thinking of this as something different from their teaching. In addition, teacher education programs generally include considerable practice in implicit assessment as part of teaching methodology or pedagogy. However, we have found that many classroom teachers feel insecure about their ability to develop and use *explicit* classroom-based assessments. In addition, as discussed in Chapter 1, teacher-training programs typically include very little, if any, training in explicit classroom-based assessment. For these reasons, in this book we do not discuss implicit assessment; rather, we focus on the explicit mode of classroom-based assessment.

Mode	Characteristics	Purpose
Implicit	• Instantaneous • Continuous and cyclical • A part of classroom teaching • Students are unaware that assessment is taking place	<u>Formative</u> decisions, e.g.: • Correct or do not correct student's response • Change form of questioning • Call on another student • Produce a model utterance • Request a group response <u>Summative</u> decisions, e.g.: • Pass/not pass decision based partly on classroom participation or performance
Explicit	• Continuous and cyclical • Clearly distinct from teaching • Both teacher and students are aware that assessment is taking place	<u>Formative</u> decisions, e.g.: • Teacher: move on to next lesson or review current lesson • Teacher: focus more on a specific learning objective • Student: spend more time on particular area of language ability • Student: use a different learning strategy <u>Summative</u> decisions, e.g.: • Decide who passes the course or grade • Certify level of ability

Table 2.3   Modes of classroom-based assessment (adapted from Bachman & Palmer, Language Assessment in Practice, Oxford University Press, p. 29)

Continuous and cyclical

Assessment in both modes (implicit and explicit) is continuous and cyclical. Assessment is *continuous* because it is an on-going process in support of teaching and learning. In the implicit mode, the amount of time from one assessment to the next might be very little, perhaps a few seconds. In the explicit mode, however, the time from one assessment to the next is more likely to be at least a few days. Assessment is *cyclical* because it recurs over and over during the process of teaching. The cyclical nature of classroom-based assessment is illustrated in Figure 2.2.

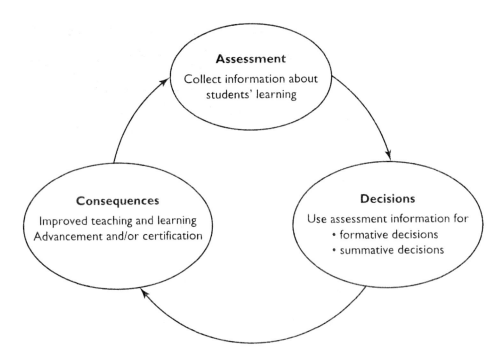

Figure 2.2 Cyclical nature of classroom-based assessment (adapted from Bachman & Palmer, Language Assessment in Practice, Oxford University Press, p. 27)

As shown in Figure 2.2, in classroom-based assessment, we use an assessment to collect information about our students' learning. We use this information to make decisions. Formative decisions lead to consequences regarding the teaching and learning tasks we use with our students. Summative decisions lead to consequences regarding what our students will do in the future, after the class, course, or grade. We then use an assessment to collect information again about our students' learning. In the case of improving teaching and learning, this information will help us find out how much the changes we or our students have made have affected their learning. In the case of advancement or certification, we may or may not receive information from any future assessments our students take.

Using classroom-based language assessments

We give an assessment in the language classroom because we want to use the information we get from students' assessment performance to help us understand something about their language ability and to make decisions. Our understandings or interpretations about students' language ability help us make decisions and these, in turn, are intended to bring about beneficial consequences. That is, we use a classroom-based assessment to help make good things happen for our students, ourselves, our school, and perhaps other individuals and institutions.

Earlier, we said that the purpose of language assessment is to collect information that will tell us something about students' language ability. When you think about how you will use this information from the assessment, you also need to think about the decisions you want to make.

➤ **Language assessment use** is the process of interpreting students' assessment performance as information that tells us something about their language ability, and using these interpretations to make decisions.

We also need to think about the beneficial consequences we want to help bring about by making these decisions. Considering all of these—interpretations, decisions, and beneficial consequences—we can define of the purpose of language assessment use as follows:

The primary purpose of using a language assessment is to:

- collect samples of students' language performance that:
  - we can interpret as indicators of their language ability
  - will help us make decisions
  - will lead to beneficial consequences for stakeholders.

Links in using classroom-based language assessments

Using a language assessment involves linking students' assessment performance to the beneficial consequences that we want to help bring about. When we give a language assessment, we present students with some language assessment tasks that they are expected to perform. We then record their performance in some way; we describe it or assign a score to it. Then we interpret these descriptions or scores as telling us something about students' language ability. We then use these interpretations to make decisions, which we intend to help bring about beneficial consequences. Using a language assessment is like making a chain. We create a series of links from students' assessment performance to assessment records, to interpretations, to decisions, to consequences. When we use an assessment in the classroom, we use the information we have obtained to achieve a specific outcome. Each link in our chain therefore includes some *information* we obtain and an *outcome* based on that information. These links between information and outcomes are illustrated in Figure 2.3.

Assessment records

For the first link in assessment use, we use the information from a student's performance on the language assessment tasks to arrive at a language assessment record, such as a verbal description, a score, or a grade or mark, that is based on his or her performance. The *information* we have obtained is the student's assessment performance, and the *outcome* is the assessment record. Assessment records are discussed in detail in Chapters 7 and 12.

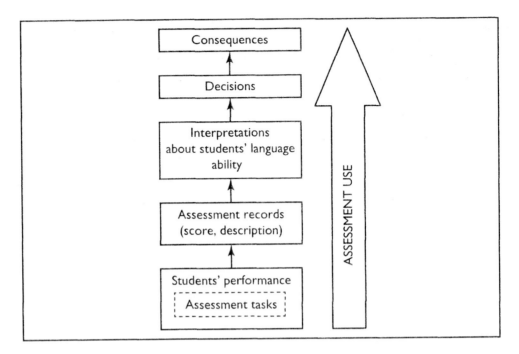

Figure 2.3 Links between assessment performance and consequences (adapted from Bachman & Palmer, Language Assessment in Practice, Oxford University Press, p. 91)

Interpretations

We then use the assessment record to make a link to an interpretation about the student's language ability. The *information* for this link is the assessment record and the *outcome* is an interpretation. Interpretations are discussed in detail in Chapter 6.

Decisions

Next, we use the interpretations about our students' language ability to make decisions. The *information* for this link is the interpretation about ability and the *outcome* is a decision. Decisions are discussed in detail in Chapter 5.

Consequences

When we make decisions in order to help bring about our intended beneficial consequences for stakeholders, we link the decisions to these consequences. The *information* for this link is the decision and the *outcome* is the consequence. Consequences are discussed in detail in Chapter 4.

To conclude this section, here is an example that illustrates the process of assessment use:

A teacher gives a vocabulary test at the end of a unit of instruction. Students have to fill in gaps in sentences with words from the unit. For each correct word they receive a point, and their score is the total of the correct words. The teacher interprets the students' scores as indicators of how well they have mastered the vocabulary in the unit. She wants to use the information from the test to help her students learn the words from the unit. So she decides to give them feedback and tells her students to review the words they did not know.

The links in this process are illustrated in Figure 2.4.

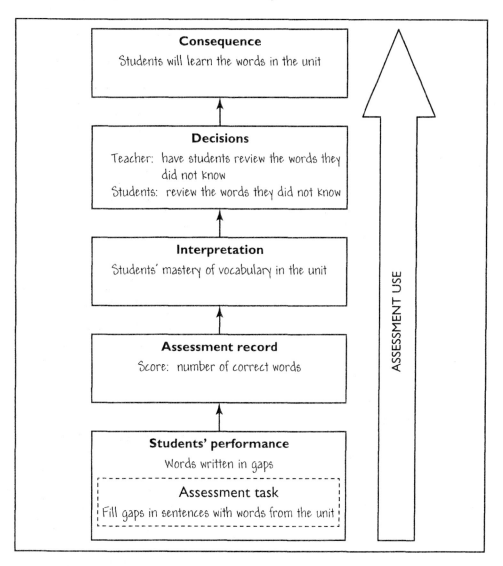

Figure 2.4 Example of links between assessment performance and consequences

Activity 2.3   Read the description of an assessment and then, using Figure 2.4 as an example, enter the relevant information in the figure.

A teacher gives a test to his students at the end of a unit of instruction on reading. The test includes three reading passages, each followed by several tasks or items in which students write short answers. The teacher gives a total score for the number of tasks completed correctly. He then interprets the scores as indicators of the students' level of achievement in reading. Next, he uses these scores, along with scores from tests of listening, speaking, and writing, to decide which students will pass the course. The teacher wants to make sure that those students who pass have mastered the material in the course and will be prepared for instruction at the next level.

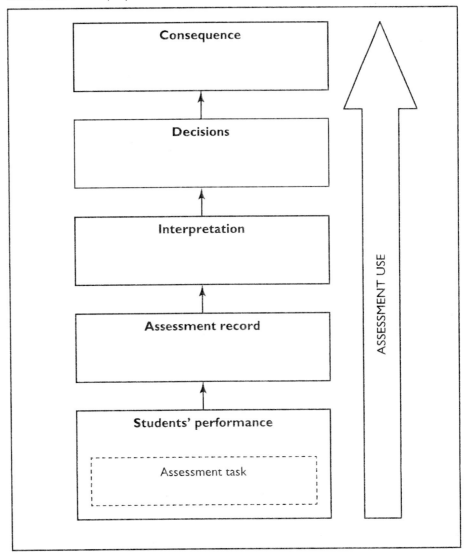

Photocopiable © Oxford University Press

(Answers to this activity are provided on page 274.)

Activity 2.4
Think of a classroom-based assessment you have used or need to develop. Following the example in Activity 2.3, describe your assessment in the space provided. Then, enter the relevant information in the figure following the example in Figure 2.4.

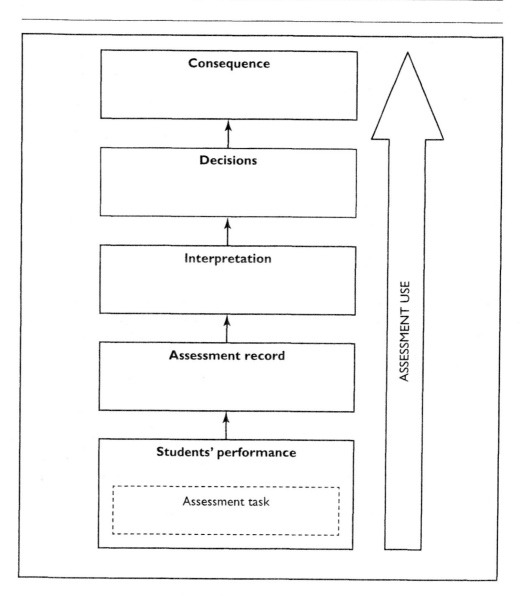

Test developers and test users

The development and use of any classroom-based assessment will involve a number of participants. As previously discussed, we have used the term "stakeholders" to refer to the people, language programs or courses, or institutions that may be affected by, or benefit from, the use of the assessment. Two stakeholders in particular perform important roles or functions in the development and use of language assessments. One stakeholder is the test user, who uses the assessment to make decisions that will affect other stakeholders. The other stakeholder who performs an important role is the test developer, who develops the assessment.

➤ The **test user** or decision-maker is the person(s) or institution that uses the information from the assessment to make decisions.

➤ The **test developer** is the person(s) or institution responsible for developing, administering, and scoring the assessment.

We think of "test user" and "test developer" as roles or functions, rather than as specific individuals, because these functions may be performed by the same or different people, or by institutions such as schools or ministries of education. In large-scale assessments, such as national school-leaving exams or standardized achievement tests, the functions of test user and test developer are typically performed by different individuals, groups of individuals, or institutions. In these assessments, the test developer might be an institution or agency outside of the school, and the test users might be the teachers, the school administration, or the outside institution.

In most classroom-based assessments, however, the roles of test developer and test user are typically performed by the same person or group of persons – a single teacher or a group of teachers. In the majority of classroom-based assessments, a single teacher is responsible for both developing the assessment and using it to make decisions. There are, of course, many situations in which several teachers may work together to develop the assessment, and also use the results of the assessment to make decisions together.

In the role of test *user*, you need to consider the intended consequences of using the assessment, and the kinds of decisions to be made. As test *developer*, you need to consider the information about students' language ability that is relevant for making the decisions, and the kinds of assessment tasks that will provide this information. For example, you might want to assess your students in order to provide them with feedback to help them improve their learning. In this case, you, as test *user*, decide to provide feedback to your students and the intended consequence is that their learning will improve. As test *developer*, you might identify your students' speaking ability as the information needed, and design a short oral interview as an assessment task.

Practicality of assessment use

A very important consideration in the context of the language classroom is to make sure that using an assessment will be practical. Several activities are involved in using an assessment, including developing the assessment, administering it to students, recording their performance, and reporting this to stakeholders. Thus, practicality is not a quality of the assessment itself, but of the entire process of assessment development and use.

When you think about the practicality of developing and using an assessment, you need to consider the resources you will need to do this. You also need to find out whether the resources that you need are available or will be available when you need them.

➢ **Practicality** is the relationship between the resources that are available and those that are needed in the development and use of the assessment.

An assessment is practical if the resources needed to develop and use the assessment are not more than those that are available. An assessment is *not* practical if more resources are needed to develop and use the assessment than are available.

Resources for assessment use

Resources include people, material, and time. People might include:

- test developers
- test users
- task writers
- scorers/graders/markers
- test administrators.

Material might include:

- space (e.g. rooms for assessment development, rooms for administering the assessment)
- equipment (e.g. paper, pen and pencils, digital recorders and players, laptops, notebooks, smartphones).

Time includes:

- development time (time from the beginning of the assessment development process to administering the assessment, and to recording students' performance to reporting the results)
- time for specific activities (e.g. designing, writing, scoring, analyzing).

Different kinds and amounts of resources will be needed at different times in the development process. For example, for developing a classroom-based assessment for making relatively low-stakes decisions, the primary resource that may be needed will be the teacher's time and a place to work. Depending on the kind of assessment, additional people and different space may be needed. In a test of speaking in which students describe pictures of animals, for example, the teacher will need time, a place to work, and access to a source of pictures of animals while developing the test. For administering the test, the teacher will require a classroom that is arranged with a specific place where the test will be given, along with a table or desk and chairs for the teacher and for the students who are taking the test. For scoring the students' responses, the teacher will require some sort of recording form.

As discussed earlier, differing amounts of resources will typically be required, depending on the importance of the decisions to be made. For most assessments that are used for low-stakes decisions, relatively few resources beyond the teacher and what is in the classroom will be required. However, assessments that are used for high-stakes decisions generally require considerably more resources. For this reason, it is particularly important for us, as test developers, to estimate the resources that we will need and those that will be available for the development and use of assessments for high-stakes decisions, to assure that they will be practical.

PART II: A SYSTEMATIC APPROACH TO CLASSROOM-BASED ASSESSMENT

In Part II, we describe the framework that underlies our approach to developing and using classroom-based assessments. In Chapter 3, we give an overview of this approach, relating it to the process of assessment use described in Chapter 2. In Chapters 3–7, we describe an assessment use argument (AUA), which provides the conceptual framework for developing and using classroom-based assessments. In each of these chapters, we describe one of the four claims in the AUA, including the outcomes and qualities of the claim, procedures for stating the claim, and possible ways to provide backing, or evidence, to support these claims.

3

OVERVIEW OF OUR APPROACH TO ASSESSMENT DEVELOPMENT

Have you ever felt that an assessment you have taken was not "fair"? What made you feel this way? Did you feel that your score was too low and did not really show how well you actually performed on the assessment? Did you feel that the content or format of the test did not enable you to show your actual ability? Did you feel that the decision that was made on the basis of the assessment was not the right one? What did you do to try to correct this situation? Or, have your students ever complained that an assessment you gave them was not fair? Why did they feel it was not fair? Did they say that the assessment did not cover what they had learned in your class? Did they feel that the responses to the assessment tasks had not been scored or marked the same way for every student? How did you respond to your students' complaints?

In this chapter, we discuss fairness and accountability as essential concerns for classroom-based language assessments. We then discuss the process of assessment justification, including specifying an assessment use argument (AUA; defined on page 30). Next, we discuss the process of assessment development, providing an example that illustrates the specification of an AUA for the links between intended consequences and assessment performance. Finally, we discuss the process of providing backing for the AUA.

Fairness and accountability

Fairness in assessment use is essential if we want stakeholders, such as our students, their parents/guardians, or school administrators, to believe in or trust the way our assessments are used. Our approach to the development and use of language assessment is aimed at assuring fair assessment use, and convincing stakeholders that the intended uses of our assessments are justified. This approach is based on the principle that fairness, or fair test use, is the most important consideration in developing and using assessments. In Chapter 2, we discussed the links in using language assessments, from the student's performance on the assessment tasks to consequences.

➢ **Fairness** is a quality of assessment use. Fairness in assessment use depends on how well each link from students' performance on assessment tasks, to assessment records, to decisions, and to consequences can be supported or justified to stakeholders. If any link cannot be justified, then the assessment use is not likely to be fair.

A concern for fairness implies a concern for the consequences of the assessment use for stakeholders. A concern for consequences, in turn, implies the need for accountability to stakeholders.

➤**Accountability** means being able to convince stakeholders that the intended uses of our assessment are justified.

Therefore, the process of developing and using an assessment must *begin* with a consideration of the consequences of assessment use.

Assessment justification

The uses, that is, the interpretations and decisions that you, as test user, make on the basis of classroom-based assessments have consequences for stakeholders. In any assessment situation, there are many possible or actual consequences that might happen as a result of using an assessment. Not all of these, however, will be consequences that you, as test developer and user, want to help bring about. For example, you would not want the use of your assessment to result in any detrimental consequences, such as providing misleading feedback to your students about their learning, or not passing a student who has actually mastered the material in the course and is ready for the next level of instruction. Therefore, as test developer and user, you need to identify those specific consequences that you intend to help bring about. You also need to specify the interpretations and decisions you need to make in order to help bring about these intended consequences. It is these intended uses of the assessment that you need to be able to justify. In other words, you need to be prepared to convince stakeholders that the intended uses of your assessment are justified. Stakeholders may include, for example, the following:

- yourself, as a teacher and as a test developer/user
- test takers (your students)
- your fellow teachers
- school administrators
- parents/guardians
- other stakeholders (e.g. government officials, the general public).

When we begin to develop an assessment, our goal is to assure that our intended uses can be justified. Thus, an essential component of assessment development and use is the process of assessment justification.

➤**Assessment justification** is the process that teachers, as test developers and test users, will follow to *demonstrate* the extent to which the intended uses of an assessment are justified.

Assessment justification includes two interrelated activities:

1 articulating an AUA that the intended uses of our assessment are justified

2 providing backing (evidence) to support the AUA.

Assessment justification is similar to the process a lawyer follows in building a legal case to convince a judge or a jury during a trial. The case that the lawyer presents to the court consists of a series of claims that, for example, the defendant in the trial is innocent of the charges that have been brought against him. In addition to these claims, the lawyer also submits evidence to the court to support her claims. In the process of assessment justification, the test developer and test user present an argument, an AUA, and backing to support the claims in the AUA. The purpose of the claims and backing is to convince stakeholders that the intended uses of the assessment are justified.

Specifying an assessment use argument (AUA)

To guide the process of assessment justification, we need a conceptual framework. An AUA provides such a framework.

➢ An **assessment use argument** (**AUA**) consists of a series of claims or statements that define the links from a student's performance on an assessment to the intended consequences of using the assessment.

➢ **Claims** are statements that the test developer and/or test user makes that specify the intended uses of the assessment, what it aims to assess, and how it intends to do this.

An AUA for a particular assessment will include four claims, about:

1 the intended consequences of using the assessment

2 the intended decisions to be made

3 the intended interpretations

4 the intended assessment records.

Each claim in an AUA has two parts: an intended *outcome* (consequences, decisions, interpretations, assessment records); and one or more *qualities* that are claimed for the intended outcomes.

In addition to guiding the development and use of the assessment, an AUA provides a statement that communicates our intentions for using the assessment to stakeholders. The outcomes and qualities of the outcomes of the claims in an AUA are illustrated in Figure 3.1. In this figure, the outcomes are italicized, and the qualities are bullet points.

When you state the claims in the AUA for a particular assessment, for each claim you will state:

• the intended outcome of the claim

• the intended quality or qualities of the outcome of that claim.

For Claims 1 and 2 (consequences and decisions), you will also state the stakeholders who will be affected by the intended outcome.

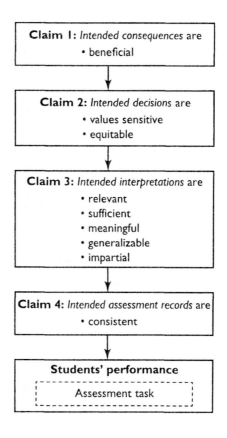

Figure 3.1 Claims, outcomes, and qualities in an AUA (adapted from Bachman and Palmer, Language Assessment in Practice, Oxford University Press, p. 104)

Assessment development

In addition to guiding the process of assessment justification, an AUA provides the conceptual framework for guiding assessment development. In Chapter 2 we said that, when we use an assessment, we begin with the students' performance and then follow the links from this to an assessment record, to interpretations, to decisions, and to consequences. In order to be able to justify making these links when we use an assessment, we need to use these same links to guide us when we develop our assessments. When we develop an assessment, the links go the other way: we begin with a consideration of consequences and then move to decisions, interpretations, and assessment records. This is illustrated in Figure 3.2.

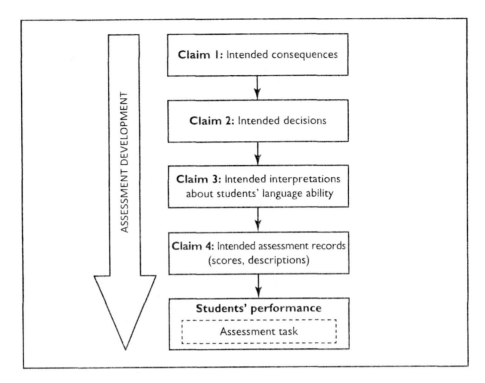

Figure 3.2 AUA for the links between intended consequences and assessment performance (adapted from Bachman & Palmer, Language Assessment in Practice, Oxford University Press, p. 91)

When we develop a language assessment, we start by asking, "What good things do we want to help make happen for our students, ourselves, our school, and perhaps other individuals and institutions?" Or, to put it another way, "What beneficial consequences do we want to help bring about?", and then describe these in Claim 1. We then ask, "What decisions do we need to make in order to help promote these beneficial consequences?", and then describe these decisions in Claim 2. Next, we ask, "What information about our students' language ability do we need in order to make these decisions?", and describe the aspects of language ability to be assessed in Claim 3. Finally, we ask, "What performance from our students will give us this information, and how will we get this?" To answer these questions, we describe the kind of assessment record, for example, a verbal description, a score, or a grade or mark, we want in Claim 4. We then specify the type of performance we want to elicit that will allow us to obtain an assessment record. And finally, we design assessment tasks that will elicit that type of performance. The four claims in an AUA including their outcomes and the qualities of these outcomes are discussed in detail in Chapters 4–7.

Here is an example assessment:

A teacher wants to use an assessment to provide feedback to her students that will guide their learning and enable them to master the aspects of reading comprehension that have been taught in a unit of instruction. She wants to obtain scores that she can interpret as indicators of her students' levels of reading comprehension. She develops an assessment task in which they must read a passage and write short answers to questions. Students' scores will be the total number of correct answers.

The claims in the AUA for this example are illustrated in Figure 3.3.

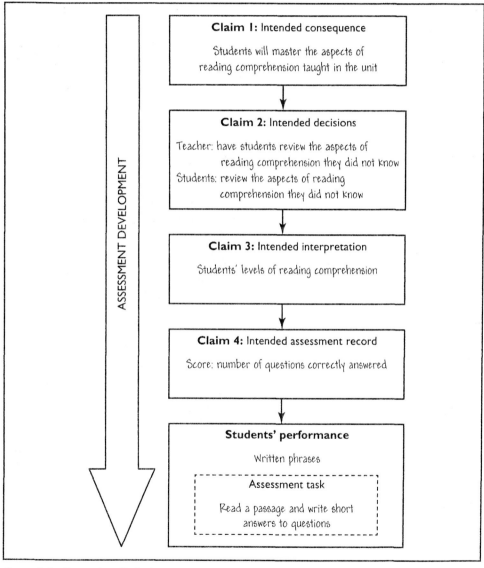

Figure 3.3 *Example of links between intended consequences and assessment performance*

Activity 3.1   Read the description of an assessment. Then, following the example in Figure 3.3, enter the relevant information in the figure.

A teacher wants to use an assessment to make sure the students who pass to the next level of instruction are prepared for instruction at that level. He wants to obtain scores that he can interpret as indicators of his students' levels of mastery of the listening material in the course. He develops an assessment task in which they must listen to a passage and select the correct answers from a list. Students' scores will be the total number of correct answers.

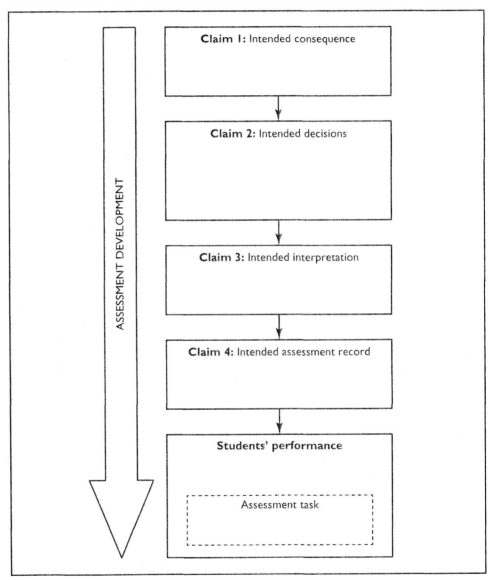

Photocopiable © Oxford University Press

(Answers to this activity are provided on page 275.)

Activity 3.2   Think of an assessment you have used or need to develop. Following the example on page 33, describe this assessment in the space provided. Then, enter the relevant information in the figure, following the example in Figure 3.3.

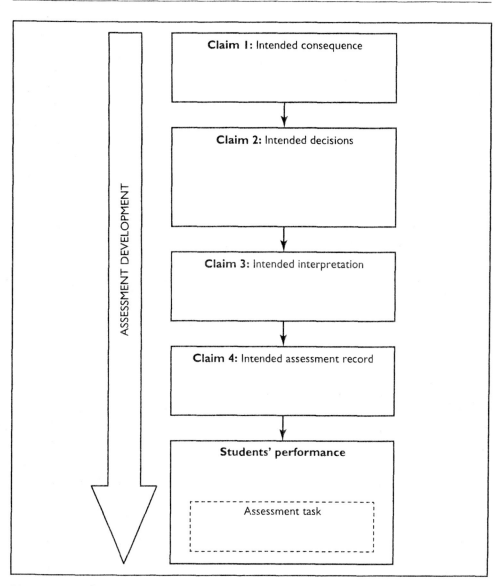

Providing backing to support the AUA

The claims in an AUA provide clear and detailed information for stakeholders about your intended uses of the assessment. However, these claims may not be enough to convince stakeholders, so you will need to provide backing, or evidence, to support these claims.

➤ **Backing** consists of evidence that the test developer and test user need to provide in order to support the claims in the AUA.

Two different kinds of backing can be provided to support the claims in an AUA:

- **Backing from procedures that are followed during the development and use of the assessment.** This kind of backing consists of the documentation of the procedures that you have followed in the development of the assessment, procedures that you follow in creating assessment tasks, administering and scoring assessment tasks, procedures for making decisions, and for reporting the assessment results to test users. The procedures that are described in Chapters 8–12, for developing and creating assessment tasks, for administering classroom-based assessments, recording students' performance, and for reporting and interpreting assessment results, will guide you in providing this kind of backing.

- **Backing that is collected during assessment development and use, specifically for the purpose of supporting claims in the AUA.** This kind of backing includes the collection of documentation such as school regulations or grading requirements, as well as analyses of students' performance, using a range of qualitative and quantitative approaches, as appropriate to the particular claim in the AUA.

Both kinds of backing can be provided at different times during the process of assessment development and use. Furthermore, the kinds and amounts of backing you need to provide will depend on the relative importance of the decisions to be made. The higher the stakes of the decision, the greater the responsibility for you, as test developer and test user, to provide evidence to support the claims in the AUA. We discuss providing backing for the four claims in an AUA in detail in Chapters 4–7.

4 CONSEQUENCES: WHY DO WE NEED TO ASSESS OUR STUDENTS?

When you need to assess your students, where do you begin? What aspects of the assessment do you consider? What kind of assessment will you use? What number of marks/points should the assessment be worth? How long should the assessment take to complete? What can you do to maintain test security?

These are all important considerations in developing and using an assessment. However, in our view, they are not the place to *start* developing an assessment. As we said in Chapter 2, the primary reason we use a language assessment is because we want to help bring about beneficial consequences for our students, ourselves as teachers, and other stakeholders. Therefore, the first question you should ask when you think about using an assessment with your students is "why do I need to assess my students?" By answering this question, you will clearly define the assessment purpose, and this will help you think through the kinds of effects your assessment might have on you and your students. That is, you will specify the beneficial consequences that you would like to help bring about by using an assessment.

In this chapter, we discuss Claim 1 of an assessment use argument (AUA), which is about the consequences that you, as a test developer and test user, want to help bring about by using the assessment. We first discuss the assessment development questions that Claim 1 addresses and the considerations that you need to make in answering them. We then describe the process of stating Claim 1, including the parts of the claim, the general version of the claim, and how you will adapt this for a particular assessment. Then, we provide a concrete example of a classroom-based assessment to illustrate this process. Finally, we discuss the kinds of backing that can be collected to support Claim 1.

Assessment development questions for Claim 1

In stating Claim 1, there are three questions you need to answer:

1 What beneficial consequences do I want to help bring about?
2 Who will be affected by these consequences?
3 What is the intended quality of these consequences?

Intended consequences

For any assessment, particularly in high-stakes settings, there are many possible consequences that could happen. Some of these might be beneficial for stakeholders and some might be detrimental. Because of the uncertainties of any assessment situation, it is almost impossible for us to think of all the possible consequences, much less try to identify and describe these. Therefore, in planning, developing, and using the assessment, you need to carefully identify and describe those consequences that you want to help bring about. These consequences are the intended consequences of using the assessment.

➢ **Intended consequences** are the effects on stakeholders that the test developer/user wants to help bring about.

There may be other consequences that you may not specifically intend to help bring about, but that might possibly result from using the assessment. Therefore, in stating Claim 1, you also need to consider these possible consequences, especially any that might be detrimental to stakeholders.

Intended consequences will be the result of the decisions that you make on the basis of the assessment. However, simply using an assessment can also have consequences. Thus, in considering the intended consequences of your assessment, you need to think about the consequences of both 1) the decisions that are made on the basis of the assessment and 2) using the assessment.

Consequences of decisions that are made

The decisions that you make on the basis of the assessment will have consequences. The decision to provide feedback to your students, for example, is intended to help them improve their language ability. This decision will affect your students, and it will also affect you, as a teacher. If you decide to make changes in your instruction on the basis of the assessment, your intention is to improve your teaching, as well as to help your students learn more effectively. This decision may also affect your students' parents/guardians, who might want to work with their children at home. Higher-stakes decisions such as deciding which students will pass to the next course or grade are intended to make sure that students who pass have mastered the learning objectives of the course they have just completed and will be ready for instruction at the next course or grade. These decisions will affect your students and you, and may also affect other stakeholders, such as the teachers in the next course or grade, the school, school administrators, and parents/guardians. If many students fail a course or grade, for example, school administrators might want to change the school budget or the curriculum. Thus, the decisions you make may have different consequences for different groups of stakeholders.

Consequence of using an assessment: Washback or impact on instruction and learning

The main consequence of using a classroom assessment that we must always consider is what language testers call "washback".

➤ **Washback** is the effect or impact of using an assessment on instruction and learning.

More specifically, washback refers to the influence of what and how we assess on the way we *teach* and the way our students *learn*. Washback can be either positive or negative.

➤ **Positive washback** happens when using an assessment leads teachers and students to engage in teaching and learning activities that are in accordance with their beliefs about teaching and learning, and about what they believe is important for students to learn.

➤ **Negative washback** happens when using an assessment leads teachers and students to engage in teaching and learning activities that are *not* in accordance with their beliefs about teaching and learning and about what they believe is important for students to learn.

Assessments can have a powerful effect on the way we teach and the way our students learn. We can all think of assessments that are used to make very high-stakes decisions about our students, such as who will graduate from school or who will be admitted to university. Many of these assessments are developed by government agencies, such as a state or provincial board of education or by a national department or ministry of education. Assessments such as these are typically given after a relatively long period of instruction and learning, such as at the end of elementary school, secondary school, or university, and thus need to assess a large amount of content. They are also given to large numbers of students, so that they must be administered and scored very efficiently. Because of these constraints, assessments such as these typically cannot include everything that we may believe is important for our students to learn. In addition, such assessments typically include tasks, such as multiple-choice items, that are very different from the teaching tasks that teachers use in the classroom. These assessments are used to make very high-stakes decisions and students want to do well on them. Therefore, they often want to study only the content that will be assessed, and practice only tasks that are like those in the assessment. As a result, teachers may feel pressured to narrow the focus of the content they teach to cover only the content of the high-stakes assessments, and to give their students multiple-choice tasks as learning tasks. It is clear that large-scale high-stakes assessments such as these can have negative washback. (We would note that, in many countries, the agencies that are responsible for developing and administering large-scale high-stakes assessments are working to assure that these include content that teachers and other educators believe is important for students to learn, and to include tasks that require students to use language, rather than simply checking boxes or filling in the bubbles on an answer sheet.)

Although washback is generally discussed in the context of assessments that are used to make high-stakes decisions, it is also important to consider the possible washback of classroom-based assessments. Many of the assessments we use to make summative decisions about our students, such as who will move to the next level in a course or to the next grade in school, are medium- to high-stakes for our students. These assessments can potentially have washback on how our students learn. Suppose, for example, that we gave two or three short tests and a longer final exam during a school year, and used these to make decisions about which students pass to the next grade. In this case, the content that we cover in these short tests and in the final exam, as well as the kinds of assessment tasks we use, are likely to have an effect on the way our students study. Because of this potential for washback, it is important that you make every effort to make sure that the assessments you develop and use for these kinds of decisions will provide positive washback on learning. Two ways in which you can do this are to make sure that:

- the content of the assessments adequately covers the content of the course – the syllabus, textbook, and teaching materials
- the kinds of assessment tasks you use correspond to the kinds of teaching tasks you use in the classroom.

The approach to developing assessments that we describe in this book is aimed at enabling you to develop classroom assessments that will have a strong potential for providing positive washback on your students' learning.

Who will be affected by the consequences?

As with consequences, for any assessment, particularly in high-stakes settings, there are many stakeholders that might be affected by the use of the assessment or by the decisions that are made. However, it is very unlikely that any single assessment could affect all of these stakeholders. Therefore, you need to identify and describe those specific stakeholders that you want to be affected by the use of the assessment. These stakeholders are the intended stakeholders.

➤ **Intended stakeholders** are the people, programs, or institutions that the test developer/user wants to be affected by the use of the assessment.

As we indicated in Chapter 2, intended stakeholders will always include ourselves, as test developer/user, and our students, as test takers.

In addition to the intended stakeholders, there may be other stakeholders who might be affected by the use of the assessment, so you also need to consider these. These may include your fellow teachers, school administrators at various levels, parents/guardians, government officials, potential employers, and the general public. You need to pay particular attention to any stakeholders who might be affected detrimentally by the use of the assessment. Because there may be many different intended stakeholders and stakeholder groups who might be affected by the use of a particular assessment, it is essential, in stating Claim 1, that you indicate who the specific intended stakeholders are.

Quality of the intended consequences

We use classroom assessments because we want to help bring about beneficial consequences. That is, we want to help make good things happen for our students, ourselves, our school, and perhaps other individuals and institutions. The quality of our intended consequences is beneficence.

➢ **Beneficence** is the degree to which the consequences of using an assessment and of the decisions that are made promote good and are not detrimental to stakeholders.

When you begin to plan and develop an assessment you need to ask, "What beneficial consequences do I want to help bring about?" For example, you might ask:

- In what specific ways will my students benefit from the use of the assessment?
- In what specific ways will I benefit from using the assessment?
- In what specific ways will others benefit from using the assessment?
- How might using an assessment be detrimental to my students and others?

Some possible beneficial consequences of using a classroom language assessment might include:

- My students will become better language learners and will improve their language ability.
- My students will be better able to master the learning objectives of their content (e.g. science, math) courses.
- I will revise the content of my teaching materials.
- I will improve my teaching and become a more effective teacher.
- Other teachers will find it easier to teach my students.
- My students' parents/guardians will be pleased that their children are succeeding in school.
- The school's record of achievement will improve.

Note: A checklist of things to think about to help guide you in developing and using classroom-based assessments is given in Appendix 1 for easy reference.

Summary: Intended consequences and stakeholders in classroom-based assessments

There are three types of intended consequences that we may want to help promote by using classroom-based assessments:

- improving instruction and learning
- assuring that students are ready for instruction at the appropriate level
- assuring that students who are certified at a given level of ability have actually achieved that level of ability.

These intended consequences will generally affect the same groups of stakeholders. Table 4.1 summarizes these intended consequences and the groups of stakeholders whom we may intend to be affected by the classroom-based assessments we use.

Intended consequences	Stakeholder groups affected
Students will improve their language ability and learning.	• Students • Teachers • Parents/Guardians
The teacher will improve his/her teaching	• Students • Teacher
Students will be ready to receive instruction at the appropriate level.	• Students • Teacher in the current level • Teachers in the next level
Students who are certified at a given level of ability have actually achieved that level of ability.	• Students • Teachers • School • University • Possible employers

Table 4.1   Typical intended consequences and stakeholders in classroom-based assessments

Stating Claim 1

Claim 1 includes the following parts:

1 a brief descriptive label for the assessment

2 a list and descriptions of the intended consequences

3 a list of and descriptive labels for the stakeholders whom we intend to benefit from the use of the assessment.

The general version of Claim 1 is given as follows, with the parts in *italics*:

> General version of Claim 1: The *consequences* of using *the assessment* made will be beneficial to *stakeholders*.

In stating Claim 1 for your own specific assessment, you will need to adapt the parts in italics in the general version of Claim 1. Here is an extract of stating Claim 1 for a specific assessment from Example 1 (see page 169).

Example of stating Claim 1
Setting:

A teacher in an ESL/EFL classroom in a primary/elementary school needs to develop a classroom assessment for his beginning level students. This assessment will be used for two different purposes. One purpose is to make sure that the students who pass the grade are prepared for instruction at the next level. In order to do this, the teacher will use the results of this assessment, along with other assessments given during the course of the school year, to make summative decisions about which students will pass to the next grade. The second purpose is to help his students improve their speaking and to improve his teaching. In order to do this, the teacher will also use the results of this assessment to make formative decisions about his teaching and to provide feedback to his students. The assessment will be based on a unit of instruction in the course, and this is one task from the assessment, in which students describe animals from pictures by speaking.

Claim 1: Intended consequences

The consequences of using the classroom speaking assessment will be beneficial to stakeholders as indicated in Tables 4.2 and 4.3.

Assessment: Describing animals from pictures by speaking	
Intended consequences	**Intended stakeholders**
1a Students who have mastered the learning objectives of the entire term will benefit by receiving appropriate instruction at the next level.	Students ESL/EFL teachers in the next level
1b Students who have not mastered the learning objectives of the entire term will benefit by receiving appropriate instruction at the same level.	Students ESL/EFL teachers in the current level
2 Students will improve their speaking.	Students Teacher
3 The teacher will improve his teaching.	Students Teacher

Table 4.2   Intended consequences and intended stakeholders

Other possible consequences	**Stakeholders who might be affected**
Teachers will be able to teach students who are prepared for their level.	ESL/EFL teachers in the current level ESL/EFL teachers in the next level
There will be fewer complaints from teachers, students, and parents/guardians.	School administrators
The reputation of the school will improve.	The school
Parents/Guardians will be satisfied with their children's speaking and help their children continue to improve.	Parents/Guardians, students, teachers

Table 4.3   Other possible consequences and stakeholders who might be affected

Activity 4.1

For the assessment outlined in the setting, state Claim 1 following the example of stating Claim 1 on page 42. Then, enter the relevant information in the table.

Setting:

A teacher in an ESL/EFL classroom in a secondary school or university needs to develop a classroom assessment for her advanced-level students. This assessment will be used for two different purposes. One purpose is to make sure that the students who pass the grade are prepared for instruction at the next level. In order to do this, the teacher will use the results of this assessment, along with other assessments given during the course of the school year, to make summative decisions about which students will pass to the next grade. The second purpose of the assessment is to help her students improve their writing and to improve her teaching. In order to do this, the teacher will use the results of this assessment to make formative decisions about her teaching and to provide feedback to her students. The assessment will be based on a unit of instruction in the course and this is one task from the assessment, in which the students write a letter of application for a job.

Claim 1: Intended consequences

The consequences of using _____ will be beneficial to stakeholders as indicated in the following table.

Assessment:	
Intended consequences	**Intended stakeholders**
Other possible consequences	**Stakeholders who might be affected**

Photocopiable © Oxford University Press

(Answers to this activity can be found in Example 8 on page 243.)

Activity 4.2 Think of an assessment that you have used or that you need to develop. Describe the setting for this assessment in the space provided, then state Claim I following the example of stating Claim I on page 42. Finally, enter the relevant information in the table.

Setting:

_____

_____

_____

_____

_____

Claim I: Intended consequences

The consequences of using _____ will be beneficial to stakeholders as indicated in the following table.

Assessment:	
Intended consequences	**Intended stakeholders**
Other possible consequences	**Stakeholders who might be affected**

Providing backing for Claim 1

As we discussed in Chapter 3, it will be necessary to provide some backing to support the claims in our AUA. For Claim 1 (intended consequences), the backing will be aimed at assuring stakeholders that the use of the assessment and of the decisions that are made are, in fact, helping promote the intended consequences. In Chapter 3, we indicated that because the intended consequences cannot occur until the assessment is used, we cannot collect backing during the process of assessment development, but can only collect backing for intended consequences after the assessment has been used. Backing that can be provided for Claim 1 might include, for example:

- For washback and/or formative decisions to improve teaching/learning: notes on how the teacher changed instructional practice; peer observations of classroom teaching; feedback from students; observations of, and interviews with, teachers and students.

- For summative decisions: follow-up with teachers in the next grade on how students who moved on to the next course/grade are succeeding; follow-up with teachers in same grade on how students who did not move to the next grade are succeeding.

Some possible backing for the example of stating Claim 1

- Students receiving instruction at the appropriate level:
  - teacher talks with ESL/EFL teachers in the next course/grade about how well students who moved on to the next course/grade are performing in speaking
  - teacher talks with ESL/EFL teachers in the same course/grade about how well students who did not move to the next grade are performing in speaking.

- Students' improvement in speaking:
  - teacher observes students' speaking performance in class
  - teacher talks with students about their use of feedback from the assessment to improve their speaking
  - teacher asks the students to answer a questionnaire on how they have improved their speaking
  - teacher compares students' performance on the next speaking assessment with their performance on this one.

- Teacher's improvement in teaching:
  - teacher makes notes on how he changed his instruction for speaking activities.
  - teacher gets feedback from students through a survey or questionnaire
  - teacher asks one or two fellow ESL/EFL teachers to observe his classroom teaching.

Activity 4.3   List the kinds of backing you might need to provide for the assessment in Activity 4.1 (on page 44).

_____

_____

_____

_____

_____

Photocopiable © Oxford University Press

(Answers to this activity can be found in Example 1 on page 170 (note that the backing for Examples 8 and 1 are the same).)

Activity 4.4   List the kinds of backing you might need to provide for the assessment in Activity 4.2 (on page 45).

_____

_____

_____

_____

_____

Photocopiable © Oxford University Press

5

DECISIONS: WHEN DO WE NEED TO ASSESS OUR STUDENTS?

Have you ever wondered if you are assessing your students too much or too often, or that you are not assessing them often enough? We can address the questions of when and how often we need to assess our students by considering the kinds of decisions we need to make and when these decisions need to be made. Since the purpose of assessment is to collect information to help us make decisions, we may need to assess our students whenever we need to make a decision. Or, to put it another way, we only need to assess our students if we need to make a decision.

In this chapter, we discuss Claim 2 of an assessment use argument (AUA), which is about the decisions that you, as test developer and test user, need to make. We first discuss the assessment development questions that Claim 2 addresses and the considerations that you need to make in answering them. We then describe the process of stating Claim 2, including the parts of the claim, the general version of the claim, and how you will adapt this for a particular assessment. Next, we provide a concrete example of a classroom-based assessment to illustrate this process. Finally, we discuss the kinds of backing that can be collected to support Claim 2.

Assessment development questions for Claim 2

In stating Claim 2, there are five questions you need to answer:
- What decisions need to be made?
- Who will be affected by these decisions?
- Who will make these decisions?
- When do these decisions need to be made?
- What are the qualities of the intended decisions?

What decisions need to be made?

If you want to help bring about the beneficial consequences that you have stated in Claim 1, you need to do something. You cannot just wait and hope that these beneficial consequences will happen on their own. It is not very likely that these beneficial consequences will occur if you are just patient and wait long enough. Therefore, if you want to increase the chances that these consequences will occur, you need to take action; you need to make decisions. Thus, the decisions that you need to make are aimed at helping bring about the beneficial consequences that you have specified in Claim 1.

➤ **Intended decisions** are specific actions that the test developer or test user takes in order to help promote the beneficial consequences that are specified in Claim 1.

In Chapter 2, we discussed two kinds of decisions—formative and summative—that we need to make in the classroom, in terms of their *purpose*, or the kinds of beneficial consequences they are intended to help bring about. In Chapter 2, we also discussed the *relative importance*—low-stakes, medium-stakes, and high-stakes—of the decisions that we need to make and that others may make on the basis of our assessments. Most of the formative decisions you make on the basis of classroom-based assessments will be low-stakes, while the summative decisions you make will be medium- to high-stakes.

Other decision makers may also use the grades or marks you give to your students at the end of a school year or a period of instruction, e.g. at secondary school, to make high-stakes decisions about university entrance or employment. Because these decisions may be intended for different purposes and be at different levels of importance, it is essential, in stating Claim 2, that you specify both the intended purpose and the relative importance of decisions that will be made on the basis of the information from the assessment. We would note that it is sometimes possible to use a single assessment for both low-stakes formative decisions and for medium- to high-stakes summative decisions.

Who will be affected by the intended decisions?

The intended stakeholders who might be affected by the intended decisions to be made are the same as those discussed in Chapter 4 for consequences. These intended stakeholders will always include ourselves, as test developer/user and our students, as test takers. In addition, the intended stakeholders may include our fellow teachers, school administrators at various levels, parents/guardians, universities, government officials, potential employers, and the general public. Because there may be many different stakeholders and stakeholder groups who might be affected by the decisions that are made, it is essential, in stating Claim 2, that you specify who the intended stakeholders are.

Who will make the intended decisions?

Depending on the purposes of the intended decision, different individuals will be responsible for making them. Formative decisions, aimed at improving instruction and learning, will generally be made by the teacher and the students. The teacher will make decisions, for example, about changing the kinds of instructional tasks to present to students, changing the amount of time or emphasis to be placed on certain learning objectives, or changing the content of a lesson. Students may decide to change the way they study, modify the learning strategies they use, or change the amount of time they spend on specific learning objectives. Summative decisions will typically be made by teachers and school administrators. In high-stakes settings, the decisions may be made by a state department of education or a ministry of education, an admissions officer at a university, or an employer. Because different kinds of decisions may be made by different individuals, it is essential, in stating Claim 2, that you specify who will be responsible for making these decisions.

When do the intended decisions need to be made?

The decisions need to be made in time for them to help bring about the intended beneficial consequences. Formative decisions may be made before, during, or after a period of instruction. This may typically range from a lesson or unit of instruction, to a semester or school term, or to an entire year-long course. Since these decisions are aimed at improving instruction and learning, they need to be made in time to achieve this purpose. Thus, if a teacher wants to improve his teaching, then decisions about modifying learning tasks, changing the amount of time spent on learning objectives, or changing course content need to be made in time for him to implement these in his instruction. Similarly, if the teacher wants to provide feedback from the assessment to help his students improve their learning, then this feedback needs to be given in time for students to make use of it. Summative decisions that are made after a period of instruction are typically aimed at helping bring about future beneficial consequences for stakeholders. For example, decisions about which students pass to the next unit of instruction or the next grade are intended to assure that students who pass will be prepared for, and be able to benefit from, instruction at the next unit or grade. The decision to certify students' language ability at a particular level may be intended to qualify them for admission to university, or for future employment. Because the timing of the decisions we make is critical to achieving the intended beneficial consequences, it is essential in stating Claim 2 that you specify when the decisions will be made.

The qualities of the intended decisions

If you want the decisions you make to help bring about the intended beneficial consequences, then these decisions need to be values-sensitive and equitable. The qualities of the intended decisions are values-sensitivity and equitability.

Values-sensitivity

➢ **Values-sensitivity** is the degree to which the use of an assessment and the decisions that are made take into consideration existing educational and societal values and relevant laws, rules, and regulations.

In considering values-sensitivity, you need to ask, "What values and regulations do I need to consider when making these decisions?" For example, you might ask:

- Are these decisions consistent with my own values as a teacher?
- Are these decisions consistent with the values of the test takers, my students? Are these decisions consistent with the educational values, rules, and regulations of my school?
- Are these decisions consistent with the values of my students' parents/guardians, and of the community? (For example, in some countries, having students repeat the same grade or the same course, especially in elementary school and secondary school, almost never happens. Thus, in these countries, a decision to have a student repeat the same grade or course would not be consistent with the educational values of the school, the parents/guardians, or the community. Such a decision would need to be made very carefully, if it were ever made.)
- If there are conflicting values among different groups of stakeholders, how can I best address these in using the assessment to make decisions?

Equitability

➤ **Equitability** is the degree to which different test takers who are at equivalent levels on the ability to be assessed have equivalent chances of being classified into the same group.

Equitability is a concern primarily in summative decisions when the decisions will be used to classify test takers into different groups, such as classes at different levels of ability, "progress" and "not progress", "pass" and "not pass", "certify" and "not certify". For assessments that will be used to classify students into groups, the test developer/user will need to specify one or more "cut scores" for making the classification decisions.

➤ A **cut score** is the score, grade, or mark on the assessment that is used as a basis for classifying students into different groups, such as "pass" and "not pass".

In considering equitability, you need to do the following:

- carefully set the cut score(s) for classifying test takers
- inform all stakeholders about the cut scores and how these were set
- make sure that the same cut scores are used for classifying all test takers, for instance:
  - if students with the same score are classified differently, the decision is not equitable
  - if students with different scores are classified the same, the decision is not equitable.

Note: A checklist of things to think about to help guide you in developing and using a classroom-based assessment is given in Appendix 1 for easy reference.

Summary: Relating intended consequences to decisions in classroom-based assessments

The kinds of decisions we need to make will be determined by the intended consequences of the assessment. Thus, for each intended consequence, one or more decisions will need to be made. The relationship between intended consequences and decisions to be made on the basis of classroom-based assessments is shown in Figure 5.1.

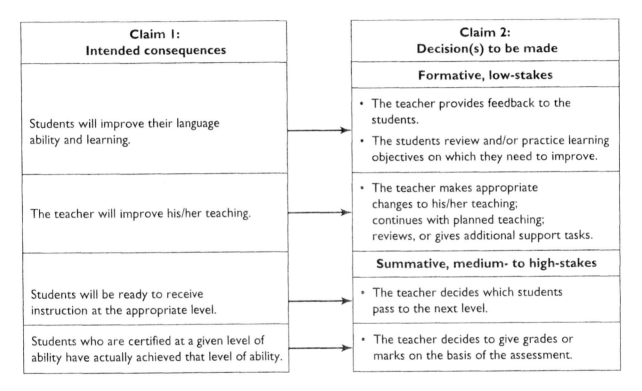

Figure 5.1 *Typical intended consequences and decisions that need to be made*

Stating Claim 2

Claim 2 includes the following parts:

1 a list and descriptions of the decisions to be made

2 a list and descriptive labels for the intended stakeholders

3 a list of who will be responsible for making these decisions

4 a list of when the decisions need to be made

5 the intended qualities of the decisions.

The general version of Claim 2 is given as follows, with the parts in *italics* and the intended qualities in **bold**.

General version of Claim 2: The *intended decisions* are made by the *decision-maker(s)*, are made *at a time when needed*, and will affect the *intended stakeholders*. The decisions are **values-sensitive** and **equitable** for the *intended stakeholders*.

In stating Claim 2 for your own specific assessment, you will need to adapt the parts in italics in the general version of Claim 2. Here is an extract of stating Claim 2 for a specific assessment from Example 1 (see page 169).

Example of stating Claim 2
Setting:

(The setting is the same as in the example in Chapter 4.)

A teacher in an ESL/EFL classroom in a primary/elementary school needs to develop a classroom assessment for his beginning level students. This assessment will be used for two different purposes. One purpose is to make sure that the students who pass the grade are prepared for instruction at the next level. In order to do this, the teacher will use the results of this assessment, along with other assessments given during the course of the school year, to make summative decisions about which students will pass to the next grade. The second purpose is to help his students improve their speaking and to improve his teaching. In order to do this, the teacher will also use the results of this assessment to make formative decisions about his teaching and to provide feedback to his students. The assessment will be based on a unit of instruction in the course and this is one task from the assessment, in which students describe animals from pictures by speaking.

Claim 2: Intended decisions

The high-stakes summative decisions are made by the teacher at the end of the school year. The low-stakes formative decisions are made by the teacher and the students before the next unit of instruction. These decisions affect the stakeholders as indicated in Table 5.1. The decisions take into consideration the educational values of the school and the societal values of the community, and follow the rules and regulations of the school. They are equitable for the stakeholders listed in Table 5.1.

Decision(s) to be made	Individual(s) who will make the decision(s)	When the decision(s) will be made	Stakeholders who will (or might be) affected by the decision(s)
Summative, high stakes			
Decide which students pass to the next grade (scores from this assessment will count as part of students' total grade for the term)	Teacher	At the end of the school term	Students Teachers (Future teachers) (School administrators) (The school) (Parents/Guardians)
Formative, low stakes			
Provide students with feedback on their speaking performance	Teacher	Immediately after the assessment	Students Teachers (Parents/Guardians)
Make appropriate changes to teaching	Teacher	Before the next unit of instruction	Students Teachers (Parents/Guardians)
Continue with planned teaching; review, or give support tasks	Teacher	Before the next unit of instruction	Students Teachers (Parents/Guardians)
Review and/or practice learning objectives on which students need to improve	Students	After they receive the teacher's feedback	Students Teachers (Parents/Guardians)

Table 5.1   Intended decisions to be made for the example of Claim 2

Activity 5.1

For the assessment outlined in the setting, state Claim 2 following the example of stating Claim 2 on page 53. Then, enter the relevant information in the table.

Setting:

A group of ESL/EFL teachers in the same grade in a secondary school need to develop a classroom assessment for their intermediate-level students. This assessment will be used for two different purposes. One purpose is to make sure that the students who pass the grade are prepared for instruction at the next level. In order to do this, the teachers will use the results of this assessment, along with other assessments given during the course of the term, to make summative decisions about which students will pass to the next grade. The second purpose is to help their students improve their writing and to improve their teaching. In order to do this, the teachers will use the results of this assessment to make formative decisions about their teaching and to provide feedback to their students. The assessment will be based on a unit of instruction in the course. This is one task from the assessment, in which the students write a descriptive paragraph about a musical instrument.

Claim 2: Intended decisions

_____

_____

_____

_____

_____

Assessment:			
Decision(s) to be made	**Individual(s) who will make the decision(s)**	**When the decision(s) will be made**	**Stakeholders who will (or might be) affected by the decision(s)**
Summative, high-stakes			
Formative, low-stakes			

Photocopiable © Oxford University Press

(Answers to this activity can be found in Example 6 on page 224.)

Activity 5.2   Think of an assessment that you have used or that you need to develop. Describe the setting for this assessment, state Claim 2 following the example of stating claim 2 on page 53, and enter the relevant information in the table.

Setting:

_____

_____

_____

_____

Claim 2: Intended decisions

_____

_____

_____

_____

Assessment:			
Decision(s) to be made	Individual(s) who will make the decision(s)	When the decision(s) will be made	Stakeholders who will (or might be) affected by the decision(s)
Summative, high-stakes			
Formative, low-stakes			

Providing backing for Claim 2

As we discussed in Chapter 3, it will be necessary to provide some backing to support the claims in our AUA. For Claim 2, the backing will be aimed at assuring stakeholders that the decisions that are made are values-sensitive and equitable for stakeholders. Backing that can be provided for Claim 2 might include, for example:

- for consideration of values-sensitivity: notes from meetings with different stakeholder groups, e.g. students, fellow teachers, school administrators, parents/guardians; for rules and regulations: documentation on relevant rules and regulations
- for equitability: documentation of procedures for 1) setting standards and cut scores; 2) monitoring how these are implemented in practice; and 3) informing students and other stakeholders about these.

As we mentioned in Chapter 3, the higher the stakes of the decision, the greater our responsibility to provide backing to support the claims in the AUA. Thus, we will need to provide more backing for relatively high-stakes decisions than for low-stakes ones.

Some possible backing for the example of stating Claim 2
Values-sensitivity

- High-stakes summative decisions:
  - the teacher meets with students, fellow teachers, school administrators, and parents/guardians to discuss the relevant values that need to be considered in the decisions to be made
  - the teacher reviews school rules and regulations regarding the use of assessments for decisions about which students will pass to the next grade.
- Low-stakes formative decisions:
  - the teacher considers how consistent the decisions to be made are with the their own values and beliefs about effective instructional practice.

Equitability

- High-stakes summative decisions:
  - the teacher documents procedures for 1) setting standards and cut scores based on all of the assessments given during the course of the school year; 2) monitoring how these are implemented in practice; and 3) informing students and other stakeholders about these.
- Low-stakes formative decisions:
  - equitability is not a concern in low-stakes formative decisions because these are not made for the purpose of classifying students into groups.

Note that in this example, the summative decisions are relatively high-stakes, so the teacher needs to provide considerably more backing to support these than for the low-stakes formative decisions.

Activity 5.3

List the kinds of backing you might need to provide for the assessment in Activity 5.1 (on page 54).

_____

_____

_____

_____

_____

Photocopiable © Oxford University Press

(Answers to this activity can be found in Example 1 on page 170.)

Activity 5.4

List the kinds of backing you might need to provide for the assessment in Activity 5.2 (on page 55).

_____

_____

_____

_____

Photocopiable © Oxford University Press

6

INTERPRETATIONS: WHAT AND HOW SHOULD WE ASSESS?

When you begin to develop a language assessment, how do you decide *what* you want to assess? Where do you find the content you want to assess? How do you decide *how* you should assess? How do you know what kinds of assessment tasks you should use? We can address the question of *what* to assess by identifying the kinds of information about our students' language ability we need in order to make our intended decisions, and then defining those areas of language ability we need to assess. We can address the question of *how* we should assess by identifying and describing the kinds of language use tasks our students need to perform in these settings or contexts.

In this chapter, we discuss Claim 3 of an assessment use argument (AUA), which is about the interpretations of students' language ability that you, as a test developer and test user, want to arrive at on the basis of the assessment. We first discuss the assessment development questions that Claim 3 addresses and the considerations that you need to make in answering these. We then describe the process of stating Claim 3, including the parts of the claim, the general version of the claim, and how you will adapt this for a particular assessment. Next, we provide a concrete example of a classroom-based assessment to illustrate this process. Finally, we discuss the kinds of backing that can be collected to support Claim 3.

Assessment development questions for Claim 3

In stating Claim 3, there are two sets of questions you need to answer:

1 *What* should I assess?

- What information about my students' language ability do I need in order to make the intended decisions? How will I identify this?
  - How will I assure that this information is *relevant* to the intended decisions?
  - Will this information be *sufficient* to make the intended decisions?
- How will I define the areas of language ability I need to assess?
- Where will this definition come from? What will be the source or sources of this definition?
  - How can I assure that this definition is *meaningful* to my students and other stakeholders?

2 *How* should I assess?
- What kind of performance do I need to obtain from my students?
- What kinds of assessment tasks should I use? Where do I find tasks that I can use as a basis for developing assessment tasks?
    - How can I assure that my interpretations of language ability will be *generalizable*?
    - How can I assure that my interpretations of language ability will be *impartial*?

We will address the first question, about *what* we need to assess, by considering the intended decisions we have specified in Claim 2 and then identifying the information about students' language ability that we need to collect in order to make these decisions. The information about language ability that we identify becomes the basis for our intended interpretations. By identifying the interpretations we need in order to make the intended decisions, we are helping assure that these interpretations are relevant. We will also need to consider whether these interpretations will provide enough, or sufficient, information for making the intended decisions. Relevance and sufficiency are two of the qualities of interpretations that we discuss later (see page 61).

Since we want to arrive at interpretations about our students' language ability, we need to specify and define the areas of language ability we want to assess. We also need to identify and describe the source of our definitions of ability. Our definition of the specific areas of language ability to be assessed and our description of the source of this definition provide the basis for assuring that our intended interpretations will be meaningful to stakeholders. Meaningfulness is one of the qualities of interpretations that we discuss later (see page 64).

We will address the second question, about *how* we should assess, by identifying and describing the contexts, or domains, beyond the assessment itself, in which our students will need to use the language ability to be assessed. We will refer to these as target language use (TLU) domains (discussed on page 65). Examples of TLU domains include the language classroom, academic classes in school, classes in a university, or a job in the workplace.

For classroom-based assessments, the primary TLU domain is the language classroom itself. We need to describe this TLU domain because we want our interpretations about our students' language ability to extend, or generalize, to the language class. We will also identify and describe the specific language use tasks that our students need to perform in the language class. We describe these language use tasks because they will guide us in designing and creating assessment tasks. By developing assessment tasks that correspond to language use tasks in the language classroom, we help assure that our interpretations will be generalizable. Generalizability is one of the qualities of interpretations that we discuss later (see page 66).

We know that personal attributes of our students and the characteristics of the assessment tasks we present them can either facilitate or hinder their opportunity to demonstrate their language ability on an assessment. Thus, in deciding how to assess, we need to consider factors that may affect students' performance on the assessement, for example: the personal attributes of our students, such as their age, their cognitive, emotional, and social development, their prior knowledge of topical content, or their native language(s). We also want to make sure that the assessment tasks we use do not favor or disfavor any particular groups of students. By doing this, we help assure that our interpretations will be impartial to all our students. Impartiality is one of the qualities of interpretations that we discuss later (see page 66).

What do we need to assess? Intended interpretations

As we indicated in Chapter 2, our interpretations will be based on the assessment records—verbal descriptions or test scores—that we arrive at on the basis of our students' performance on an assessment. In order to interpret these assessment records as indicators of our students' levels of language ability, we will need to define the specific area or areas of language ability we want to assess. These definitions will constitute our intended interpretations.

➢ An **intended interpretation** is the understanding about our students' language ability, which we want to arrive at on the basis of their assessment records.

Identifying the interpretations we need for making decisions: relevance and sufficiency

In the language classroom, there are many different kinds of decisions that we need to make about our students and about our teaching and these decisions need to be informed by interpretations about our students' language ability. The kinds of interpretations we need to provide will thus be determined by the kinds of decisions we need to make. That is, our intended interpretations need to be relevant to the decisions we intend to make.

➢ **Relevance** is the degree to which the intended interpretations provide the information the test user needs to make the decision.

In considering relevance, we need to think about how useful the intended interpretation will actually be for making the intended decisions. For formative decisions aimed at providing feedback to our students and to ourselves for improving learning and instruction, we need to provide interpretations about how well students have mastered specific learning objectives. For summative decisions, such as which students will pass or not pass a language course, we need to provide interpretations about how well students have mastered the learning objectives of the entire course. For decisions about students' readiness to use the language in contexts outside of the language class, we need to provide interpretations about their ability to use the language needed in these contexts.

To help assure the relevance of our interpretations, we need to do the following:

- think about or consult with other test users about the intended decisions
- identify interpretations about our students' language ability that we believe will help us make the decisions to be made.

In addition to relevance, we need to think about whether the intended interpretation will be sufficient for making the intended decisions.

➤ **Sufficiency** is the degree to which the intended interpretations provide *enough* information for the test user to make a decision.

In considering sufficiency, we need to think about whether or not a single assessment will provide enough information for making the decisions. For low-stakes formative decisions based on a single lesson, a single interpretation from a single assessment based on the content of that lesson or unit might be sufficient. For high-stakes summative decisions, such as passing or not passing a grade, however, multiple assessments are likely to be necessary to assess an entire year's achievement. For decisions such as these, we might give our students several short assessments during the year and one larger assessment at the end of the year, and then combine the results of these to arrive at an interpretation, typically reported as a grade or mark, which will be sufficient for the intended decision.

To address the sufficiency of your interpretations, you need to do the following:

- think about, or consult with other test users about all the information that you will need to make the intended decisions
- identify interpretations about our students' language ability that you will need in order to make the intended decisions:
  - Can I obtain these interpretations from a single assessment?
  - If not, what additional assessments will I need?

Source of ability definitions

If we want to be able to define the specific areas of language ability we need to assess, we need to identify and describe a specific *source* for these definitions. The specific source we identify for any given assessment will depend upon the specific kinds of interpretations we need in order to make the intended decisions. If we need interpretations about how well students have mastered specific learning objectives, or the learning objectives of an entire course, we will base our definitions of ability on the content of the course.

By identifying and describing the source or sources of our ability definitions, we accomplish two things. First, these descriptions provide a frame of reference for our students and other stakeholders to understand our definitions of the ability to be assessed. Second, they provide backing for our claims about the meaningfulness and generalizability of our intended interpretations. For classroom-based assessments in a language class, the content of the language course itself is the primary source for defining the abilities we need to assess.

Content of a language course

In most classroom-based assessments, we are interested in finding out how well our students are learning or have mastered the content covered in a particular course of instruction. This might consist of a single lesson, a unit of instruction, a marking period, a school term, a school year, or an entire level (e.g. elementary school, secondary school, university) of instruction. The ability that we want to assess will therefore be defined in terms of the content of that course of instruction. The "content" of a course can be specified in many different ways, or different places, including the following:

- a list of learning objectives
- course outline, syllabus, or curriculum
- textbooks
- content of lesson plans
- content of teaching and learning materials
- content of teaching and learning tasks and activities.

Any or all of these are possible sources for defining the areas or aspects of language ability we want to assess. The more specific we can be in relating individual assessment tasks to particular parts of the course content, the more likely it will be that stakeholders will be able to understand our definitions of the ability to be assessed, and the more likely they will be convinced by our claims about meaningfulness.

Areas of language ability needed in contexts outside the language course

In many situations, our students will be learning the language because they will need to use it in a context outside of the language class, such as in their academic content courses in school, in future courses they may take, either in school or at university, or in the workplace. (We use the term "target language use (TLU) domain" for these contexts. TLU domain is defined on page 65.) In situations like these, if the learning objectives of the language course are aimed at preparing students to use language outside of the classroom, then we should be able to base the content of our assessment on the content of the language course. If, for example, the institution is using a content-based instruction or content and language integrated learning approach to language teaching, then the content of the language class will be integrated with the content of the academic class. In this case, the language teacher and the academic content teacher may want to collaborate to develop classroom-based assessments that reflect the integrated content of the language class. Our students may also be learning the language because it is needed for their future academic or professional careers. In many countries, for example, the language that is taught in secondary school may be "academic" in that it is aimed at preparing students for university studies. In this case, the content of the language course is likely to be based, in part, on the kind of language our students will need in their university studies. In other situations, the language class may be aimed at preparing students for a professional career. In this case, the content of the language course may focus on language for specific purpose instruction, so that the content of the language classroom can be used as a basis for developing classroom-based assessments. Thus, in the vast majority of situations, even though our students may need to use the language outside of the language class, we will use the content of the language class itself as the source of our ability definitions.

Defining the areas of language ability to be assessed: Meaningfulness

After we have identified and described the source for our ability definitions, we need to define the areas of language ability we intend to assess with reference to the contexts in which our students need to use language. This will help assure that our interpretations will be meaningful to students and other stakeholders.

> ➤ **Meaningfulness** is the degree to which the intended interpretation 1) provides stakeholders with information about the ability to be assessed and 2) conveys this information in terms that they can understand and relate to.

To help assure the meaningfulness of our interpretations we need to do the following:

1 Define the areas of language ability we want to assess and describe the source of our ability definition:

   a using terms that we, the test developer and user, will understand,
      e.g. specific terms used in the textbook or by the teacher

   b using terms that other stakeholders, such as parents/guardians, will understand.

When we define the areas of language ability to be assessed and describe the source of this definition, we may need to use different terms and phrasings, depending on the audience. Thus, for ourselves, as test developers, we may use technical terms such as, "ability to recognize and comprehend paragraph-level cohesive markers in a written text", "control of rhetorical organization in writing a three-paragraph essay", or "effective use of conversational markers and appropriate register in speaking", as these will provide the level of detail we will need to create assessment tasks. For our students, we will most likely use the terminology that is in the textbook or that we have used in class. For other audiences, such as parents/guardians, however, terms such as these may not be understandable, so that we may use more common terms such as, "ability to read and comprehend paragraphs of written texts", "ability to write a well-organized essay", or "ability to participate in a spoken conversation".

We want to point out that there is no single "correct" way to define the ability to be assessed. In the Examples in Part IV, we have not always used exactly the same terms or phrases to define the same ability in different examples. For instance, in Example 1 we define the ability as "using accurate grammar, vocabulary and pronunciation in speaking", while in Example 3 we define it as "using correct grammar and vocabulary and accurate pronunciation in spoken language". In each example, the ability to be assessed is defined in a way that will be understandable to the stakeholders. Therefore, when you define the ability to be assessed for your own assessments, it is not necessary to use the same wording as in the Examples in Part IV. What is important is that you define the ability to be assessed using words and phrases that are appropriate to your own specific situation.

2 Make sure that the areas of language ability that are assessed by the assessment tasks adequately represent the areas of language ability in either the course content or that students need in their TLU domains.

Even though we may carefully define the areas of language ability we want to assess and describe the sources of these ability definitions, we must also make sure that the tasks we include in the assessment adequately represent or cover these. Adequate or representative coverage of the content to be assessed is a particular concern when the content domain is an entire course of instruction. This is because it is seldom practical to assess every learning objective in a course of instruction, or every area of language ability that may be needed in students' TLU domains. For example, in any given language course, there will most likely be a large number of different learning objectives, each focusing on a specific area of language ability. In most situations, the time and resources that are available for developing and using the assessment will not be enough for us to assess all of these learning objectives. We therefore must select which ones to include in the assessment. When we do this, we must try our best to make sure that the areas of language ability we include are representative of the learning objectives in the course content.

How should we assess? Assessment tasks

When we use an assessment, we are not really interested in how our students perform on the assessment itself. What we are interested in is the information that their assessment performance provides us about their ability to use language, or to perform language use tasks in contexts beyond the assessment itself. That is, we want our interpretations about language ability to extend or generalize to one or more TLU domains beyond the assessment itself.

➤ A **target language use (TLU) domain** is a specific context outside the assessment itself in which students need to perform language use tasks.

Different students may have different TLU domains and any given student may have more than one TLU domain.

An important way to help assure that our interpretations generalize beyond the assessment is to develop and use assessment tasks that correspond to TLU tasks.

➤ A **target language use (TLU) task** is a language use task that students may need to perform in one or more of their TLU domains.

Generalizability of interpretations

We describe the TLU domains of our test takers and the TLU tasks from these to help assure that our interpretations will be generalizable.

➤ **Generalizability** is the degree to which the assessment-based interpretations apply or extend to our students' TLU domains.

To help assure the generalizability of our interpretations, we need to do the following:

- identify and describe the TLU domain(s) of our students
- identify and describe the TLU tasks that our students need to perform
- select TLU tasks that we can use as a basis for creating assessment tasks.

Identifying TLU domains and TLU tasks

For classroom-based language assessments, the primary TLU domain to which we want our interpretations of our students' language ability to generalize is the language classroom itself. In the language classroom, we present our students with a wide variety of learning tasks. Each of these tasks can potentially serve as a basis for developing an assessment task. For example, if we engage our students in a short oral interaction, we can describe this task and then use this description for developing assessment tasks that are similar to this task.

In many situations, there are also contexts outside of the language class in which our students will need to use the language. These are the TLU domains that we discussed on page 60 as possible sources of ability definitions. If our class is intended to prepare students to use the language in other TLU domains, then the content of the course and the kinds of language use tasks we present to our students are likely to be based on those needed in these other TLU domains. For example, if our students need to use the language in their academic classes, then tasks we use in the language class will be based, in part, on the TLU tasks in this TLU domain, and these can be used to develop assessment tasks. Or, if our class is aimed at preparing our students for jobs after they finish their schooling, the tasks we use in our class will reflect the kinds of TLU tasks they need to perform in the workplace, and these can be used as a basis for developing assessment tasks. The process of creating assessment tasks on the basis of TLU tasks is described in Chapters 8 and 9.

Impartiality of interpretations

When we use a language assessment, we want to be able to interpret our students' assessment records as indicators of their levels of language ability. However, as we mentioned earlier, students' performance on language assessments can be affected by many other factors, including their individual personal attributes and the characteristics of the assessment tasks themselves. If students' performance on the assessment tasks is affected by personal attributes such as age, ethnicity, native language, disabilities, prior familiarity with particular topical content, or with the formats of the assessment tasks, then our interpretations about their language ability are likely to be biased. If the assessment tasks include content that is topically, culturally, or linguistically inappropriate and may be offensive or cause anxiety to some students, then these tasks may be biased against some students. Similarly, if the formats of the assessment tasks are unfamiliar or too cognitively demanding for some students, then these tasks may be biased. Finally, we need to assure that our students are treated impartially in all aspects of the assessment procedure. Thus, we need to develop and use assessment tasks and assessment procedures that are unbiased, or impartial.

> **Impartiality** is the degree to which the format and content of the assessment tasks and all aspects of the administration of the assessment are free from bias that may favor or disfavor some students.

In order to help assure that your interpretations are impartial, you need to do the following:

- avoid content that may be offensive (topically, culturally, or linguistically inappropriate) for some students, and hence affect their performance
- avoid using task types or response formats that may be unfamiliar to some students and hence affect their performance
- make sure that all students are treated impartially during the assessment procedure.

Qualities of interpretations

The qualities of interpretations are provided in Figure 6.1 for easy reference.

> **Relevance** is the degree to which the intended interpretations provide the information the test user needs to make the decision.

> **Sufficiency** is the degree to which the intended interpretations provide enough information for the test user to make a decision.

> **Meaningfulness** is the degree to which the intended interpretations 1) provide stakeholders with information about the ability to be assessed and 2) convey this information in terms that they can understand and relate to.

> **Generalizability** is the degree to which the assessment-based interpretations apply or extend to our students' TLU domains.

> **Impartiality** is the degree to which the format and content of the assessment tasks and all aspects of the administration of the assessment are free from bias that may favor or disfavor some students.

Figure 6.1 Qualities of interpretations

Relating Claim 3 to Claims 1 and 2

The ability to be assessed needs to be relevant to the decisions to be made. These decisions, in turn, are determined by the intended consequences of using the assessment. The relationship between Claim 3 and Claims 1 and 2 is illustrated in Figure 6.2.

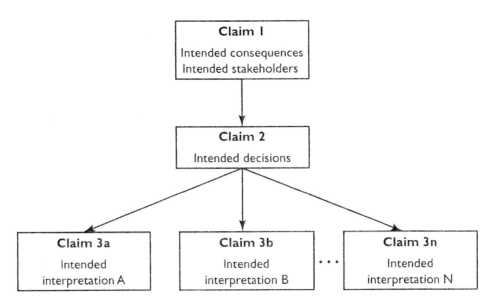

Figure 6.2 Relationships between Claim 3 and Claims 1 and 2

Figure 6.2 also illustrates a situation in which different intended interpretations can be used to make the same intended decisions. Suppose, for example, that the language class you are teaching includes speaking, listening, and reading. If you wanted to give an assessment at the end of the year to help you decide which students pass to the next grade, you would want to include assessments of all three of these areas of language ability.

Stating Claim 3

Claim 3 includes the following parts:

1 a descriptive label for the area(s) of language ability to be assessed (the descriptive label you use needs to be understandable for the intended audiences of stakeholders)

2 a list and description of the source(s) for the definition of the ability to be assessed

3 a list and description of students' TLU domains

4 the intended qualities of the interpretations.

The general version of Claim 3 is given as follows, with the parts in *italics* and the intended qualities in **bold.**

> General version of Claim 3: The interpretations *about the areas of language ability to be assessed* are relevant to the decisions to be made, **sufficient/not sufficient** to the decisions to be made, meaningful with respect to *the source(s) of the definition of the ability to be assessed*, **generalizable** to *the students' TLU domains*, and **impartial** to all students.

In stating Claim 3 for your own specific assessment, you will need to adapt the parts in italics in the general version of Claim 3. Here is an extract of stating Claim 3 for a specific assessment from Example 1 (see page 169).

Example of stating Claim 3

Setting:

(The setting is the same as in the example in Chapters 4 and 5.)

A teacher in an ESL/EFL classroom in a primary/elementary school needs to develop a classroom-based assessment for his beginning level students. This assessment will be used for two different purposes. One purpose is to make sure that the students who pass the grade are prepared for instruction at the next level. In order to do this, the teacher will use the results of this assessment, along with other assessments given during the course of the school year, to make summative decisions about which students will pass to the next grade. The second purpose is to help his students improve their speaking and to improve his teaching. In order to do this, the teacher will also use the results of this assessment to make formative decisions about his teaching and to provide feedback to his students. The assessment will be based on a unit of instruction in the course, and this is one task from the assessment, in which students describe animals from pictures by speaking.

Claim 3: Intended interpretations

The interpretations about three aspects of students' speaking ability—accurate grammar, vocabulary, and pronunciation—are relevant to the formative and summative decisions to be made. The interpretations are sufficient for the low-stakes formative decisions to be made, but not sufficient for the high-stakes summative decisions. These summative decisions will be made on the basis of this assessment and other classroom assessments that will be given during the course of instruction. The interpretations are meaningful with respect to the content of the course and of the current lesson, generalizable to the current language class, and are impartial to all students.

Activity 6.1

For the assessment outlined in the setting, state Claim 3 following the example of stating Claim 3 on page 69.

Setting:

A teacher in an ESL/EFL classroom in a secondary school or university needs to develop a classroom assessment for her advanced level students. This assessment will be used for one purpose. She wants to make sure that the students who pass the grade are prepared for instruction in the next grade. In order to do this, the teacher will use the results of this assessment, along with other assessments given during the course of the school year, to make summative decisions about which students will pass to the next grade. The assessment will be based on a unit of instruction in the course and this is one task from the assessment, in which students read a written text with gapped sentences and then choose the correct sentences from a list that best fit in the gaps.

Claim 3: Intended interpretations

_____

_____

_____

_____

_____

Photocopiable © Oxford University Press

(Answers to this activity can be found in Example 2 on page 183.)

Activity 6.2

Think of an assessment that you have used or that you need to develop. Describe the setting for this assessment and state Claim 3, following the example of stating Claim 3 on page 69.

Setting:

_____

_____

_____

_____

_____

Claim 3: Intended interpretations

_____

_____

_____

_____

_____

Photocopiable © Oxford University Press

Providing backing for Claim 3

As we discussed in Chapter 3, it will be necessary to provide some backing to support the claims in your AUA. For Claim 3, the backing will be aimed at assuring stakeholders that the interpretations are relevant, sufficient, meaningful, generalizable, and impartial. Backing that can be provided for Claim 3 might include, for example:

- Relevance and sufficiency (for high-stakes decisions): notes from meetings with decision makers during the assessment development process about the interpretations that will be relevant for making the decisions; notes from follow-up studies or meetings with decision makers on how helpful the interpretations actually are for making the decisions; reports on the results of including additional assessments or assessment tasks.

- Meaningfulness: documentation of the assessment development procedures that were followed; relevant course materials; analysis showing the links or articulation between specific assessment tasks and course content or TLU tasks.

- Generalizability: analysis of the TLU domain and the characteristics of TLU tasks; independent expert judgment about the degree of correspondence between the characteristics of assessment tasks and those of TLU tasks; students' perceptions of the degree of correspondence between assessment tasks and TLU tasks.

- Impartiality: results of bias reviews of assessment tasks; surveys of students.

Some possible backing for the example of stating Claim 3

Relevance and sufficiency:

- teacher meets with ESL/EFL teachers in the current and next levels during the development of the assessment to discuss the interpretations of speaking ability that will be relevant for making the decisions about which students will pass the course

- teacher conducts follow-up meetings with these ESL/EFL teachers on how useful the interpretations actually were in making these decisions.

Meaningfulness:

- teacher provides documentation of relevant instructional materials, e.g. course syllabus, textbook, teaching notes, instructional activities, and lists of the learning objectives of the course, with the specific assessment tasks that are linked to these

- teacher collects feedback from students and other relevant stakeholders about their understanding of the areas of speaking ability to be assessed.

Generalizability:

- teacher provides an analysis of the administrative procedures and task characteristics (TCs) of the instructional tasks in the current classroom
- teacher compares the administrative procedures and TCs of these instructional tasks with those of the assessment tasks
- teacher collects feedback from students and fellow teachers about the degree of correspondence between target language use (TLU) tasks and assessment tasks.

Impartiality:

- teacher carefully reviews the assessment tasks for possible sources of bias
- teacher asks fellow teachers to review the assessment tasks for possible sources of bias
- teacher collects feedback from students about assessment tasks that they felt were possibly biased.

Activity 6.3   List the kinds of backing you might need to provide for the assessment in Activity 6.1 (on page 70).

_____

_____

_____

_____

_____

Photocopiable © Oxford University Press

(Answers to this activity can be found in Example 2 on page 183.)

Activity 6.4   List the kinds of backing you might need to provide for the assessment in Activity 6.2 (on page 70).

_____

_____

_____

_____

Photocopiable © Oxford University Press

7 ASSESSMENT RECORDS: HOW CAN WE RECORD OUR STUDENTS' ASSESSMENT PERFORMANCE?

When we give a classroom-based assessment, there are typically many aspects of the assessment procedure and assessment tasks that can differ. We might administer the assessment to individual students or to pairs or groups of students. We might administer it at the beginning, in the middle, or at the end of a unit of instruction (e.g. a class period, term or semester, or year). Or, without realizing it, we might allow our students a little more or a little less time to take the assessment from one administration to the next. Have you ever thought about whether and how these differences in the way the assessment is administered might affect students' performance?

The assessment tasks we give to our students can also differ in many ways. The input or the material that students need to process and respond to may differ across assessment tasks: the input may be longer in some tasks than in others, the language used in some tasks may be more complex than in other tasks, or tasks may differ in their topical content. In a reading assessment, for example, students might be given several different written passages to read. Some of these passages might be longer than others, some might include language that is more complex, in terms of grammar, vocabulary, and cohesion, than others, and the passages might be about different topics. The way students are expected to respond to the assessment task can also vary: for some tasks they may select an answer from several choices, while for other tasks they may speak or write their answers.

Have you ever thought about how these differences in the assessment tasks and how students are expected to respond to these might affect their performance? If students perform differently on different tasks because of differences in the tasks, rather than because they are at different levels of ability, how does this affect their assessment records? How will this affect the interpretations we make about their levels of ability?

The way we record or score students' responses can also differ. For selected response tasks such as multiple-choice or matching, even though we may use a scoring key, we, as human beings, can make mistakes in the way we use this when scoring many different assessments. For assessment tasks that require students to *produce* some language, such as short answer questions, or an oral assessment or a written exam, we need to read or listen to the language that students produce in order to record their performances on tasks such as these. When we do this, do we always pay attention to the same features of the language that students produce? Are we ever influenced by features of their answers that may not necessarily be related to the area of language ability we want to assess? If different teachers score the answers, do they differ in the criteria they use to score the responses? For example, does one teacher focus primarily on correct grammar and vocabulary, while another pays more attention to the content?

In this chapter, we discuss Claim 4 of an assessment use argument (AUA), which is about the assessment records you, as a test developer and test user, will arrive at on the basis of students' performance on the assessment. We first discuss the assessment development questions that Claim 4 addresses and the considerations that you need to make in answering these. In particular, we discuss consistency and the considerations you need to make in order to assure that the assessment records you arrive at are as consistent as possible. We then describe the process of stating Claim 4, including the parts of the claim, the general version of the claim, and how you will adapt this for a particular assessment. Next, we provide a concrete example of a classroom-based assessment to illustrate this process. Finally, we discuss the kinds of backing that can be collected to support Claim 4.

Assessment development questions for Claim 4

In stating Claim 4, there are two questions you need to answer:

1 What kind(s) of assessment records—descriptions, scores, or grades or marks— do I need?
   • What kind of assessment record will be most appropriate for the intended uses of my assessment?

2 What is the intended quality of the assessment records I will use?
   • What are the potential sources of inconsistency for my assessment?
   • What can I do to minimize these sources of inconsistency?

Assessment records

As indicated in Chapter 2, we will arrive at assessment records from the students' assessment performance.

➢ **Assessment performance** is what students do in response to an assessment task. These responses might be actions, marks on an answer sheet, or samples of writing or speaking, or any combination of these.

➢ An **assessment record** is a written or verbal description or a score that is assigned to a student's performance on an assessment task.

➢ A **score** is an assessment record that is reported as a number or a letter. A score can be reported in different ways, for example, as the number of correct responses, a rating, a percentage, or a grade or a mark (e.g. A, B, C, or 1, 2, 3).

The specific ways in which we arrive at assessment records—descriptions or scores—will be specified in the recording or scoring method for the assessment tasks we create and use. (See Chapter 12 for a discussion of scoring students' assessment performance.)

Identifying the types of assessment records we need

There are two types of assessment records: a written or verbal description and a score. The type of assessment record we need will depend on the intended use of the assessment. In general, when we intend to use an assessment primarily for low-stakes formative decisions, the most appropriate type of assessment record will be written or verbal. This might include comments on the students' performance with feedback indicating areas in which their performance meets expectations and areas in which they can improve. For example, if a teacher uses a short quiz at the end of a lesson as a way to collect feedback on his teaching, as well as to provide feedback to his students, then he would most likely give the students comments and feedback, either verbal or written, on their assessment performance. The teacher might also give his students scores for such an assessment, in order to provide them with general feedback on how well they have achieved the learning objectives of the lesson as a whole. We would note that such scores can provide only general feedback and cannot give the kind of detailed and focused feedback that can be provided by a verbal or written assessment record.

When we intend to use an assessment primarily for medium- to high-stakes summative decisions, a score, a set of scores, or a grade or mark is most likely to be the most appropriate kind of assessment record to report. For example, for an assessment given at the end of a school year to make decisions about which students will pass on to the next grade in school, the most appropriate kind of assessment record would be a score, typically reported as a grade or mark. This is for several reasons. First, an assessment such as this is likely to cover a large area of content, so that there might not be sufficient information from the students' performance to provide diagnostic feedback on specific learning objectives. Second, because the decisions to be made come at the end of the instructional period, students are less likely to be able to use verbal or written feedback to improve their learning. Finally, in the vast majority of schools with which we are familiar, teachers are required, by either the school regulations or the administrators, to give assessments that are scored so that they can give percentage scores or grades or marks to their students at the end of the school year.

Quality of the assessment records

When we give an assessment and arrive at an assessment record, we want to be sure that a student's performance will yield essentially the same assessment record, irrespective of when, where, or how the assessment is administered, and irrespective of which particular assessment tasks they are given. In other words, we want our assessment records to be consistent across different aspects of the assessment procedure and different assessment tasks.

Consistency

> **Consistency** is the degree to which students' performances on different assessments (e.g. different administrations, different tasks, and different scorers/raters) of the same area of language ability yield essentially the same assessment records.

Although we will do our best to make sure that the assessment records are consistent, it is essential for us to understand that no assessment record, not even if it is a score, is perfectly consistent. This is because in every assessment situation there are many potential sources of *inconsistency*. These include differences in the way the assessment is administered, differences in the assessment tasks themselves, and differences in how students' performances are reported. For example, in an assessment of listening, if the tasks are read aloud to students, different administrators might read these at different speeds, with different clarity, or with different pronunciation or intonation. Different kinds of test tasks, for example, multiple-choice, short answer, oral presentation, or written composition, can affect students' performance. Differences in the way the students' performances are reported or scored (for example, verbal or written feedback, scoring key, and ratings) are also a potential source of inconsistency.

In order to help assure the consistency of your assessment records, you need to do two things:

1 identify the specific possible sources of inconsistency for your particular assessment

2 specify the ways in which you will try to minimize the effects of these sources of inconsistency on your assessment records.

Identifying possible sources of inconsistency

1 Inconsistencies in the way the assessment is administered:

   a at different times

   b to different groups of students

   c by different teachers.

2 Inconsistencies across different assessment tasks:

   a in the types of assessment tasks (e.g. short answer, completion, oral response, written response)

   b in the input—or information—students need to process and respond to across different assessment tasks of the same task type:

     i in the length

     ii in the language (e.g. grammar, vocabulary, organization)

     iii in the topical content.

Because of these inconsistencies across different assessment tasks, a score based on a single assessment task is not likely to be very consistent. When the assessment record consists of a score, then the size of the sample of the students' performance we obtain in the test can affect the consistency of scores. In general, the larger the sample of performance we obtain, the more consistent our scores will be. A score based on a single assessment task gives us only a small sample of performance, and is thus not likely to be very consistent. This is of particular concern with tests used for medium- to high-stakes decisions, which is why these tests typically include more than one assessment task. (Consistency of test scores is discussed in detail in Chapter 12.)

3 Inconsistencies in how we score student's assessment performance:

   a in how the scoring criteria and procedures for arriving at a score are followed (e.g. the teacher might be overly influenced by one student's high performance on one area of language ability, and give him a high score on others as well, even though he might not be as high in these aspects)

   b in how responses rated (e.g. oral or written responses):

      i in the ratings of the same rater

         a) at different times

         b) for different tasks

         c) for different students

      ii in the ratings of different raters.

Minimizing the effects of sources of inconsistency

It is not possible to completely eliminate the effects of the various sources of inconsistency in an assessment. However, we can *minimize* the effects of these sources of inconsistency by doing the following:

1 Clearly specify the procedures for administering the assessment. Then make sure that the assessment is always administered in the same way at different times, with different groups of students, and by different teachers. (Procedures for administering assessments are discussed in detail in Chapter 11.)

2 Prepare specifications or an assessment task template for each assessment task type. Make sure that all tasks that are developed follow this template. (Procedures for developing assessment task templates are discussed in Chapter 8.) Include enough assessment tasks in the assessment to obtain scores that are consistent.

3 Clearly specify the scoring method for each assessment task type. Make sure that the scoring method—including a scoring key or rating scale—is followed consistently. (Procedures for scoring students' performance are discussed in Chapter 12.)

4 If raters score the assessment:

    a develop clear and understandable rating scales

    b train raters in the use of these rating scales if there will be multiple raters

    c periodically monitor ratings for consistency.

5 Include a sufficient number of assessment tasks in the assessment to arrive at scores that are consistent.

Stating Claim 4

Claim 4 includes the following parts:

1 the type(s) of assessment records you intend to obtain

2 the potential sources of inconsistency in the assessment procedure and assessment tasks

3 the different groups of students for whom the assessment is intended.

The general version of Claim 4 is given as follows, with the parts in *italics*:

> General version of Claim 4: The *assessment records* are consistent across *different aspects of the assessment administration*, *different assessment tasks* and *different assessors*, and across *different groups of students*.

In stating Claim 4 for your own specific assessment, you will need to adapt the parts in italics in the general version of Claim 4. Here is an extract of stating Claim 4 for a specific assessment from Example 1.

Example of stating Claim 4

Setting:

(The setting is the same as in the example in Chapters 4, 5, and 6.)

A teacher in an ESL/EFL classroom in a primary/elementary school needs to develop a classroom-based assessment for his beginning level students. This assessment will be used for two different purposes. One purpose is to make sure that the students who pass the grade are prepared for instruction at the next level. In order to do this, the teacher will use the results of this assessment, along with other assessments given during the course of the school year, to make summative decisions about which students will pass to the next grade. The second purpose is to help his students improve their speaking and to improve his teaching. In order to do this, the teacher will also use the results of this assessment to make formative decisions about his teaching and to provide feedback to his students. The assessment will be based on a unit of instruction in the course, and this is one task from the assessment, in which students describe animals from pictures by speaking.

Administrative procedures for assessment task:

The assessment takes place during a class period. It is given as a paired speaking activity between two students, with the teacher observing and listening, in a "Speaking Corner" of the classroom. The teacher calls the first pair of students to be assessed and explains the assessment task to make sure that the students understand the procedure. The teacher gives the first student a picture of an animal and allows him or her to take half a minute to think about how he or she will describe it. Then the student has one minute to describe the animal to his or her partner. After the first student has finished, the teacher follows the same assessment procedure with the second student. While each student is speaking, the teacher scores his or her performance using the Rating Scale, and enters these scores on the Recording Form. The teacher also enters notes for feedback on the student's speaking on the Recording Form. At the end of the assessment, the two students return to the class. The teacher then calls the next pair of students for their assessment.

Scoring method:

The scoring method for this example is given in Table 7.1.

Scoring method
    <u>Criteria</u>: (See the Rating Scale in Table 7.2.)
    For each aspect: exceeds expectations – 3; meets expectations – 2; needs
        improvement – 1
    <u>Score reported</u>: total score = accurate grammar + accurate vocabulary +
        accurate pronunciation
    <u>Procedures</u>: the teacher listens to individual students' responses and enters a
        score for each aspect of speaking in the Rating Scale for each student. The
        teacher then adds up the scores to arrive at a total score and enters this on
        the Recording Form. The teacher also enters written feedback on the student's
        speaking on the Recording Form. This is given back to the students in the next
        lesson.

Table 7.1 Scoring method

Explanatory note: The teacher rates students' performances on this task using the Rating Scale on the Recording Form in Table 7.2. In this example, the Rating Scale is given in the four columns to the left, with the aspects of speaking to be assessed specified in the first column. The descriptors of the three scale levels are given in the next three columns to the right.

In deciding which level to rate a student's speaking, the teacher needs to consider two things: 1) the specific learning objectives that are being assessed and 2) the level of speaking that he or she believes demonstrates that the student has *minimally* achieved these learning objectives. If the student's speaking is at this level, the rating is "meets expectations – 2". If the student's speaking is below this level, then the rating is "needs improvement – 1". If the student's performance is above this level, then the rating is "exceeds expectations – 3".

Recording Form

Assessment task: Speaking, describing the physical characteristics of an animal

Student name: _____   Date: _____

Student paired with: _____

Animal picture: _____

Rating Scale: Aspect of speaking	Needs improvement 1	Meets expectations 2	Exceeds expectations 3	Feedback on student's speaking
Accurate grammar				
Accurate vocabulary (especially adjectives)				
Accurate Pronunciation				

Total score: _____

Table 7.2 Recording Form

Claim 4: Assessment records

The scores from the speaking assessment are consistent across different times and days of administration and across different administrations to different groups of students. Students' scores are consistent across the pictures of different animals and different pairs of students. Students' performances are scored consistently by the teacher, according to the Rating Scale. The possible sources of inconsistency for this assessment are listed in Table 7.3.

Possible sources of inconsistency in scores
1 Inconsistencies in the administration of the assessment • different times or days of administration • different administrations to different pairs of students • different administrations to different groups of students
2 Inconsistencies across different assessment tasks • different animals in the pictures • differing amounts of detail in the pictures • differences between the students who make up the pair
3 Inconsistencies in how students' performances are scored • different applications of the Rating Scale from one student to the next • different applications of the Rating Scale from one pair to the next

Table 7.3 Possible sources of inconsistency in scores

Activity 7.1

For the following assessment, state Claim 4, following the Example of stating Claim 4 on page 78. Then fill in the table with the possible sources of inconsistency.

Setting:

A teacher in an ESL/EFL classroom in a secondary school needs to develop a classroom assessment for one purpose. He wants to make sure that the students who pass the grade are prepared for instruction at the next level. In order to do this, the teacher will use the results of this assessment, along with other assessments of other skills, to make summative decisions about which students will pass to the next grade. The assessment will be based on a unit of instruction in the course. This is one task from the assessment in which the students listen to four different speakers talking about the best times of their lives.

Administrative procedures for the assessment task:

The assessment takes place during one class period in the classroom. The teacher explains the assessment at the beginning of the class period. The assessment is administered to the class as a group, with students working individually. Students are given an answer sheet, which is a table with the speakers' names and blanks for information that each speaker mentions in his or her talk. Students then listen to an audio recording with four short talks by four different speakers. Then the students are given three minutes to write short answers in the blanks for each speaker. The students listen to the interviews again and are given three minutes to correct their answers.

Scoring method:

Students' answers are scored according to the amount of correct information provided. The Scoring Key is given in Table 7.4.

Scoring Key:

What was the best moment of his or her life?		Points
Mark	birth, daughter	I point each (2 points total)
Jenny	pass(ed) driving test	I point
Peter	got job	I point
Isabel	retire(d)	I point
Why was this the best moment of his or her life?		
Mark	first moments, amazing	I point each (2 points total)
Jenny	felt/was free	I point
Peter	brilliant job	I point
Isabel	having fun	I point
	Total points	10

Table 7.4 Scoring Key

Claim 4: Assessment records

_____

_____

_____

_____

The possible sources of inconsistency for this assessment are given in the following table.

Possible sources of inconsistency in scores
I Inconsistencies in the administration of the assessment
2 Inconsistencies across different assessment tasks
3 Inconsistencies in how students' performances are scored

Photocopiable © Oxford University Press

(Answers to this activity can be found in Example 5 on page 213.)

Activity 7.2	Think of an assessment that you have used or that you need to develop. Following the Example of stating Claim 4 on page 78, describe the setting, the assessment task, and the scoring method for this assessment. Then state Claim 4 and fill in the table with the possible sources of inconsistency.

Setting:

_____

_____

_____

_____

Assessment task:

_____

_____

_____

_____

Scoring method:

_____

_____

_____

_____

Claim 4:

_____

_____

_____

_____

The possible sources of inconsistency for this assessment are given in the following table.

Possible sources of inconsistency in scores
1　Inconsistencies in the administration of the assessment
2　Inconsistencies across different assessment tasks
3　Inconsistencies in how students' performances are scored

Photocopiable © Oxford University Press

Providing backing for Claim 4

As we discussed in Chapter 3, it will be necessary to provide some backing to support the claims in our AUA. For Claim 4, you need to assure stakeholders that the assessment records are consistent. You will do this by providing backing to show that the relevant sources of inconsistency are minimized. Backing that can be provided for Claim 4 might include, for example:

- Consistency in assessment administration: *Documentation*: specification of administrative procedures to be followed (e.g. "Notes for assessment administrators" or "Assessment administration manual"); notes from administering the assessment or from observing administrations of the assessment; feedback from students; *Backing that is collected*: results of appropriate analyses to estimate consistency of scores across different administrations of the test.

- Consistency in assessment tasks: *Documentation*: task specifications for assessment tasks, procedures for creating assessment tasks from task specifications; notes on analyses of how well assessment tasks follow task specifications; *Backing that is collected*: results of appropriate analyses to estimate consistency of scores.

- Consistency in recording students' performance:

  o Criteria and procedures: *Documentation*: scoring criteria and procedures for scoring

  o Raters: *Documentation*: rating scales and instructions for raters; documentation of procedures followed to train different raters; *Backing that is collected*: results of appropriate analyses to estimate rater consistency.

For discussions of backing that is collected to estimate consistency, see Bachman (2004) and Carr (2011) in *Suggestions for further reading* (page 284).

Some possible backing for the Example of stating Claim 4

The possible sources of inconsistency and possible backing that can be provided to assure the consistency of the assessment records are given in Table 7.5.

Possible sources of inconsistency	Possible backing to assure consistency
1 Inconsistencies in the administration of the assessment • *different times or days of administration* • *different administrations to different pairs of students* • *different administrations to different classes of students*	• *Documentation: administrative procedures to be followed.* • *Teacher's notes from administering the assessment at different times during the class period, on different days, with different pairs of students, and with different classes of students*
2 Inconsistencies across different assessment tasks • *different animals in the pictures* • *differing amounts of detail in the pictures* • *differences between the students who make up the pair*	• *Documentation: task specifications for the pictures to be used in the assessment* • *Teacher's notes on any differences that were observed in how different pictures may have affected students' performances* • *Teacher's notes on how the attributes of students who were paired may have affected their performances*
3 Inconsistencies in how students' performances are scored • *different applications of the Rating Scale from one student to the next* • *different applications of the Rating Scale from one pair to the next*	• *Documentation: Rating Scale, Recording Form, and instructions for scoring* • *Teacher's notes on how the Rating Scale may have been applied differently from one student to the next or across pairs of students.*

Table 7.5 Possible backing to assure the consistency of scores in the example

Activity 7.3

Following the example given in Table 7.5, list the kinds of backing you might need to provide for each possible source of inconsistency for the assessment in Activity 7.1 (on page 81).

Possible sources of inconsistency	Possible backing to assure consistency
1 Inconsistencies in the administration of the assessment	
2 Inconsistencies across different speakers	
3 Inconsistencies in how students' performances are scored	

Photocopiable © Oxford University Press

(Answers to this activity can be found in Example 5 on page 213.)

Activity 7.4

List the kinds of backing you might need to provide for each possible source of inconsistency for the assessment in Activity 7.2 (on page 83).

Possible sources of inconsistency	Possible backing to assure consistency
1 Inconsistencies in the administration of the assessment	
2 Inconsistencies across different speakers	
3 Inconsistencies in how students' performances are scored	

Photocopiable © Oxford University Press

PART III: APPLYING THIS APPROACH IN YOUR CLASSROOM

In Part III, we describe procedures that can be used to develop assessment tasks based on the assessment use argument (AUA) described in Part II. In Chapter 8, we discuss procedures for developing an assessment task template, which links the assessment tasks to the AUA. In Chapter 9, we describe how to create multiple assessment tasks from a single assessment task template, while in Chapter 10 we describe how to combine individual assessment tasks to make a classroom-based assessment. In Chapter 11, we discuss considerations and procedures for administering classroom-based assessments, and in Chapter 12, we discuss procedures for scoring students' performance and reporting the results.

8 DEVELOPING ASSESSMENT TASK TEMPLATES

A classroom-based assessment typically consists of a number of language assessment tasks, or items. (We will generally use the term "task", but may sometimes use "item" with essentially the same meaning.) For example, if you wanted to assess your students' mastery of the vocabulary presented in a lesson, you could develop a sufficient number of assessment tasks to be able to determine whether your students have mastered the vocabulary presented in the lesson. Assessment tasks are the basic building blocks of an assessment. It is through assessment tasks that you will realize the qualities that you have stated in Claims 3 and 4 in the AUA. In order to justify your claim about the *meaningfulness* of your interpretations of ability, you will need to develop assessment tasks that engage the ability you want to assess. In order to justify your claim about the *generalizability* of interpretations, you will need to develop assessment tasks that correspond to target language use (TLU) tasks and that elicit performance that generalizes to them. In order to justify your claim about the *consistency* of assessment records, you will need to develop procedures for administering the assessment tasks and for scoring students' responses that will minimize sources of inconsistency. Finally, in developing assessment tasks, you must consider *practicality*, in terms of the resources that may be required to administer and use the tasks.

The key link between the claims you make in your AUA and the assessment tasks you develop and use is what we call an assessment task template, which includes detailed specifications for creating multiple assessment tasks. (We define "assessment task template" on page 98.) The process that you will follow in developing an assessment task template is to first identify a TLU task that engages the ability you want to assess. Then you will describe the activities and procedures to be followed in the task and the task characteristics (TCs) of that TLU task. ("Task characteristics" are defined on page 92.) In most cases, the TLU task itself will not be suitable as it is to use as an assessment task, so you will need to modify it. This modified task then becomes an assessment task template that you can use for creating multiple assessment tasks. This process is illustrated in Figure 8.1.

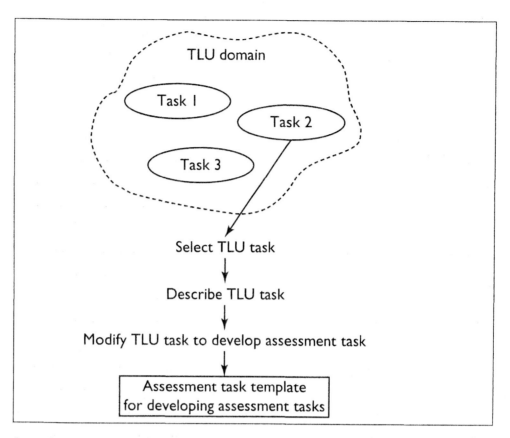

Figure 8.1 Process for creating assessment task templates (adapted from Bachman & Palmer, Language Assessment in Practice, Oxford University Press, p. 294.)

When you develop an assessment task, you need to keep several things in mind. The assessment task should:

- elicit performance that engages the ability to be assessed. This will help assure that your intended interpretations will be *meaningful.*

- correspond to TLU tasks. This will help assure that your intended interpretations are *generalizable.*

- avoid content that may be offensive (topically, culturally, or linguistically inappropriate) for some students; avoid using task types or response formats that may be unfamiliar to some students. This will help assure that your intended interpretations are *impartial.*

- provide assessment records that are *consistent.*

- be *practical* to develop, administer, and use in the classroom.

In this chapter, we discuss a process for creating assessment task templates that can be used to develop assessment tasks that will address considerations of meaningfulness, generalizability, impartiality, consistency, and practicality.

Here are the steps you will follow in developing assessment task templates:

1 Select a TLU task that might serve as a basis for developing assessment tasks.

2 Describe this TLU task.

3 Modify the TLU task to provide the basis for an assessment task template.

4 Develop a method for recording the students' performance for the assessment task template.

5 Evaluate the assessment task template in terms of assessment qualities of meaningfulness, generalizability, impartiality, consistency, and practicality.

With respect to practicality, we would point out that although developing an assessment task template may seem like a lengthy process, it does not need to be repeated for every assessment you develop. In Chapter 9, we discuss ways in which multiple assessments can be created from a single assessment task template.

Using TLU tasks to develop assessment task templates

Step 1: Selecting a TLU task

In Claim 3, you defined the area(s) of language ability you want to assess. This is the ability that you want your assessment tasks to engage. That is, you want your assessment task to elicit performance from students that you can interpret as evidence of the ability you want to assess. This will provide support for your claim about the meaningfulness of your interpretations. In Claim 3, you have also identified the TLU domain to which you want your interpretations of ability to generalize. By selecting a language use task from that TLU domain, you will provide support for your claim about the generalizability of your interpretations.

In step 1, you will provide:

a a short descriptive label for the TLU task

b a short descriptive label for the area of language ability that is engaged by the TLU task. (In most cases this will be the same label you have used in Claim 3, when you defined the ability to be assessed.)

In many situations, there may be several TLU tasks that are very similar, or that differ very little in their TCs.

Here is an extract of selecting a TLU task from Example 1 (see page 169).

Example of selecting a TLU task for a speaking assessment task

Step 1 TLU task selected for development of assessment task

1 Short descriptive label for TLU task: Describing animals orally in groups in the language classroom.

2 Areas of language ability the TLU task engages: Using accurate grammar, vocabulary, and pronunciation in speaking.

Step 2: Describing TLU tasks

In order to justify your claim to *generalizability*, you need to demonstrate that your assessment tasks correspond to TLU tasks. To determine how well your assessment tasks correspond to TLU tasks, you need to be able to describe these tasks. You will do this in two ways: describe the activities and procedures to be followed and describe the TCs of the TLU task.

Step 2: Describe the TLU task(s) that you have identified in Step 1. Describe:

a the activities and procedures to be followed

b the TCs of the TLU task.

Step 2a: Describing activities and procedures

Describing the activities and procedures of the TLU task is illustrated in Table 8.1.

Activities and procedures for the TLU task

1 Activities and procedures to be followed:

   a The teacher explains the speaking activity to the class.

      i Each group will get a picture of an animal to describe.

      ii Group members will describe parts of their animal orally to the class.

      iii The other students in the class will try to guess which animal the group has.

   b Students are arranged in groups of three to four.

   c The teacher gives each group a picture of an animal and tells the students not to show their picture to the other groups.

   d Students work on descriptions of animals in their groups, taking notes, as needed.

   e The teacher moves around and helps groups.

   f Each student in each group has about half a minute to present a part of their group's description orally to the class.

   g The other students in the class may ask questions after each presentation and guess the animal.

   h The teacher provides verbal feedback on the quality of the descriptions.

Table 8.1 Activities and procedures for TLU task

Step 2b: Describing the TCs of the TLU task

Whenever we use language, whether this is in the language classroom or in a TLU domain outside of the classroom, we perform many different kinds of language use tasks. If we think about the different kinds of language use tasks we perform, we realize that these tasks differ in many ways. For some language use tasks we may need to process the same kind of information, but might have to respond to this in very different ways. For example, in some situations, we might need to read a text and then tell someone what it is about, while in other situations, we may need to read a text and write some notes or a summary of it. Another way in which tasks can differ is in their topical content, or what they are about. Thus, the information to be processed might be a reading passage, and the content of the reading may differ from one passage to another. For example, if we were planning a trip, we might need to read different sources of information, some about the location and things to do, others about the weather, and others about places to stay. For other language use tasks, we may need to provide a spoken explanation to a group of individuals, such as our students, while in other situations we may engage in an oral interaction that requires both speaking and listening to another person. Thus, in order to describe language use tasks, we need to think of them not as single entities, but as bundles of features, or characteristics.

Assessment tasks are language use tasks, so they consist of sets of characteristics that can be used to describe them. In order to develop assessment tasks that correspond to TLU tasks, we need to be able to describe these tasks precisely enough to determine how closely the assessment task corresponds to the TLU task. We also need to specify the characteristics of our assessment task precisely enough to guide the creation of multiple assessment tasks that are consistent with these characteristics, or template.

In order to describe both TLU and assessment tasks precisely and to provide a template for developing assessment tasks, we can use a set of task characteristics (TCs).

➤ **Task characteristics (TCs)** are aspects or features of language use tasks that provide a way to describe the task with more precision than simply giving it a label.

Tasks that are very similar will share many TCs; tasks that are very different may share few, if any, TCs.

We can use three sets of TCs to systematically describe TLU tasks and assessment tasks: these TCs will make it possible for us to compare TLU and assessment tasks, in order to help us assure that our interpretations generalize to the TLU domain. The three sets of TCs are: the setting, the input, and the expected response. These are defined below.

1 **Setting**: the setting of a task consists of the circumstances under which the assessment takes place. The characteristics of the setting include:

   a the <u>physical circumstances</u> (e.g. arrangement of the classroom, how students are seated, equipment/materials)

   b the <u>participants</u> who will engage in the task (e.g. teacher and students, pairs or groups of students) c the <u>time of the task</u> (which part of the class period, and the amount of time the task requires).

2 Input: the input is any material contained in the task itself which students are expected to process and to which they are expected to respond. The characteristics of the input include:

a <u>Form</u>: this may be aural, visual, or both; language or non-language, or both.

   i Aural input may be either spoken language or non-language (sounds), or both.

   ii Visual input may be either written language or non-language (e.g. pictures, figures, charts, gestures, or physical actions), or both.

b <u>Language</u>: if the input is language, then the language is either the students' native language or the language to be assessed. This will also include a brief description of the language of the input (e.g. level of vocabulary, the grammar, and the length). In most situations, the language of the input will be the language to be assessed. However, in some situations, the language of the input may be the students' native language. For example, suppose we wanted to assess students' writing, and the input is a reading passage. If we are not sure whether the students' reading comprehension in the language to be assessed is sufficient, we may want to provide the input in their native language. Otherwise, their written responses may be affected by the fact that they did not understand the input. In other words, their responses might indicate as much about their reading as it does about their writing. In this case, we could not interpret their responses as evidence, only their writing. There are two reasons why we need to describe the language of the input:

   i This will help us assure that the language of the input in the assessment task is comparable to that in the TLU task, which will support our claim that the interpretation is generalizable.

   ii This will help us assure that the language that students need to process is consistent from one assessment task to another, which is related to our claim that the assessment records are consistent. For example, if the input of an assessment task were a reading passage, we would want to make sure that the reading passages for different tasks were comparable in the amount and kind of language used.

c <u>Topical content</u>: what the input is about.

3 Expected response: the expected response is the language or non-language performance we want to elicit from the students. The reason we call this "expected response" is that students do not always respond in the way we want them to. The characteristics of the expected response include:

a <u>Form</u>: this may be oral, visual, or both; language or non-language, or both.

   i Oral expected responses will be spoken language.

ii Visual expected responses will be either language (written) or non-language, e.g. drawing pictures, figures, charts, or physical actions such as gestures.

b <u>Language</u>: if the expected response is language, then the language is either the students' native language or the language to be assessed. This will also include a brief description of the characteristics of the language of the expected response, e.g. level of vocabulary, the grammar, and the length. In most situations, the language of the expected response will be the language to be assessed. There are three reasons why we need to describe the language of the expected response:

i We want students to produce language that we can evaluate or score. In order to score the student's language response, that response needs to demonstrate that the student is able to produce the kind of language that we have specified in the criteria for correctness in our scoring method. (See "Recording Method" below.) This is related to the meaningfulness of our interpretations.

ii We want the students to produce samples of the kind of language that they need to use in their TLU domain, which is related to the generalizability of our interpretations.

iii We want to assure that the language of the expected response is consistent from one task to another. For example, if the expected response were a short oral presentation, then we would want to make sure different students' responses were comparable in the amount and kind of language used.

c <u>Topical content</u>: what the expected response is about.

These TCs are summarized in Table 8.2. (A fourth set of TCs, the recording method, will apply only to assessment tasks and is described later on page 106.)

Setting	<u>Physical circumstances</u> (arrangement of the classroom, how students are seated, equipment/materials) <u>Participants</u> who engage in the task (e.g. teacher and student, pairs of students, groups of students) <u>Time of the task</u> (part of the class period and the amount of time the task requires)
Input	<u>Form</u> (aural, visual, or both; language, non-language, or both) <u>Language</u> (students' native language or the language to be assessed; quality and length of the language) <u>Topical content</u> (what the input is about)
Expected response	<u>Form</u> (oral, visual, or both; language, non-language, or both) <u>Language</u> (students' native language or the language to be assessed; quality and length of the language) <u>Topical content</u> (what the expected response is about)

Table 8.2 Summary of TCs

As discussed above, in Step 2a you will have described the activities and procedures to be followed in the TLU task. In Step 2b, you will describe the TCs of the TLU task. Table 8.3 is an extract from Example 1, illustrating describing the TCs of the TLU task (see page 176).

TLU Task: Speaking, describing animals in groups	
Areas of language ability the TLU task engages: using accurate grammar, vocabulary, and pronunciation in speaking.	
Setting	<u>Physical circumstances</u>: teacher in front of classroom; students in groups of 3–4 *Equipment/materials*: pictures of animals; paper and pencil <u>Participants</u>: teacher and students (young learners, beginning level) <u>Time of the task</u>: during the class; two class periods will be required
Input	<u>Form</u>: *Aural*: *Teacher*: description of the task, questions and comments *Students*: descriptions of animals and questions *Visual*: a picture of an animal for each group; words and phrases that the students may write on paper <u>Language</u>: English *Teacher*: short utterances describing and explaining, questions; simple grammar and vocabulary *Other students*: fairly short utterances describing their pictures; questions and answers; simple grammar and vocabulary *Length*: *aural*: short utterances; *visual*: short (single picture) <u>Topical content</u>: physical characteristics of animals
Expected response	<u>Form</u>: *Oral*: students' descriptions of the animals; students' questions; students' responses to teacher's and other students' questions *Visual*: words, phrases, and sentences students write on paper to support their speaking <u>Language</u>: English; short descriptive utterances, adjectives, and questions *Length*: about half a minute per student <u>Topical content</u>: physical characteristics of animals

Table 8.3   Task characteristics for the example TLU task

Activity 8.1

Here is a description of a TLU task. After reading it, complete the table with the TCs for this task, following the example given in Table 8.3.

1 TLU task selected for development of an assessment task: writing a letter of application for a job.

2 Areas of language ability the TLU task engages: task achievement – following the format of a formal letter application for a job, using appropriate range of grammar, vocabulary and cohesion.

3 Activities and procedures to be followed:

   a The teacher explains the writing activity to the class.

      i Students are arranged in groups of three to four.

      ii Students in groups write a letter of application for a job. This letter will follow the format of a formal letter of application that was discussed in class.

      iii Students are given a job description.

      iv Students decide on how to divide up the writing assignment in their groups.

   b Students work on the letter collaboratively in their groups, taking notes, as needed.

   c The teacher moves around and helps the groups.

   d Each group presents its letter orally to the class.

   e The other students in the class give feedback on the writing in the letter.

   f The teacher provides verbal feedback on the writing in the letter.

   g Students discuss the feedback in their groups and rewrite their letters in the next lesson, taking the feedback into consideration.

Setting	Physical circumstances: Participants: Time of the task:
Input	Form: Language: Topical content:
Expected response	Form: Language: Topical content:

Photocopiable © *Oxford University Press*

(Answers to this activity can be found in Example 8 on page 247.)

Step 3: Modifying a TLU task to develop an assessment task template

In virtually all situations, the TLU task itself will not be suitable for use as an assessment task. There are a number of reasons why we may need to modify TLU tasks to develop an assessment task.

- **The TLU task itself might not be practical to use as is as an assessment task.** A TLU task not may be practical to use as an assessment task if it requires too much time, special materials or equipment, or complicated procedures for administration or scoring. For example, asking students to write a term paper or make a long speech might not be practical because it requires too much time, while the procedures for playing a board game or preparing a meal together might not be practical to use for an assessment because this might require either special equipment or materials.

- **The TLU task itself cannot be used as is because it does not enable us to arrive at assessment records for *individual* students.** Suppose, for example, that a TLU task involves oral interactions and collaboration among students in groups, and we want to assess *individual* students' speaking ability. If we administer the assessment task to students in groups, it will be difficult to use for assessing individual students. This is because it might not be possible to distinguish each individual student's performance from the group's performance.

- **It might be necessary to give the assessment tasks in a secure way, so that students cannot share their answers or information about the assessment with other students either prior to or during the assessment.** When we need to obtain information about individual students' language ability, we need to be sure that each student's performance is based on his or her own level of ability and not on prior knowledge of the specific content of the assessment. This is particularly a concern in assessments that will be used to make medium to high-stakes decisions. For example, in the speaking assessment illustrated in Table 8.4, if the teacher wanted to make sure that students who have finished the assessment do not share their experience with their classmates, he or she would need to arrange to keep the other students from communicating with each other during the assessment process. In an assessment that is administered to a group of students at the same time, the test administrator would need to make sure that students do not share their answers with each other during the assessment.

- **The TLU task itself cannot be used as is because of the students' prior familiarity with the task's topical content.** We know that students' familiarity with the topical content of the input can affect their performance on a language assessment. For example, students who are familiar with the topical content of a reading passage may perform better than students who are not familiar with the topical content, even though they are at the same level of reading ability. Or, if all students are already familiar with the topical content of the assessment task, they may all perform well in part because of this, so that their performance reflects not only their language ability, but also their topical knowledge. It is for this reason that we generally do not want to use the same texts for assessment tasks that are used for instructional tasks.

For these reasons, you will need to modify the TLU task in some way in order to use it for creating assessment tasks. Like the TLU task, the modified task will consist of a set of TCs. These TCs of the modified task, along with a recording method, can be used as a specification, or assessment task template, for creating different assessment tasks. These assessment tasks will share many of the TCs in the assessment task template, but will also differ in specific ways. Creating multiple assessment tasks from a single assessment task template is discussed in Chapter 9. (A summary example of a complete assessment task template is provided in Appendix 2.)

➤ An **assessment task template** provides the basis for creating different assessment tasks that have many activities and procedures and TCs in common. It consists of 1) a set of activities and procedures to be followed in administering the assessment, 2) a set of TCs, and 3) a recording method.

Assessment tasks that are created from the same template will be consistent in their TCs and recording method.

In modifying a TLU task to develop a template for creating assessment tasks, you need to make sure that assessment tasks that are created from this template will:

- elicit performance that engages the ability to be assessed
- correspond to TLU tasks
- provide assessment records that are consistent
- be practical to develop, administer, and use in the classroom.

Therefore, when you modify a TLU task to develop a template for creating assessment tasks, you need to ask the following questions:

- How well will the assessment tasks elicit the ability I want to assess?
- How closely will the assessment tasks correspond to the TLU task?
- How consistent will the assessment records be?
- Will the assessment tasks be practical?

In Step 3 you will modify the TLU task that you have described in Step 2. You will proceed as follows:

1 TLU activities and procedures

   a specify the reasons for making the modifications to the TLU task

   b make the modifications to the TLU task.

2 TLU TCs

   a specify the reasons for making the modifications to the TLU TCs

   b make the modifications to the TLU task TCs.

Step 3a: Modifying the activities and procedures of the TLU task

Modifying the activities and procedures of the TLU task to create an assessment task template for the Example speaking assessment task is illustrated in Table 8.4. The TLU task is a collaborative group activity, and the teacher needs to obtain speaking scores for individual students. Thus, the reason these activities and procedures of the TLU task were modified was to make it possible to obtain speaking scores for individual students.

Description of the modified task: speaking individually, describing an animal from a picture, in pairs.

Areas of language ability to be assessed: using accurate grammar, vocabulary, and pronunciation in speaking.

I Activities and procedures to be followed

  a On the day before the assessment the teacher tells the students:

    i They will have an assessment of their speaking the next day.

    ii The purposes of the assessment are:

      a) to give each student a grade or mark that will count as part of his or her grade or mark for the school year

      b) to provide feedback to individual students about their speaking ability.

    iii The teacher will assign the students to pairs for the assessment.

    iv The test will be given individually to each student in the pair.

      a) One student in the pair will be given a picture of an animal that will be different from the ones they described in class. The other student cannot see this student's picture.

      b) The first student will be given half a minute to prepare his or her description.

      c) The first student will then have one minute to describe the animal in the picture to his or her partner. The other student will be asked to guess the animal. This will not be scored.

      d) Then the test will be given to the second student in the pair, following the same procedure as with the first student.

  b On the day of the assessment, the teacher assesses each student in each pair individually.

    i The teacher briefly explains the assessment task again.

    ii The teacher makes sure the students understand the procedure.

    iii The teacher calls the names of the students in the first pair.

    iv The teacher and these two students go to the Speaking Corner of the classroom.

    v The teacher shows the first student a picture of an animal.

    vi The first student takes half a minute to think about his or her description.

    vii Then the first student takes about one minute to describe the animal orally to his or her partner. The other student guesses the animal.

    viii The teacher scores the first student's performance using the Rating Scale on the Recording Form and also makes notes for feedback on the student's speaking using the Recording Form.

> ix The teacher then administers the assessment to the second student,
>   following the same procedure as with the first student.
> x   The teacher lets the two students go back to the class and calls the next pair
>   of students for the assessment.
> c During the next lesson after the assessment:
>   i   The teacher gives the students their Recording Forms with their scores and
>   written feedback.
>   ii The teacher gives the class general feedback on their areas of strength and
>   the areas in which they need to improve.
>   iii The teacher also provides suggestions for ways in which students can
>   improve their speaking.

Table 8.4 Activities and procedures for modified assessment task/assessment task template

In order to illustrate some reasons for making specific modifications to a TLU task, we first discuss the differences between the activities and procedures in the TLU task illustrated in Table 8.1 and the modified task illustrated in Table 8.4. If we compare the activities and procedures of the two tasks, we can see several differences:

- In the TLU task, the teacher explains the speaking activity to the whole class before starting the task. In the modified task, the teacher explains the assessment procedure to the entire class on the day before the assessment, and then explains it again to each pair of students before the assessment begins. This modification was made because the teacher needs to assure that each student has adequate and equal information about the procedures for administering the test (impartiality).

- In the TLU task, students work collaboratively, interacting with each other, taking notes, and interacting with the teacher. Individual students will have about half a minute each to speak. In the modified task each student in the pair has about half a minute to prepare for his or her description after seeing the picture he or she is to describe. The two students are not allowed to take notes, and each student has about one minute to speak. Students are kept apart, before and after the assessment. These modifications were made to assure that the assessment is administered in the same way to each student (consistency), to make it possible to provide a score for each individual student (meaningfulness) and to assure that students do not share their answers with each other during the time of the assessment (impartiality). Administering the assessment in pairs of students, rather than individually, requires less time (practicality).

- The pictures used in the TLU task and the modified task are different. This modification was made to assure that students' performance on the assessment reflected their speaking ability and not their prior familiarity with the specific animals in the pictures (meaningfulness).

- In the TLU task the students are given sufficient time to prepare their answers, so that the amount of preparation time may differ from one student to the next. In the modified task, each student is given only half a minute to prepare. This modification was made to assure that the assessment is administered in the same way to each student (consistency). It also requires less time to administer the assessment task than the TLU task (practicality).

Step 3b: Modifying the TCs of the TLU task

Modifying the TCs of the TLU task to develop an assessment task for Example 1 (see page 169) is illustrated in Table 8.5. The TLU task is a collaborative group activity, and the teacher needs to obtain speaking scores for individual students. Thus, the reason these TCs of the TLU task were modified to make it possible to obtain speaking scores for individual students.

Assessment task: Speaking individually, describing an animal from a picture, in pairs.	
Areas of language ability to be assessed: Using accurate grammar, vocabulary, and pronunciation in speaking	
Task characteristics	
Setting	<u>Physical circumstances</u>: the teacher with a pair of students in the Speaking Corner of the classroom *Equipment/materials*: pictures of animals; Recording Form, pen or pencil (for the teacher); table and three chairs for the teacher and students <u>Participants</u>: teacher and a pair students (young learners, beginning level) <u>Time of task</u>: during the class period; task requires more than one class period depending on the number of students
Input	<u>Form</u>: *Aural*: teacher's description of the task *Visual*: one picture per student of an animal that is different from the ones used in the TLU task <u>Language</u>: English *Teacher*: short spoken description and explanation; simple grammar and vocabulary *Length*: *aural*: short utterances; *visual*: short (single picture) <u>Topical content</u>: physical characteristics of animals
Expected response	<u>Form</u>: *Oral*: student's description of the animal in the picture *Visual*: (none) <u>Language</u>: English; short descriptive utterances, adjectives *Length*: about one minute per student; two minutes per pair of students <u>Topical content</u>: physical characteristics of animals

Table 8.5   TCs of the modified task/assessment task template

To illustrate some reasons for making specific modifications to a TLU task we also discuss the differences in the TCs of the TLU task illustrated in Table 8.3 and the modified task/assessment task template illustrated in Table 8.5. These differences are illustrated in Table 8.6. The differences in TCs are highlighted in grey.

	TLU Task: Speaking, describing animals in groups	Modified task/assessment task template: Speaking individually, describing an animal from a picture, in pairs
Setting	Physical circumstances: the teacher in front of classroom; students in groups of 3–4 Equipment/materials: pictures of animals; paper and pencils Participants: the teacher and students (young learners, beginning level) Time of the task: during the class period; two class periods will be required	Physical circumstances: the teacher with a pair of students in the Speaking Corner of the classroom Equipment/materials: pictures of animals; Recording Form, pen or pencil (for the teacher); table and three chairs for the teacher and students Participants: the teacher and a pair of students; (young learners, beginning level) Time of the task: during the class period; task requires more than one class period depending on the number of students
Input	Form: Aural: Teacher: description of the task, questions and comments Students: descriptions of animals and questions Visual: a picture of an animal for each group; words and phrases that the students may write on paper	Form: Aural: teacher's description of the task Visual: one picture per student of an animal that is different from the ones used in the TLU task
	Language: English Teacher: short utterances describing and explaining, questions, simple grammar and vocabulary Other students: fairly short utterances describing their pictures; questions and answers; simple grammar and vocabulary Length: aural: short utterances; visual: short (single picture) Topical content: physical characteristics of animals	Language: English Teacher: short spoken description and explanation; simple grammar and vocabulary Length: aural: short utterances; visual: short (single picture) Topical content: physical characteristics of animals

Expected response	Form: *Oral*: students' descriptions of the animals; students' questions; students' responses to teacher's and other students' questions *Visual*: words, phrases, and sentences students write on paper to support their speaking Language: English; short descriptive utterances, adjectives, and questions *Length*: about half a minute per student Topical content: physical characteristics of animals	Form: *Oral*: student's description of the animal in the picture *Visual*: (none) Language: English; short descriptive utterances, adjectives *Length*: about one minute per student; two minutes per pair of students Topical content: physical characteristics of animals

Table 8.6   Differences in TCs of TLU and modified task/assessment task template

If we compare the TCs of the two tasks we can see several differences. These are highlighted in grey in Table 8.6 and summarized as follows:

- Setting: The main difference in the setting is in the participants. In the TLU task, the teacher interacts with groups of students and the students interact with each other in their groups, and with other students. In the modified task, two students describe their pictures to each other. The teacher listens to each student's description in order to assess his or her individual performance. The equipment is also different between the two tasks. In the TLU task, students have paper and pencils to use for taking notes, while in the modified task, only the teacher has a pen or pencil for filling in the Recording Form.

- Input: There are several differences between the two tasks in the input. The input in the TLU task is much more extensive and varied than it is in the modified task, and includes both aural description, explanation, and questions from the teacher, as well as aural descriptions and questions from the other students. The pictures of animals in the modified task are different from the ones used in the TLU task. Finally, the visual input in the TLU tasks includes the notes that the students write in their groups to support their speaking, while in the modified task, the students do not take notes.

- Expected response: As with the input, there are several differences in the expected response between the two tasks. The expected response in the TLU task is more extensive and varied than it is in the modified task, and includes both the students' spoken questions and their spoken responses to the teacher's and other students' questions. It also includes the notes that the students write in their groups to support their speaking. In the TLU task, the amount of time each individual student has to speak is about half a minute, while in the modified task, each student is given one minute to speak.

At the same time, there are some important similarities between the two tasks:

- Setting: In both tasks the materials used include pictures of animals, the place is the classroom, and the time of the task is during the class period.

- Input: The input for both tasks includes the teacher's description of the task. The language of the teacher's input and the topical content, the physical characteristics of animals, are essentially the same for both tasks.

- Expected response: The expected response – a spoken description of an animal, is the same, as is the kind of language of the expected response. The topical content is also the same across the two tasks.

Activity 8.2

Here is a description of the activities and procedures for a modified task. After reading it, complete the table with the TCs for this task, following the example in Table 8.5.

1 Description of modified task: writing a formal letter of application for a job.

2 Areas of language ability to be assessed: task achievement—following the format of a formal letter of application for a job—using appropriate range of grammar, vocabulary, and cohesion.

3 Activities and procedures to be followed:

a The teacher explains the writing assessment to the class.

b Students will have the whole class period to complete their letter.

c The teacher reviews the Rating Scale with the students, reminding them to pay attention to the features of writing that are included in the Rating Scale.

d Students are given the writing prompt, and are allowed time to read this and ask clarification questions.

e Students work individually on their letters.

4 Assessment task:

Teacher's description of the task:

"Here's the prompt for your writing test." (The teacher gives students the writing prompt.) "Read it through and let me know if you have any questions." (Teacher allows time for students to read the prompt.) "Are there any questions?" (The teacher answers any clarification questions the students may have.) "You'll have 45 minutes to complete your letter. You may begin now."

Writing prompt:

"Suppose you have read the following job description in the newspaper:"

Summer job: Sales Assistant

If you are a motivated and outgoing person who is looking for a great summer job that offers flexible hours and good income, join our team at "The Market Place"! Working hours are Monday through Friday from 9.00 am–5.00pm. You will receive benefits such as discounts on merchandise and food.

Your duties will be to assist the sales manager in the following:

- Answering customers' queries about merchandise needs
- Offering recommendations based on customers' needs and interests
- Restocking inventory
- Processing cash and card payments
- Dealing with customer refunds
- Dealing with customer complaints

Please apply in writing to the Human Resources Department at: *The Market Place, 132 Baker Street, St Louis, MI, 63105*

"You would like to apply for this job. Write a letter of application (**150–200 words**) to the human resources department of the store. Use the same structure for your letter that we have been using in class. Include all the necessary information. Your letter will be scored according to the Rating Scale we discussed in class. You have **45 minutes** to complete your letter."

5 Task characteristics of the modified task/assessment task template:

Setting	Physical circumstances: Participants: Time of the task:
Input	Form: Language: Topical content:
Expected response	Form: Language: Topical content:

Photocopiable © Oxford University Press

(Answers to this activity can be found in Example 8 on page 249.)

Step 4: Developing a method for recording/scoring students' performance

In order to use the modified task as an assessment task template for creating assessment tasks, you will need to develop a method for recording the students' responses. This recording method will specify the type of assessment record. If the students' responses are to be scored, you will also need to specify a scoring method, the procedures for scoring, and the person who will score students' assessment performance. Step 4—specifying a recording method for the Example speaking assessment task—is illustrated in Table 8.7.

Recording method for assessment task	Assessment task: Speaking, describing an animal from a picture
	Types of assessment record: score and written feedback
	Aspects of ability: three aspects of speaking: use of accurate grammar, vocabulary (adjectives), and pronunciation
	Scoring method
	  Criteria: (See the Rating Scale in Table 8.8.)
	  For each aspect: needs improvement – 1; meets expectations – 2; exceeds expectations – 3
	  Score reported: total score = accurate grammar + accurate vocabulary + accurate pronunciation
	  Procedures: the teacher listens to individual students' responses and enters a score for each aspect of speaking in the Rating Scale for each student. The teacher then adds up the scores to arrive at a total score and enters this on the Recording Form. The teacher also enters written feedback on the student's speaking on the Recording Form. This is given back to the students during the next lesson.

Table 8.7   Recording method for example speaking assessment task

Specifying a scoring method

Since students' responses in Example 1 will be scored or rated by the teacher, the recording method needs to include a scoring method. (Different scoring methods are discussed in detail in Chapter 12.) The scoring method for Example 1 is a rating scale, and is specified on the Recording Form in Table 8.8. The aspects of speaking to be rated are given in the first column. The descriptors of the three scale levels are given in the next three columns to the right. This rating scale specifies that each aspect of speaking of each student's performance will be scored from 1 to 3, depending on whether it is "Needs improvement – 1", "Meets expectations – 2", or "Exceeds expectations – 3". There is also space for the teacher to write his feedback for each aspect of speaking.

Recording Form

Assessment task: Speaking, describing the physical characteristics of an animal

Student name: _____   Date: _____

Student paired with: _____

Animal picture: _____

Rating Scale: Aspect of speaking	Needs improvement 1	Meets expectations 2	Exceeds expectations 3	Feedback on student's speaking
Accurate grammar				
Accurate vocabulary (especially adjectives)				
Accurate pronunciation				
Total score: _____				

Table 8.8   Recording Form

Step 5: Evaluating the modified task/assessment task template in terms of assessment qualities

In Step 5 you need to address the following questions:

- How well will the assessment tasks based on this template elicit the ability I want to assess? (meaningfulness)
- How closely will the assessment tasks based on this template correspond to the TLU task? (generalizability)
- How well will the assessment tasks based on this template avoid sources of bias? (impartiality)
- How consistent will the assessment records be? (consistency)
- How practical will the assessment tasks be to administer and score? (practicality)

Evaluating the assessment task template in terms of assessment qualities, for the Example speaking assessment task, is discussed below.

Meaningfulness

The main modification that affects the meaningfulness of the interpretations is the increased time for the students to speak in the modified task. This modification was made so as to obtain a longer sample of each student's speaking, which means that the teacher has more of the student's performance on which to base his or her scores. There is a possible source of partiality, or bias, in the pictures. Although all the pictures are of animals, some students might already be familiar with some of the animals, so that their prior familiarity would favor them. In this case, the scores may reflect the student's topical knowledge as much as his or her speaking ability, so that the scores might not be meaningfully interpreted as indicators of the ability to be assessed – speaking.

Generalizability

Given the relatively minor modifications in the setting, input, and expected response, the teacher can be reasonably confident that his or her interpretations will generalize to the TLU domain—the ESL/EFL classroom.

Impartiality

Assessment tasks based on the assessment task template are likely to be impartial for several reasons:

- The content of the assessment tasks will be based on the content of the course, which we can assume is free of any content that may be offensive to some students.

- The teacher is very familiar with the sociocultural backgrounds of his students, and thus will be sensitive to any content that might be offensive to some students.
- The assessment tasks will be very similar in their input format and expected responses to tasks in the language classroom, so that students will be very familiar with these.

Consistency

Several of the procedures in the modified task are intended to help minimize sources of inconsistency in assessment records. In assessment tasks based on the assessment task template, the assessment would be administered in the same way: the teacher's descriptions and explanations of the procedures would be the same, the pictures would all be of animals, and the students would each be given the same amount of time to prepare and to speak. Finally, the teacher would use the same scoring procedure for scoring all the students' responses.

At the same time, there are several possible sources of inconsistency in the modified task that need to be considered, and ways found to minimize these.

Inconsistencies across pictures

Some pictures might be more complex than others. For example, some animals might be multicolored, or have body parts, such as an elephant's trunk and tusks, that might be more difficult to describe. Or, some pictures might include more detail or be of better quality than others. In order to minimize this source of inconsistency, the teacher could try to make sure that the pictures are equally detailed and of the same quality.

Inconsistencies in how students' performance is evaluated

Although the teacher would follow the same administrative procedure for each student, after testing many students, the teacher's attention might not be exactly the same as it was for the first students, which could affect his or her scoring. In addition, the teacher's scoring might be influenced by a "h alo effect". This happens when the order in which students are tested affects the teacher's scoring. For example, if the teacher tests several very good students and then tests an average student, that student's performance may appear to be very weak, and the teacher might give him or her a lower score than he or she deserves. Or, after testing several weak students, and then testing an average student, the teacher might give this student a higher score than he or she deserves.

Practicality

In Example 1, the resources that are required and available are shown in Table 8.9.

	Required	**Available?**
Human	Teacher, students	Yes
Material	Classroom space, pictures, paper and pencils, Recording Form	Yes
Time	Teacher's time for development: one day	Yes
	Teacher's time for administration, scoring, and providing feedback: about 2 ½ hours (24 students at five minutes per pair of students, plus time for setting up and administration time)	Yes
	Each student's time for taking the assessment: half a minute for preparation, one minute for speaking	Yes

Table 8.9 Practicality of example assessment tasks

From Table 8.9, we can see that the resources that are required are available, so we can say that assessment tasks created from this template would be practical to develop, administer, and score. The teacher's time for development might include activities such as selecting the pictures to use for the assessment and developing the scoring method and Recording Form. We would note that this would only need to be done once, irrespective of how many times this assessment is used. If the teacher wanted to use this assessment with different classes of students, or from one year to the next, for example, virtually no additional development time would be needed. If the teacher wanted to create assessment tasks with different topical content, such as describing a place, a building, or a person, this could be done with relatively little additional development time.

Once you have determined that assessment tasks developed from the assessment task template will support the qualities of meaningfulness, generalizability, impartiality, and consistency, and that these tasks will be practical, this template can be used for developing multiple assessment tasks. Creating assessment tasks is discussed in Chapter 9.

9 CREATING LANGUAGE ASSESSMENT TASKS

In Chapter 8, we described how to develop an assessment task template. In this chapter, we discuss how you can use an assessment task template to create multiple assessment tasks. The aims are to:

- guide you through the process of creating multiple assessment tasks from a single assessment task template
- provide examples of classroom assessments for the language use activities of writing, speaking, listening, and reading in order to illustrate the process of creating assessment tasks
- provide you with example templates that you can use in creating your own assessment tasks
- provide activities that enable you to practice applying the steps in the process.

Creating multiple assessment tasks from templates

As we indicated in Chapter 2, a language assessment typically includes many assessment tasks. The reason you need more than one assessment task is that a single assessment task is not likely to be adequate for providing scores that are consistent, or interpretations that are meaningful and generalizable. As discussed in Chapter 7, a single assessment task is generally not sufficient for providing scores that are consistent. Similarly, a single assessment task may not elicit enough performance for score-based interpretations to be meaningful. Finally, a single assessment task may not adequately sample the different tasks in the TLU domain, so that interpretations based on scores from this task may not generalize to the TLU domain. Issues about the meaningfulness and generalizability of interpretations are of particular concern when several aspects of language ability are to be assessed and when the teacher uses a wide variety of instructional tasks. In order to create assessments of the same ability, you can develop multiple tasks from a single assessment task template. The assessment task template defines an assessment task type.

➢ An **assessment task type** is defined by the activities and procedures, TCs and a scoring method in an assessment task template. Multiple assessment tasks that are created by changing some of the TCs of the same assessment task template belong to the same assessment task type.

You can create multiple assessment tasks to assess the same areas of language ability from a single assessment task template by changing some of the TCs from one task to the next. This process is illustrated in Figure 9.1.

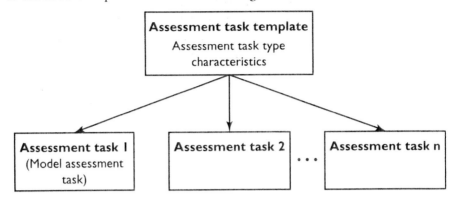

Figure 9.1 Creating multiple assessment tasks from a single template (adapted from Bachman & Palmer, Language Assessment in Practice, Oxford University Press, p. 314.)

To create multiple assessment tasks from a single assessment task template, you will do the following:

1   Create one task following the assessment task template. That is, for each assessment task template, you will create one model assessment task that follows the assessment task template.

➢ A **model assessment task** is an assessment task that is created following the specifications in an assessment task template. This assessment task then serves as a basis for creating additional assessment tasks.

2   Create additional tasks by:

   a   keeping the definition of the ability to be assessed the same

   b   keeping the attributes of the students (e.g. age, ability level, etc.) the same

   c   changing one or more of the TCs.

Examples of developing multiple assessment tasks of the same ability

In this section, we present four examples of assessment tasks extracted from the Examples in Part IV. Each example includes the following parts:

- a setting
- the TCs for the assessment task template
- the recording method, including a rating scale or a scoring key
- three example tasks: one model assessment task that follows the assessment task template and two that have one or more TCs from the template changed to create additional tasks.

After each example, there is an activity for you to create additional tasks by modifying the TCs of the assessment task template.

Example 9.1: Writing a descriptive paragraph

Setting

ESL/EFL class in a secondary school; students – intermediate-level teens. (See Example 6 on page 222 for the complete description of this assessment task.)

Task characteristics of assessment task template

The TCs for the assessment task template for Example 9.1 are given in Table 9.1.

Assessment task: Writing a descriptive paragraph about a musical instrument	
Areas of language ability to be assessed: Task achievement in descriptive writing, using appropriate range of grammar, vocabulary, and correct mechanics	
Task characteristics	
Setting	<u>Physical circumstances</u>: teacher in front of classroom, students in groups of four *Equipment/materials*: pen/pencil, paper (or computer), pictures of musical instruments <u>Participants</u>: teacher and students in groups of four (teens, intermediate level) <u>Time of the task</u>: during the class period; one class period required
Input	<u>Form</u>: *Aural*: teacher's spoken description of the task *Visual*: a list with pictures of musical instruments <u>Language</u>: English *Teacher*: short utterances describing and explaining, simple grammar and vocabulary *Length*: *aural*: short utterances; *visual*: long (several pictures) <u>Topical content</u>: musical instrument
Expected response	<u>Form</u>: *Visual*: a written descriptive paragraph about a musical instrument <u>Language</u>: English: organized with fairly simple grammar and vocabulary *Length*: one paragraph (100–130 words) <u>Topical content</u>: musical instrument

Table 9.1   TCs for the assessment task template for Example 9.1

Recording method for modified task/assessment task template

The recording method for Example 9.1 is given in Table 9.2, the Rating Scale is given in Table 9.3, and the Recording Form is given in Table 9.4.

Recording method for assessment task	<u>Type of assessment record</u>: score and written feedback <u>Aspects of ability</u>: four aspects of writing: task achievement, grammar, vocabulary, and mechanics <u>Scoring method</u>: <u>Criteria</u>: (See the Rating Scale in Table 9.3) *For each aspect*: 1–4, according to the Rating Scale <u>Score reported</u>: total score = task achievement + grammar + vocabulary + mechanics <u>Procedures</u>: the teacher reads the students' paragraphs and arrives at scores according to the Rating Scale, entering their scores on the Recording Form, and then adds up the scores to arrive at a total score and enters this on the Recording Form. The teacher provides written feedback on the Recording Form. This is given back to the students during the next lesson.

Table 9.2 Recording method for Example 9.1

Points	Task Achievement	Grammar	Vocabulary	Mechanics
4	• Includes all content points • Meets all descriptive paragraph requirements	• Wide range of grammar structures with very few inaccuracies	• Wide range with very few inaccuracies	• Very few errors in English writing conventions • Very few errors in punctuation and spelling
3	• Includes most content points • Meets most descriptive paragraph requirements	• Good range of grammar structures with occasional inaccuracies	• Good range of vocabulary with occasional inaccuracies	• Few errors in English writing conventions • Few errors in punctuation and spelling
2	• Includes some content points • Meets some descriptive paragraph requirements	• Limited range of grammar structures with frequent inaccuracies	• Limited range of vocabulary with frequent inaccuracies	• Frequent errors in English writing conventions • Frequent errors in punctuation and spelling
1	• Includes few content points • Meets few descriptive paragraph requirements	• Very limited range of grammar structures with very frequent inaccuracies	• Very limited range of vocabulary with very frequent inaccuracies	• Very frequent errors in English writing conventions • Very frequent errors in punctuation and spelling

Table 9.3   Rating Scale for Example 9.1

Recording Form

Assessment task: Writing a descriptive paragraph about a musical instrument

Student name: _____   **Date:** _____

Rating Scale: Aspect of speaking	Score	Feedback on student's writing
Task achievement		
Grammar		
Vocabulary		
Mechanics		

Total score: _____

Photocopiable © Oxford University Press

Table 9.4   Recording Form for Example 9.1

Multiple Assessment tasks

Task 1: Model assessment task

Writing prompt:

(Students are given a list of five musical instruments.)

Choose a musical instrument from the list and write a descriptive paragraph about it in **100–130 words**. Use the same structure for your paragraph that we have been using in class. You will receive a score on the structure of your paragraph, according to the Rating Scale we discussed in class. You have **45 minutes** to complete your descriptive paragraph. Are there any questions? (Teacher answers any questions.) You may begin.

Task 2: Different topical content from Task 1

Writing prompt:

Choose a piece of laboratory equipment that you are using or have used in your science (e.g. biology, chemistry, physics) class. Write a description (**100–130 words**) that includes the following:

- a physical description of the equipment
- the way the equipment works
- the purpose for which the equipment is used.

You have **45 minutes** to complete your descriptive paragraph.

Scoring method:

Since Task 2 assesses the same ability—four aspects of writing—as Task 1, the scoring method will be the same (as in Tables 9.2–9.4).

Task 3: Different genre of writing and topical content from Task 1

Writing prompt:

Choose a famous person you have read or heard about. Write a short biography in **100–130 words** of this person for the school newspaper. Follow the format and content of a biography that we have studied in class.

You have **45 minutes** to complete your descriptive paragraph.

Scoring method:

Since Task 3 assesses the same ability—four aspects of writing—as Task 1, the scoring method will be the same (as in Tables 9.2–9.4).

Activity 9.1

Look at Example 8 on page 242. Create two new assessment tasks based on the assessment task template in that Example. Indicate which TCs you will change and provide the writing prompt for each.

Task 1

TC(s) changed: _____

Writing prompt: _____

_____

_____

_____

Scoring method: _____

_____

_____

_____

Task 2

TC(s) changed: _____

Writing prompt: _____

_____

_____

Scoring method: _____

_____

_____

_____

Photocopiable © Oxford University Press

Example 9.2: Discussing an environmental issue

Setting

Content-based ESL/EFL class in a secondary school or university; students – advanced-level teens or adults. (See Example 7 on page 232 for the complete description of this assessment task.)

Task characteristics of assessment task template

The TCs for the assessment task template for Example 9.2 are given in Table 9.5.

Assessment task: Speaking, paired discussion of an environmental issue	
Areas of language ability to be assessed: Task achievement, knowledge of topical content, use of accurate grammar, vocabulary, and pronunciation in speaking	
Task characteristics	
Setting	<u>Physical circumstances</u>: teacher with a pair of students seated at a table in the Speaking Corner of the classroom *Equipment/materials*: paper and pencils for taking notes (for the students); Recording Form, pen or pencil (for the teacher) <u>Participants</u>: teacher and a pair of students (teens or adults, advanced level) <u>Time of the task</u>: during the class period; task requires more than one class period depending on number of students
Input	<u>Form</u>: *Aural*: teacher's spoken description of the task *Visual*: words and phrases that the students may write on paper <u>Language</u>: English *Teacher*: short spoken description and explanation; simple grammar and vocabulary *Length*: *aural*: short utterances; *visual*: short (words and phrases) <u>Topical content</u>: an environmental issue
Expected response	<u>Form</u>: *Visual*: students' notes for their discussion *Oral*: students' discussion of an environmental issue <u>Language</u>: English; medium to long utterances; advanced grammar and vocabulary, questions and answers *Length*: *visual*: one minute to read and think about their discussion; *oral*: about five minutes for each pair to discuss the issue <u>Topical content</u>: an environmental issue

Table 9.5   TCs for the assessment task template for Example 9.2

Recording method for modified task/assessment task template

The recording method for Example 9.2 is given in Table 9.6, the Rating Scale is given in Table 9.7, and the Recording Form is given in Table 9.8.

Recording method for assessment task	<u>Type of assessment record</u>: score
	<u>Aspects of ability</u>: five aspects of speaking: task achievement, knowledge of topical content, grammar, vocabulary, and pronunciation
	<u>Scoring method</u>:
	  <u>Criteria</u>: (See the Rating Scale in Table 9.7.)
	    For each aspect: 1 – Few/Limited; 2 – Some/Moderate;
	      3 – Most/Good; 4 – All/Wide
	  <u>Score reported</u>: total score = task achievement + knowledge of topical content + grammar + vocabulary + pronunciation
	  <u>Procedures</u>: the teacher listens to students' discussions and enters a score for each aspect of speaking in the Rating Scale for each student; he/she then adds up the scores to arrive at a total score and enters this on the Recording Form. This is given back to the students during the next lesson.

Table 9.6 Recording method for Example 9.2

Points	Task Achievement	Knowledge of topical content	Grammar	Vocabulary	Pronunciation
4	Meets all discussion requirements	Wide knowledge of the assigned topic	Wide range of grammar structures with very few inaccuracies	Wide range of vocabulary with very few inaccuracies	High degree of control, very few errors
3	Meets most discussion requirements	Good knowledge of the assigned topic	Good range of grammar structures with occasional inaccuracies	Good range of vocabulary with occasional inaccuracies	Good control, some errors
2	Meets some discussion requirements	Moderate knowledge of the assigned topic	Moderate range of grammar structures with frequent inaccuracies	Moderate range of vocabulary with frequent inaccuracies	Moderate control, frequent errors
1	Meets few discussion requirements	Limited knowledge of the assigned topic	Limited range of grammar structures with very frequent inaccuracies	Limited range of vocabulary with very frequent inaccuracies	Limited control, very frequent errors

Table 9.7   Rating Scale for Example 9.2

Recording Form

Assessment task: Speaking, discussing an environmental issue

Student name: _____ Date: _____

Student paired with: _____

Number of the prompt chosen: _____

Rating Scale: Aspect of speaking	Few/Limited 1	Some/Moderate 2	Most/Good 3	All/Wide 4
Task achievement				
Knowledge of topical content				
Grammar				
Vocabulary				
Pronunciation				

Total score: _____

Table 9.8   Recording Form for Example 9.2

Multiple assessment tasks

Task 1: Model assessment task

Speaking prompt:

(Students have been studying environmental issues in their science class, and have been discussing possible solutions to these in their ESL/EFL class. During the class before the assessment, the teacher has told the students that for the assessment task they will discuss, in pairs, a question about an environmental issue that will be different from the one that was discussed in class. They will need to discuss this question with each other.)

Teacher: "Here is a question about an environmental issue that I want you to discuss between the two of you." (Teacher chooses one of the prompts from a list and gives it to the students.) "Now, take a minute to make notes to guide your discussion." (Teacher waits for one minute.) "OK. You'll now have five minutes to discuss this issue together. You may begin now."

Task 2: Different type of dialogue (debate versus discussion) and topical content

Speaking prompt:

(Students have been studying environmental issues in their science class, and have been debating different points of view about some of these in their English class. They have previously been told that for the assessment task they will debate, in pairs, two statements about an environmental issue that is different from the one that was discussed in their ESL/EFL class. Each student will have to argue in favor of one statement and against the other.)

Teacher: "Here are two statements that express different points of view about water pollution:

1 Reducing the amount of polluted water should be <u>mainly the responsibility of governments</u>.

2 Reducing the amount of polluted water should be <u>mainly the responsibility of individuals</u>.

[Student 1], you will argue in favor of statement 1 and [Student 2] you will argue in favor of statement 2." (The teacher gives each student a printed version of his or her statement.) "You can do this the way we did it in class. Now, take a minute to make notes to guide your arguments." (Teacher waits for one minute.) "OK. You'll have five minutes to debate this issue. You may begin now."

Scoring method:

Since Task 2 assesses the same ability—five aspects of speaking—as Task 1, the scoring method will be the same (as in Tables 9.6–9.8).

Task 3: Different function and topical content

Speaking prompt:

> (Students have been studying ancient cultures in their history class and have been discussing some of these in their EFL/ESL class. They have previously been told that for the assessment task they will discuss, in pairs, the similarities and differences between two ancient cultures that are different from the ones that were discussed in class.
>
> Teacher: "Here is a question about two ancient civilizations. I want you to discuss the question between the two of you." (Teacher gives the students the question on a piece of paper and also reads it aloud.) "What are the similarities and differences between the culture of ancient Rome and that of ancient China? Now, take a minute to make notes to guide your discussion." (Teacher waits for one minute.) "You will have five minutes to discuss this question. You may begin now."

Scoring method:

> Since Task 3 assesses the same ability—five aspects of speaking—as Task 1, the scoring method will be the same (as in Tables 9.6–9.8).

Activity 9.2   Look at Example 1 on page 169. Create two new assessment tasks based on the assessment task template in that Example. Indicate which TCs you will change and provide the speaking prompt for each.

Task 1:

TC(s) changed: _____

Speaking prompt: _____

_____

_____

Scoring method: _____

_____

Task 2:

TC(s) changed: _____

Speaking prompt: _____

_____

_____

Scoring method: _____

_____

Example 9.3: Listening for specific details

Setting

ESL/EFL class in a secondary school; intermediate-level students. (See Example 4 on page 200 for the complete description of this assessment task.)

Task characteristics of assessment task template

The TCs for the assessment task template for Example 9.3 are given in Table 9.9.

Assessment task: Listening and answering questions	
Areas of language ability to be assessed: Comprehension of specific details in listening	
Task characteristics	
Setting	<u>Physical circumstances</u>: teacher in front of classroom, students are seated individually *Equipment/materials*: audio playback equipment (e.g. computer, digital player, CD player), questions on answer sheet, pen/pencil <u>Participants</u>: teacher and all students (teens, intermediate) <u>Time of the task</u>: during the class period, task requires 20 minutes to complete

Input	<u>Form</u>:
	  Aural: *teacher*: description of the task, a prerecorded conversation
	  Visual: questions on paper about the conversation
	<u>Language</u>: English
	  Teacher: utterances from teacher: spoken text, fairly simple grammar and vocabulary
	  Students: short, written answers
	  Length: *aural*: short prerecorded conversation; *visual*: fairly short answers to questions
	<u>Topical content</u>: talking about free-time activities

Expected response	<u>Form</u>:
	  Visual: questions; students write the correct answers according to the conversation between two people they have heard
	<u>Language</u>: English
	  Length: long sentences and phrases with fairly simple grammar and vocabulary
	<u>Topical content</u>: talking about free-time activities

Table 9.9 TCs for the assessment task template for Example 9.3

Recording method for modified task/assessment task template

The recording method for Example 9.3 is given in Table 9.10.

Recording method for assessment task	Type of assessment record: score
	Aspects of ability: Comprehension of specific details in listening
	Scoring method:
	    Criteria: (See the Scoring Key on page 126.)
	    Score reported: total score = 1 point for each correct
	        response according to the Scoring Key (15 maximum)
	    Procedures: the teacher reads each student's answers,
	        assigns the points according to the Scoring Key, adds these
	        up to get a total score, and enters this on the student's
	        answer sheet. The answer sheets with the scores are given
	        back to the students in the next lesson.

Table 9.10 Recording method for Example 9.3

Multiple Assessment tasks

Task 1: Model assessment task

Instructions for the assessment task:

Students are given an answer sheet with questions and room for their short answers, as illustrated in Table 9.11.

Questions and answers (Write your answers in the box after each question.)		Score/possible points
1 Where is Austin going?		__ /1
2 Why does Bev hesitate when Austin asks her to go with him to the café?		__ /1
3 What kind of team is Bev on?		__ /1
4 When is Bev allowed to eat according to her coach?		__ /2
5 What does the coach allow Bev to drink?		__ /3
6 What does Bev do on the day before the game?		__ /2
7 When did Bev train for the big game?		__ /1
8 What time does Bev's game start?		__ /1
9 On what day of the week is Bev's game?		__ /1
10 Why can't Austin go to Bev's game?		__ /2
	Total score	__ /15

Table 9.11 Answer sheet for the assessment task in Example 9.3

Teacher's description of the task:

"First, you will listen to a conversation between two people. While listening to the conversation, you will write your answers to the questions on the answer sheet provided. You will have 10 minutes to complete your answers. Then you will listen to the conversation again and will have three minutes to correct your answers. Your score on this part will be the number of correct answers."

Audio Script:

Bev: Hi, Austin

Austin: Hi, Bev. I'm going to the café. Would you like to come?

Bev: I'd love to…but I'm not allowed to eat anything unhealthy right now. Well, I can have water or juice, I guess. And we can talk.

Austin: Are you on a ….? I can't think of the word. It's when you eat only special food.

Bev: A diet?

Austin: That's it. Are you on a diet?

Bev: Sort of. I'm doing some training. I'm on the baseball team and we have a big game tomorrow. The coach is making us eat special food at certain times.

Austin: Wow. So when are you allowed to eat?

Bev: The coach lets us eat at normal mealtimes—breakfast, lunch, and dinner—but not snacks. And he won't let us drink soda, only water, juice, or milk.

Austin: So are you doing exercise, too?

Bev: Not today. He doesn't make us exercise the day before a game. We always take a break. He lets us rest because we've exercised and done training every day this week.

Austin: What time is the game?

Bev: It's at 4 o'clock. Can you come?

Austin: No, I can't. I'm not allowed to go out on Thursday afternoons. My mom makes me stay at home and practice the violin!

Scoring Key:

The Scoring Key for Example 9.3 is given in Table 9.12.

Question	Answer	Point(s)
1	café	1 point
2	She can't eat unhealthy (food).	1 point
3	(a) baseball	1 point
4	(at) normal meal times / breakfast, lunch, and dinner	1 point each (2 points total)
5	water / juice / milk	1 point each (3 points total)
6	(take) a break from exercise / rest	1 point each (2 points total)
7	every day this week, except today	1 point
8	4 o'clock	1 point
9	Thursday	1 point
10	stay home / practice violin	1 point each (2 points total)
	Total possible points:	15

Table 9.12 Scoring Key for Example 9.3

Multiple assessment tasks

Task 2: Different topical content from Task 1

Possible adaptation for the assessment task:

> One adaptation of this listening task could present students with a conversation between two people describing their plans for their upcoming holiday. The questions could ask the students to provide specific details about each person's holiday plans, e.g. where they will go, how they will get there, how long they will stay and what they will do.

Recording method and scoring key:

> Since Task 2 assesses the same ability as Task 1, the recording method and scoring key will follow the same format (as in Tables 9.9–9.12).

Task 3: Different function (description versus discussion) and topical content

Possible adaptation for the assessment task:

> Another adaptation of this listening task could present students with a conversation between two people discussing the advantages and disadvantages of purchasing merchandise online versus purchasing it at local stores.

Recording method and scoring key:

> Since Task 2 assesses the same ability as Task 1, the recording method and scoring key will follow the same format (as in Tables 9.9–9.12).

Activity 9.3   Look at Example 5 on page 210. Describe two possible assessment tasks based on the assessment task template in that Example. Indicate which TCs you will change, what the listening text would include, and what the questions would be.

Task 1:

TC(s) changed: _____

Listening text: _____

_____

_____

_____

Questions: _____

_____

_____

_____

Task 2:

TC(s) changed: _____

Listening text: _____

_____

_____

_____

Questions: _____

_____

_____

_____

Photocopiable © Oxford University Press

Example 9.4: Reading for cohesion

Setting:

ESL/EFL class; secondary school or university; advanced-level students. (See Example 2 on page 181 for the complete description of this assessment task.)

Task characteristics of assessment task template

The TCs for the assessment task template for Example 9.4 are given in Table 9.13.

Assessment task: Reading and filling in gapped sentences	
Areas of language ability to be assessed: Comprehension of cohesion and coherence in reading	
Task characteristics	
Setting	<u>Physical circumstances</u>: teacher in front of classroom, students are seated individually *Equipment/materials*: reading text with gaps, pen/pencil <u>Participants</u>: teacher and all students (teens or adults, advanced level) <u>Time of the task</u>: during the class period, students will have 20 minutes to complete the assessment
Input	<u>Form</u>: *Aural*: teacher's description of the task *Visual*: reading text with six gaps; eight sentences <u>Language</u>: English *Teacher*: short utterances explaining and describing; simple grammar and vocabulary *Length: aural*: short sentences and phrases; *visual*: medium: reading text with one paragraph; list of eight sentences <u>Topical content</u>: Greenwich Village
Expected response	<u>Form</u>: *Visual*: students write the numbers of sentences from the list that match the gaps in the paragraphs <u>Language</u>: non-language *Length: visual*: short (only numbers) <u>Topical content</u>: Greenwich Village

Table 9.13 TCs for the assessment task template for Example 9.4

Recording method for modified task/assessment task template

The recording method for Example 9.4 is given in Table 9.14.

Recording method for assessment task	<u>Type of assessment record</u>: score <u>Aspects of ability</u>: comprehension of cohesion and coherence in reading <u>Scoring method</u>: <u>Criteria</u>: (See the Scoring Key on page 130.) *For each correct gap completion*: 1 point <u>Score reported</u>: number of correct choices for gaps (6 maximum) <u>Procedures</u>: the teacher reads each student's answers and assigns the points according to the Scoring Key, adds these up to get a total score and enters this on the student's paper. The papers with the scores are given back to the students in the next lesson.

Table 9.14 Recording method for Example 9.4

Multiple assessment tasks

Task 1: Model assessment task

Instructions for the assessment task:

Students are given an answer sheet with a reading text and a list of sentences.

Teacher's description of the task:

"Here's your reading text and answer sheet. Choose the correct sentence from the ones below that best fits in each gap. Write the number of that sentence in the gap. There are two sentences that you do not need .You will have 20 minutes for this task. Are there any questions?" (Teacher answers any clarification questions the students may have). "You may begin now."

Reading text and answer sheet:

I'm a Greenwich Villager and proud of it

I live in Greenwich Village, New York, which is in the "downtown" (southern) part of Manhattan and includes Washington Square Park, New York University, and a maze of picturesque little streets. A) ___ So why do I like it so much? It's an artistic and intellectual neighborhood with people playing chess in the park, artists selling paintings on the sidewalk, and students discussing life in coffee shops. B) ___ There's a surprise around every corner – maybe a brand new restaurant that wasn't there last week, a snoring down-and-out sleeping in the doorway, or a celebrity being pursued by paparazzi and fans. A sense of history pervades Greenwich Village. It was first inhabited by Native Americans, then Dutch settlers, and then the British, who in 1713 named it "Greenwich" after a town in England. The Village really was a small, rural village until the 1800s, when people escaping outbreaks of disease began moving there. C) ___ Many famous people have lived in Greenwich Village, including the writer Jack Kerouac, the singer Bob Dylan, and the actress Uma Thurman. D) ___ The heart of the Village is an area of pretty, twisting streets west of Sixth Avenue, where there are endless theatres, used bookstores, coffee shops, trendy boutiques, and of course restaurants. E) ___ The Village is packed with food shops and restaurants from every region of the world. Mouth-watering aromas are everywhere from first thing in the morning until late at night. The Village is a genuine 24/7 part of the town. F) ___ They flock from every corner of the world to sit on the benches or beside the fountain, talking, playing musical instruments, and celebrating the freedom of friendship and youth. My mother, who grew up in New York City, used to say that Times Square is for tourists, but the Village is the real New York.

Sentences:

1 A large part of the Village experience has to do with food.

2 Washington Square Park is like a magnet for young people.

3 I still remember the corner stores everywhere around here from when I was a child.

---

4 Ever since, the Village has been a haven for artists, writers, poets, and musicians.

5 Life in the Village is never dull.

6 Tourists always visit Times Square.

7 It's my favorite part of town.

8 The popular sitcom *Friends* was set here, and busloads of tourists looking for places mentioned in the show come here every weekend.

Scoring Key:

A 7   B 5   C 4   D 8   E 1   F 2

Task 2: Different topical content from Task 1

Possible adaptation for the assessment task:

One adaptation of this reading task could present students with a paragraph about a topic from their history or social studies class with several gaps, and a list of sentences. Students would match the sentences with the gaps.

Recording method and scoring key:

Since Task 2 assesses the same ability as Task 1, the recording method and scoring key will follow the same format (as in Table 9.14 and above).

Task 3: Different topical content, genre, and different expected response (matching sentences versus matching headings)

Possible adaptation for the assessment task:

Another adaptation of this reading task could present students with six short paragraphs that explain different steps in the activity of a hot air balloon ride and a list of possible headings. Students would match the headings with the paragraphs.

Recording method and scoring key:

Since Task 3 assesses the same ability as Task 1, the recording method and scoring key will follow the same format (as in Table 9.14 and above).

Activity 9.4

Look at Example 9 on page 253. Describe two possible reading assessment tasks based on the assessment task template in that Example. For each task, indicate which TCs you will change. Then describe briefly what the reading text would include, what the questions, the recording method, and scoring key would be.

Task 1:

TC(s) changed:_____

Reading text: _____

_____

_____

Questions: _____

_____

_____

_____

Recording method and scoring key: _____

_____

_____

_____

Task 2:

TC(s) changed: _____

Reading text:_____

_____

_____

_____

Questions: _____

_____

_____

_____

Recording method and scoring key: _____

_____

_____

_____

When you create multiple assessment tasks for an assessment, you need to have a set of specifications that will indicate how many and what kinds of assessment tasks you need in order to obtain scores from the assessment that are consistent, and interpretations that are meaningful and generalizable. We discuss procedures for preparing specifications for combining assessment tasks to make an assessment in Chapter 10.

10 COMBINING ASSESSMENT TASKS TO MAKE CLASSROOM-BASED ASSESSMENTS

In most situations, you need to develop classroom-based assessments that include more than a single assessment task. The larger and more varied the amount of instructional content to be assessed, the more assessment tasks you will need. Thus, for a short quiz over a single lesson, you may only need two or three assessment tasks. For an assessment covering a whole unit of instruction, you will most likely need more assessment tasks, and for an assessment that covers an entire school term or year, you will need even more assessment tasks. In some situations, you and your fellow teachers may need to develop assessments of the same abilities for students who are in different classes at the same level. There may also be times when you need to develop similar assessments, or different forms of an assessment with the same characteristics, to give your students at different times during a period of instruction, or from one year to the next.

When you want to develop assessments with multiple tasks, or different forms of an assessment, you need to prepare a set of assessment specifications, also known as a "blueprint". This blueprint will guide you in the development of the assessment. It will help you make sure that the areas of ability to be assessed are, in fact, covered in the assessment, that the kinds of assessment tasks included correspond to instructional tasks in the TLU domain, and that assessment reports will be consistent from one assessment to the next.

In addition to guiding your development of assessments, a blueprint enables you to maintain quality control as you develop assessments. When you develop assessments from the same blueprint, you can compare the different assessment tasks within an assessment or different forms of the assessment to determine the degree to which they are comparable. In this way, a blueprint can be used as a document to provide backing for your claims about the qualities of your interpretations and assessment records.

In this chapter, we first describe a blueprint for developing assessments and discuss the components that need to be included in this blueprint. We then describe some different situations in which a blueprint can be used to guide assessment development. Finally, we briefly discuss how a blueprint can be used to provide quality control during the development of assessments.

What is a blueprint?

Specialists in language assessment and educational assessment use the term "blueprint" for a set of specifications that can be used for developing assessments.

➤ A **blueprint** is a detailed plan that specifies the content and format of an assessment, and the procedures and instructions for administering an assessment.

A blueprint includes the components listed in Table 10.1.

| 1 Assessment specifications |
| a Numbers and descriptive labels of the parts |
| b Numbers and descriptive labels of the tasks per part |
| c Relative importance of the parts and tasks |
| d Time allowed for each part and overall |
| 2 Procedures and instructions for the whole assessment |
| a Procedures |
| b General instructions |
| 3 Assessment task template (for each task type) |
| a Activities and procedures to be followed |
| b Assessment TCs |
| c Recording method |
| d Task-specific instructions |

Table 10.1 Components of a blueprint

Following the structure shown in Table 10.1, an example blueprint for listening and reading assessments is illustrated in the next section. When you develop your own assessment, you will include the areas of language ability that you want to assess. In the example blueprint, we have indicated that the assessment would include two listening tasks and two reading tasks. However, to save space, we have included only one task each for listening and reading. When you develop your own assessment, you will include as many assessment tasks as you need in order to support the claims in your AUA.

Example of an assessment blueprint

1 Assessment specifications

Part	Ability tested	Tasks		Relative importance (%)	Time allowed (minutes)
I	Listening	Listening task 1 (Listen to audio input and select answers to questions from a list)		25	10
		Listening task 2 (Listen to different audio input and write short answers to questions)		25	10
			Total	50	20
II	Reading	Reading task 1 (Read and match headings with paragraphs)		25	10
		Reading task 2 (Read a different text with gaps and choose the sentence from a list that correctly fills the gap.)		25	10
			Total	50	20
			Test total	100	40

2 Procedures and instructions for the whole assessment

a Procedures:

1 The teacher reads the general instructions to the students.

2 The teacher reads the instructions for each task and follows the activities and procedures described in the assessment task template.

b General instructions:

This is a test of your listening and reading. There are two parts in the test and each part has two tasks. You will begin with Part I, Listening. After you finish the two listening tasks, you may begin Part II, Reading. There are two reading tasks in Part II and you will have 20 minutes to complete this part. Are there any questions? OK. Let's begin.

3 Assessment task templates

Part I: Listening

Listening task 1: Assessment task template

a Activities and procedures to be followed:

  i A week before the assessment the teacher tells the students:

    a) they will have an assessment of their listening ability the following week

    b) the purpose of the assessment is to give each student a mark that will count as part of his or her grade to pass the course

    c) they will listen to a conversation between two speakers

    d) they will then answer listening comprehension questions.

  ii On the day of the assessment:

    a) the teacher briefly explains the listening activity to the class

    b) students are given an answer sheet with questions on the conversation they will listen to

    c) students listen to a short conversation about free-time activities and write their answers to questions about the conversation on the answer sheet.

b Assessment task TCs

Task: Listening and answering questions	
Areas of language ability to be assessed: Comprehension of specific details in listening	
Task characteristics	
Setting	<u>Physical circumstances</u>: teacher in front of classroom, students are seated individually *Equipment/materials*: audio playback equipment (e.g. computer, digital player, CD player), questions on paper, pen/pencil <u>Participants</u>: teacher and all students (teens, intermediate) <u>Time of the task</u>: during the class period, task requires 20 minutes to complete
Input	<u>Form</u>: *Aural*: teacher's description of the task, a pre-recorded conversation *Visual*: questions on paper about the conversation <u>Language</u>: English *Teacher*: spoken text, fairly simple grammar and vocabular *Students*: short: written answers *Length: aural*: pre-recorded conversation of two minutes; *visual*: fairly short answers to questions <u>Topical content</u>: free-time activities
Expected response	<u>Form</u>: *Visual*: questions; students, written answers to questions <u>Language</u>: English *Length*: short, with words and phrases <u>Topical content</u>: free-time activities

c Recording method

Recording method for assessment task	<u>Type of assessment record</u>: score <u>Aspects of ability</u>: comprehension of specific details in listening <u>Scoring method</u>: (See the Scoring Key below.) <u>Criteria</u>: <u>Score reported</u>: 1 point for each correct response according to the Scoring Key (15 maximum) <u>Procedures</u>: the teacher reads each student's answers, assigns the points according to the Scoring Key, adds these up to get a total score, and enters this on the student's answer sheet. The answer sheets with the scores are given back to the students in the next lesson.

d Instructions

Part I: Listening

"In this part of the test you will listen to a conversation between two people. While listening to the conversation, you will write your answers to the questions on the answer sheet provided. You will have 10 minutes to complete your answers. Then you will listen to the conversation again and will have three minutes to correct your answers if necessary. Your score on this part will be the number of correct answers. Are there any questions?" (Teacher answers students' questions.) "OK, let's begin."

(In the actual assessment, the assessment task template for Listening Task 2 would be included here. We have omitted it in this example.)

Part II: Reading

Reading task 1: Assessment task template

a Activities and procedures to be followed

   i A week before the assessment the teacher tells the students:

      a) they will have an assessment of their reading ability the following week

      b) the purpose of the assessment is to give each student a mark that will count as part of his or her grade for the school term

      c) they will have to read a text and match the paragraphs with headings.

   ii On the day of the assessment:

      a) the teacher explains the reading activity to the class

      b) students will be given a reading text with six paragraphs and a blank before each paragraph for a heading

c) students will be given eight headings and they will have to choose the ones that best suit the paragraphs.

d) students will have to fill the blanks for the headings in the reading passage by writing the numbers of the appropriate blanks for the headings in the text.

b Assessment task TCs

Assessment task: Reading and matching headings with paragraphs	
Areas of language ability to be assessed: Comprehension of major ideas in reading	
Task characteristics	
Setting	<u>Physical circumstances</u>: teacher in front of classroom, students are seated individually *Equipment/materials*: reading text with blanks for headings, pen/pencil <u>Participants</u>: teacher and all students (teens, intermediate level) <u>Time of the task</u>: during the class period, students will have 20 minutes to complete the assessment
Input	<u>Form</u>: *Aural*: teacher's description of the task *Visual*: reading text with six paragraphs and list of eight headings <u>Language</u>: English *Teacher:* short utterances describing and explaining, simple grammar and vocabulary *Length: aural*: short utterances; *visual*: long (written text with six paragraphs and a list of eight headings, simple grammar; well organized, with cohesion and coherence) <u>Topical content</u>: street art
Expected response	<u>Form</u>: *Visual*: students write the numbers of matching headings in the blanks before each paragraph <u>Language</u>: non-language *Length:* short (only numbers) <u>Topical content</u>: street art

c Recording method

Recording method for assessment task	<u>Type of assessment record</u>: score <u>Aspects of ability</u>: comprehension of major ideas in reading <u>Scoring method</u>: 　<u>Criteria</u>: 　*For each correct blank heading completion*: 1 point, according to the Scoring Key 　<u>Score reported</u>: number of correct choices for headings (6 maximum) 　<u>Procedures</u>: the teacher reads each student's answers and assigns the points according to the Scoring Key, adds these up to get a total score, and enters this on the student's paper. The papers with the scores are given back to the students in the next lesson.

d Instructions

Part II: Reading

"In this part of the test there are two tasks. For each task, there are six paragraphs and a list of possible headings for them. Match the headings from the list with the paragraphs they describe the best. Write the number of the heading in the space after the paragraph. There will be two headings that you do not need. Your score on this part will be the number of correct matches between paragraphs and headings. You will have 20 minutes for this part of the test. Are there any questions?" (Teacher answers any clarification questions the students may have.) "You may begin now."

(In the actual assessment, the assessment task template for Reading Task 2 would be included here. We have omitted this in this example.)

How can you use a blueprint to guide assessment development?

There are several situations in which a blueprint can guide you in developing an assessment:

An assessment developed by a single teacher

As discussed in Chapter 9, multiple assessment tasks can be created from a single assessment task template. Combining several assessment task templates in a blueprint can guide the development of a classroom-based assessment with multiple assessment tasks.

An assessment developed by a group of teachers or by different teachers

In some situations, you may want to collaborate with your fellow teachers to develop an assessment with many different assessment tasks. For example, if there are several teachers who teach different classes of students at the same level, they may decide to collaborate in writing an end-of-term test to be used to make pass/ not pass decisions. In situations like this, if all the teachers work from the same blueprint, they can make sure that tasks they develop will yield assessments that satisfy the need for meaningful and generalizable interpretations and consistent assessment records.

Similar assessments to be given at different times

In other situations, you may need to develop similar assessments to give to your students at different times during a period of instruction. Suppose, for example, that you need to give an assessment after each unit of instruction, and the results of these unit assessments will be used to assign grades and make pass/not pass decisions at the end of the year. If the learning objectives of your class cover essentially the same areas of language ability, but focus on different aspects of these throughout the school term, you may be able to use the same blueprint for all of your end-of-unit assessments by creating different assessment tasks to reflect the different areas of focus of the different units of instruction.

How can you use a blueprint to maintain quality control?

In addition to guiding you in the development of assessments, a blueprint helps you monitor the quality of your assessment as you develop them. You can do this by using the blueprint to compare:

1 the content assessed and characteristics of the assessment tasks with the learning objectives and characteristics of instructional tasks
2 the assessment tasks that are included in different forms of the assessment.

Comparing assessment tasks with instructional tasks

The blueprint provides a link between the learning objectives of the language classroom and the content to be assessed, and between the characteristics of the instructional tasks and those of the assessment tasks. This is illustrated in Figure 10.1.

Because the blueprint links instruction to assessment, it helps you make sure that the assessment tasks you include in the assessment adequately sample both the content to be learned and the tasks in the TLU domain, to assure that your interpretations will be meaningful and generalizable.

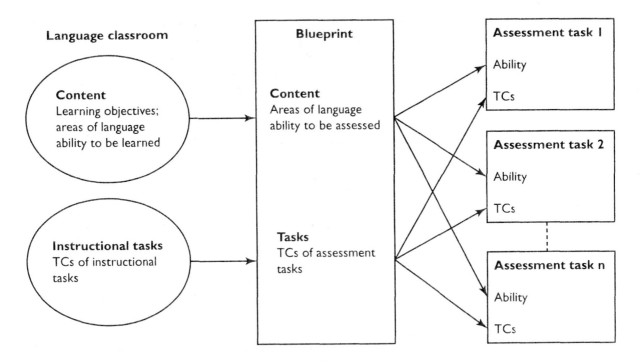

Figure 10.1 *Relationships between language classroom, blueprint, and assessment tasks*

Comparing tasks across different assessments

When you develop assessments from the same blueprint, you can compare the degree to which the different assessment tasks within an assessment or different forms of the assessment are comparable. By regularly checking the blueprint as you develop different assessment tasks or different forms of the assessment, you can quickly discover any differences between the specifications in the blueprint and the assessment tasks or different forms of the assessment, and correct these.

In summary, a blueprint guides you as you develop assessments, and also provides a way for you to monitor the quality of the assessment as you develop them. Using a blueprint to develop assessments thus helps you make sure that:

- the assessment tasks you include in the assessment adequately sample both the content to be assessed and the tasks in the TLU domain, to assure that your interpretations will be meaningful and generalizable
- the assessment will provide sufficient performance from your students to yield consistent assessment records
- different forms of an assessment are equivalent in the content they assess and in the characteristics of the tasks they include.

11 ADMINISTRATIVE PROCEDURES AND INSTRUCTIONS

When you give an assessment to your students, do you ever think about whether they can all understand what they are supposed to do? Is it always clear to your students how they are expected to respond to the tasks in the assessment? Do you tell them how their responses to the assessment tasks will be scored? Do you try to make sure they have the opportunity to perform at their best? Do you try to make sure that they are all treated fairly?

In this chapter, we discuss the roles of administrative procedures and instructions in helping us assure the quality of our assessments. We first discuss why it is important to specify the procedures for administering the assessment. Next, we discuss the activities involved in administering classroom-based assessments. Finally, we discuss the role of instructions and how to write these.

Why do we need to specify administrative procedures?

When you develop an assessment to use in the classroom with your students, you will follow procedures to assure that students' performance on the assessment will provide information about their language ability. You want to make sure that your interpretations about their language ability are impartial or unbiased. Thus, you avoid content that may be inappropriate or that may cause anxiety for some students and you avoid using tasks that may be biased against some of your students. As discussed in Chapter 6, another possible source of bias is when students are treated differently in the administration of the assessment. You also want to make sure that your students' performance is consistent. As discussed in Chapter 7, one possible source of inconsistency is when the assessment is administered differently at different times or to different groups of students.

Thus, in order to help assure that your interpretations about your students' language ability are unbiased and that their assessment records are consistent, you need to specify the procedures you will use to administer the assessment. For low-stakes assessments covering small amounts of instructional material, the administrative procedures can be relatively simple, while for high-stakes assessments, which may cover larger amounts of instructional material and consist of several different parts, they will be more extensive. However, irrespective of the importance of the decisions to be made or the amount of material covered in the assessment, you need to specify in advance how you will administer the assessment.

Administrative procedures

The administrative procedures you specify will include the following activities:

1 preparing the test setting

2 providing an encouraging testing environment

3 communicating the instructions.

Preparing the test setting

The way you prepare the test setting will follow the activities and procedures and the TCs that are specified in the assessment task template for each assessment task (see Chapter 8, pages 99 and 101). Specifically, preparing the test setting will include:

1 arranging a time, place, and the physical conditions for testing

2 making sure that the needed materials and equipment are available

3 making sure that the needed personnel for administering the assessment are available.

When the assessment is to be administered to a group of students at the same time, in the classroom, and can be administered during a single class period, then it may not be necessary to make any special arrangements for the time and place. If, on the other hand, the assessment will be administered individually or to small groups or pairs of students, then special preparations for the place and physical conditions may need to be made. For example, look at the assessment task in Example 1 on page 176, which involves administering a speaking assessment to pairs of students. The activities and procedures and the TCs of the assessment task template specify the preparations that the teacher will need to make for this assessment, which are listed in Table 11.1.

Aspects of the test setting that need to be prepared	Specific preparations for Example 1
Time of assessment	During the class period
Place	The Speaking Corner in the classroom where the language class meets
Physical conditions	A table with three chairs; two chairs facing each other across the table for the students, one chair at the end of the table for the teacher
Materials and equipment	Pictures of animals, Recording Form, pen or pencil, table and three chairs for the teacher and the students
Personnel to administer the assessment	Teacher

Table 11.1 Steps in preparing the test setting for Example 1

Providing a supportive testing environment

In keeping with the goal of enabling your students to perform at their best on the assessment, you need to make sure that the testing environment is supportive. This involves avoiding distractions and assuring that test administrators exhibit an encouraging attitude toward the test takers. Many different kinds of distractions can occur during the administration of an assessment. Some of these, such as public or school events, come from outside of the testing place itself. You can usually anticipate any such events that might be distracting to your students and schedule the assessment either before or after these take place. Some distractions may occur unintentionally within the testing place itself, and these are potentially more distracting to test takers. If the test administrators are constantly whispering to each other, shuffling papers, or walking back and forth in front of the class, this can be very distracting to test takers. Test administrators thus need to be informed or trained to be as unobtrusive as possible, and only make themselves obvious when they need to make administrative announcements or give instructions.

If you have ever taken a large-scale high-stakes assessment, or observed or helped administer one, you are probably familiar with the way test administrators in many of these tests "enforce" test security. You may also be aware of the negative environment this creates for the test takers. Glowering at or hovering over test takers while they are trying to concentrate and do their best has the effect of making it difficult for test takers to perform at their best. While maintaining test security or making sure that test takers do not "cheat" during the test is clearly a concern for such tests, we believe that this can be done without creating a negative, discouraging atmosphere. Our role as test administrators is to make sure students understand what they are supposed to do and to make them feel comfortable, rather than stressed, while taking an assessment.

Most classroom-based assessments are low- to medium-stakes and these are administered by teachers to their own students. Therefore, maintaining test security is seldom a serious concern. Nevertheless, some students may feel anxious about their ability to do well on the assessment. It is thus essential for you to maintain the same supportive attitude in administering the assessment as you do while teaching. In this way, you can help reduce any anxieties your students may have and help make the assessment a positive experience for them.

Communicating the instructions

As we discussed in Chapter 10, there will be instructions that are specific to each assessment task type. In addition, for tests that consist of multiple parts, there will be general instructions for the entire test. The instructions are usually the first part of the test that your students will hear or read. The instructions thus play a critical role in forming students' expectations about the test and in encouraging them to perform at their best. The primary purpose of the instructions is to make sure that students understand the assessment procedure, the kinds of test tasks they will encounter, how they are expected to respond to these, and how their responses will be scored. The instructions will include the following information:

- the purpose for which the test results will be used
- the areas of language ability that will be tested
- a description of the procedures and tasks
- a description of the way students' responses will be scored.

When do you give instructions?

You can give instructions about the test to your students in different ways and at different times. For a single low-stakes classroom assessment, the instructions need to include all of the information above, but you can give this orally just before the assessment. In some situations, you may want to give some general instructions about the test in advance, prior to the time when the test is given. This is particularly important for tests that will be used for medium- to high-stakes decisions, in order to give your students adequate time to prepare for the test. In this case, these advance instructions will include the purpose for which the test results will be used and the instructional content or learning objectives that will be covered in the test. Table 11.2 gives an example of advance instructions for a high-stakes test, in which students are informed of the ability to be tested and the purpose of the assessment, and are given a general description of the procedures and tasks for the assessment.

A week before the assessment, the teacher tells the students:

1 they will have an assessment of their ability to write a descriptive paragraph the following week
2 the purposes of the assessment are:
    a to give each student a mark that will count as part of his or her grade for the school term
    b to provide feedback to individual students about their writing ability
3 they will have to write a descriptive paragraph on a topic they will be given on the day of the assessment
4 they will have an entire class period to write their descriptive paragraph
5 the teacher will score their descriptive paragraphs according to the Rating Scale that he gives them and describes to them. This Rating Scale includes features of writing that have been covered in the class. The teacher explains that he will also give them written feedback.

Table 11.2 Example advance instructions

On the day the test is given, you can give your students more specific instructions including descriptions of the specific task or tasks they will be given, how they should respond to these, and how their responses will be scored. Table 11.3 shows an example of instructions to be given at the time the test is administered.

On the day of the assessment:

1 The teacher explains the writing assessment to the class.
2 Students will have the whole class period to complete their descriptive paragraph.
3 The teacher reviews the Rating Scale with the students, reminding them to pay attention to the features of writing that are included in the Rating Scale.
4 Students are given a list of musical instruments that are different from those used in the TLU task and the writing prompt.

Writing prompt:

"Choose a musical instrument from the list and write a descriptive paragraph about it in **100–130 words**. Use the same structure for your paragraph that we have been using in class. You will receive scores on the structure of your paragraph, according to the Rating Scale we discussed in class. You have **45 minutes** to complete your descriptive paragraph. Are there any questions?" (Teacher answers any questions.) "You may begin."

Table 11.3 Example instructions given when the test is administered

For tests that include several different parts, you will need to provide instructions for the entire test, as well as for each task type that is included. Table 11.4 shows an example of instructions for a test that includes two parts.

"This is a test of your reading and writing. There are two parts to the test and each part includes one task. You will begin with Part I, Reading, and will have 20 minutes to complete this part. After you finish this part, you may go on to Part II, Writing, and you will have 20 minutes to complete this part. Are there any questions?" (Teacher answers any questions.) "You may begin."

Table 11.4 Example instructions for a multi-part test

For tests with multiple parts, each part will also include specific instructions. See Table 11.5 for the instructions for the two parts of the example.

Part 1: Reading
(Teacher reads these instructions to the class.)
"In this part of the test you will be given a reading text with six gaps with sentences missing, and a list of sentences. The gaps in the text are labeled A–F, and the sentences in the list are numbered 1–8. Choose the sentence from the ones in the list that best fits in each gap. Write the letter of that sentence in the gap. There are two sentences that you do not need. Your score will be the number of correct matches between gaps and sentences. Here's your test with the reading text and list of sentences." (Teacher passes out the test papers to the class.) "You will have 20 minutes for this task. Are there any questions?" (Teacher answers any questions.) "You may begin now."

Part 2: Writing
"In this part of the test you will read a job description from a newspaper. Then you will write a letter of application for this job. Your letter should be about **100–130 words** long. Use the same format for your letter as we have studied in class. You will receive scores on the structure of your paragraph, according to the Rating Scale we discussed in class. You have **45 minutes** to complete your letter."

Table 11.5 Example instructions for multiple parts tests

How do you make instructions understandable?

The primary purpose of the instructions is to make sure that students understand exactly what they will encounter in the test and how they are expected to respond. Thus, the instructions are *not* part of the test itself. Rather, they are provided to enable students to perform at their best on the test. It is therefore critical that you do everything possible to make sure that the instructions are understandable. In doing this, there are two things you need to consider: the language of the instructions and the form of the language you will use to present the instructions.

Language

You can present the instructions in either the students' native language or the target language of the assessment. With beginning level students, making the instructions understandable can be particularly challenging. If your students all have the same native language, then the instructions should be presented in their native language if there is any doubt about whether they could understand instructions in the target language. If your students speak many different native languages, then presenting the instructions in the target language is unavoidable. In this case, it is critical that you try to make sure that the level of language in the instructions is lower than the level of language at which you are assessing.

Form

The form of language (spoken or written) through which the instructions are presented can also affect the comprehensibility of the instructions. Presenting the instructions in the same form as the input of the task can facilitate understanding.

Thus, for assessments of reading and writing, the input will typically be written so that it is most appropriate for the instructions also to be presented in writing. For assessments of listening and speaking, the input will typically be spoken, so that the most appropriate form for the instructions would also be spoken. In some cases, it may be helpful to present the instructions through both speaking and writing, as this may provide students with two ways of understanding. At the same time, you need to be aware that some students may find it distracting to have to listen to the instructions while they are reading them.

Providing examples of the tasks included in the assessment can also help students understand what to expect on the assessment. This is particularly important if you are using assessment tasks that may not be familiar to all of your students.

The role of instructions is critical to making sure your students are able to perform at their best on an assessment. The more varied your students' levels of language ability are, the more likely it is that some of them may not be able to understand either the language or the form of the language you use to present the instructions. Thus, it is very important that you try out the assessment instructions with your students before you give the assessment. This can be done by giving your students the instructions to read while you read them aloud, and then asking them if they find this helpful or not, or whether they prefer only written or only spoken instructions.

How extensive do instructions need to be?

You do not need to prepare instructions that are long or complex. You *do* want to make sure that the instructions include all the information needed and thus effectively accomplish their purpose. You also want to make sure that the instructions are efficient in that they do not take up too much assessment time. Instructions that are both effective and efficient are:

* simple enough for students to understand
* short enough not to take up too much time
* detailed enough for students to know exactly what they need to do.

The amount of information that needs to be included in the instructions depends on the following:

* how familiar the assessment tasks are to our students
* the number and variety of different task types used.

Thus, for a classroom-based assessment that includes only one or two assessment tasks that are very similar to instructional tasks, you may need to include only a minimal amount of detail in the instructions. For assessments covering longer periods of instruction and larger amounts of material, and that may be administered to different groups of students, you will most likely need to include more extensive, detailed information in the instructions.

12 SCORING STUDENTS' TEST PERFORMANCE AND REPORTING THE RESULTS

Have you ever written a test, given it to your students, and then after they have taken it, tried to figure out how to score their responses? Have you asked yourself any of these questions?

- How many points should each test task be worth?
- Should some tasks count more than others?
- Should I give multiple points (e.g. 2, 3, 4) to tasks that are more important, or should I give partial points (e.g. ½, ⅓, ¼), to tasks that are less important?
- What is the "best" way to get a total score for the test?
- How can I give my students grades or marks that appropriately reflect their achievement?
- How can I report my students' achievement in ways that their parents/guardians and other stakeholders can understand?

In this chapter, we discuss procedures for arriving at an assessment record that is a score and for reporting the results to stakeholders. We first discuss procedures for arriving at scores for individual test tasks or items. We then discuss procedures for combining item scores to arrive at a total test score that will be reported to stakeholders. We also discuss procedures for combining multiple parts of a test or multiple tests given at different times, and for arriving at scores, grades, or marks that we can report to stakeholders. Finally, we describe problems with interpreting raw scores and discuss ways for making test scores meaningful.

As discussed in Chapter 7, an assessment record can consist of a written or verbal description or a score. Written or verbal descriptions are provided primarily for the purpose of giving feedback to students. These descriptions can vary greatly, from a single word or phrase to lengthy explanations referring to specific aspects of students' performance in relationship to the particular learning objectives that were assessed. Furthermore, the content and form of this feedback needs to be tailored to the specific assessment and the individual needs of each student. For this reason, it is not possible to prescribe a set of procedures for providing written or verbal feedback on the basis of classroom-based assessments. Therefore, we do not discuss assessment records that consist of written or verbal descriptions.

Scoring individual test tasks or items

As we discussed in Chapter 8, an essential component of an assessment task template is a method for recording students' responses. If the assessment record is a score, the recording method will include a scoring method.

➤ A **scoring method** specifies how the teacher will arrive at a score on the basis of students' performances. It consists of the criteria for evaluating the correctness or quality of the students' responses, the score to be reported, and the procedures to be followed in arriving at a score.

An example of a scoring method—for a matching item in this instance—is given in Table 12.1 (see Example 2 on page 181 for the complete example). This matching item is aimed at testing students' comprehension of cohesion and coherence in reading. In this test, students read a text with six gapped sentences. Then they select the sentences that match the gaps from a list of possible sentences.

Scoring method:
  Criteria: (See the Scoring Key)
  For each correct gap completion: 1 point
  Score reported: number of correct choices for gaps (6 maximum)
  Procedures: The teacher reads each student's answers and assigns the points according to the Scoring Key, adds these up to get a total score, and enters this on the student's paper. The papers with the scores are given back to the students in the next lesson.

Table 12.1 Example scoring method

The scoring method is an essential component of the assessment task template that you will use for creating assessment tasks. Thus, you will specify the scoring method when you create the assessment task template *before* you give the assessment tasks to your students.

Considerations in deciding on a scoring method

There are different kinds of scoring methods and not all of these will be appropriate for every aspect of language ability you may want to test, or for every type of test task you may want to include in your test. Therefore, in specifying a scoring method, you will need to consider the relationships among the way you have defined the ability to be tested, the kinds of tasks you will include in the test, and the scoring method you will use.

You may want to include certain kinds of test tasks and use a particular scoring method for these because of the way you have defined the ability to be assessed. For example, if you defined the ability to be tested as "comprehension of major ideas in reading", you might present your students with several short paragraphs that discuss different aspects of some topic, and a list of possible headings for these paragraphs. Then you could ask your students to match the headings with the paragraphs, and score their responses by giving one point for each correct match. If, on the other hand, you defined the ability as "appropriate use of formal and informal registers in speaking", you might develop a task in which students perform a spoken role-play that requires them to use both formal and informal registers. You could score their performance by using a rating scale that describes several different levels of appropriate register use.

For the purpose of developing a scoring method, it is useful to think of students' expected responses in terms of three different types: selected responses, limited production responses, and extended production responses.

➤ In a **selected response**, students select one or more responses from among several possible responses that are given. Typical tasks that elicit selected responses are multiple-choice and matching items.

➤ In a **limited production response**, students' responses can vary from a single word or phrase (oral or written), to a single sentence or utterance. Typical tasks that elicit limited production responses are short answer and completion items.

➤ In an **extended production response**, students' responses are longer than a single sentence or utterance, and can vary from two sentences to longer stretches of discourse, such as a written paragraph or essay, or, in speaking, a conversation or a speech. Typical tasks that elicit extended production responses are those that are generally included in essay/composition exams or oral interviews.

As we discuss in the next section, different scoring methods will be appropriate for each of these expected response types.

Different types of scoring methods

Many different kinds of tasks are used in language tests and thus there are many different kinds of scoring methods. However, all of these can be grouped into two general types. In one type, the score consists of the number of tasks or items successfully completed. In the other type, the score is defined in terms of several levels on one or more rating scales of language ability.

Number of tasks successfully completed

When the assessment consists of items intended to test specific aspects of language ability, the students' responses will generally be either selected responses or limited production responses.

Selected response

Items aimed at eliciting a selected response can be useful for testing specific areas of language knowledge, for example, grammatical or lexical knowledge, or specific aspects of listening and reading comprehension. For scoring selected responses, the criteria for scoring will be specified in a scoring key.

➢ A **scoring key** specifies the correct responses to assessment tasks and how many points each correct response counts.

An example of a scoring key for a selected response item is given as follows: A 4 B 1 C 9 D 7 E 8 F 6. This scoring key is from an assessment that includes matching items aimed at testing students' comprehension of major ideas in reading (see Example 9 on page 253 for the complete example). In this test, students read six short paragraphs (A–F) and are given a list of nine possible headings (1–9). Students match the headings with the paragraphs they describe the best.

For selected responses, the procedure for arriving at a score is to add up the number of correct responses, according to the Scoring Key. If you believe that some items are more important than others, it is easier to arrive at a total score for the test if you give multiple points (e.g. 2, 3, 4) to these items, rather than giving partial or fractional points (e.g., ½, ⅓, ¼) to items that are less important.

The only advantage of items aimed at eliciting a selected response is that they are easy to score by using a scoring key. For each item there is only one correct response. However, there are several disadvantages. Most importantly, in our view, they do not require students to produce language and thus may not correspond very closely to instructional tasks. For this reason, they may produce negative washback on instruction. Another disadvantage is that because they are scored right or wrong, they do not allow us to give students credit for partial knowledge or partial mastery of the learning objectives. They are also difficult to create. In order to minimize the chance that students can guess the correct response, we need to provide more choices than there are correct responses. For multiple-choice items, this means providing two or three choices that are not correct responses, in addition to the correct responses. For matching items, we need to provide two or three more choices than there are correct matches. We also need to try to make sure that all of the incorrect choices we provide are responses that might be plausible to students who have not mastered the learning objectives, or that might be based on a misinterpretation of the input of the task. It can be difficult to come up with choices that are incorrect responses but also plausible for students who have not mastered the learning objectives.

Limited production response

Items aimed at eliciting a limited production response can also be used for testing specific areas of language ability. For scoring limited production responses, the criteria for scoring will be also specified in a scoring key. An example of a scoring key for a limited production response item is given in Table 12.2. This scoring key is from an assessment that includes short answer items aimed at testing students' comprehension of specific details in listening. In this test, students listen to a conversation between two people and then write short answers to 10 questions on an answer sheet. (See Example 4 on page 200 for the complete example.)

Question	Answer	Point(s)
1	café	1 point
2	She can't eat unhealthy (food).	1 point
3	(a) baseball	1 point
4	(at) normal meal times / breakfast, lunch, and dinner	1 point each (2 points total)
5	water / juice / milk	1 point each (3 points total)
6	(take) a break from exercise / rest	1 point each (2 points total)
7	every day this week, except today	1 point
8	4 o'clock	1 point
9	Thursday	1 point
10	stay home / practice violin	1 point each (2 points total)
	Total possible points	15

Table 12.2 Example scoring key for limited production response item

For limited production responses, the procedure for arriving at a score is to add up the number of points for correct responses, according to the scoring key. If you believe that some items are more important than others, it is easier to arrive at a total score for the test if you give multiple points to these items, rather than giving partial or fractional points.

Items aimed at eliciting limited production responses can be easy to score using a scoring key. In addition, there are several advantages of these items, as opposed to items aimed at eliciting selected responses. Most importantly, because these items require students to actually produce some language, they are likely to correspond more closely to instructional tasks and thus provide more generalizability than selected response items. Another advantage is that because we can create items that elicit more than a single piece of information, we can give students credit for partial knowledge. Finally, short answer and completion items are generally easier to create because we do not have to provide incorrect responses as choices.

How many points per question?

For selected responses, if the items are all aimed at testing learning objectives that are equally important, then each correct response should be given one point. In some cases, you may feel that some learning objectives are particularly important. In this case, you can include more than one question to test each of these, or you can give more points to the questions that are aimed at testing important learning objectives.

For limited production responses, students' responses to different items may be given different numbers of points. The number of points given for each item will depend on the amount of information required. For testing reading and listening comprehension, the number of points will be determined by the completeness of the information given in the response. If only a single piece of information is required, as in questions 1, 2, 3, 7, 8, and 9 in the example in Table 12.3, then the item should be given one point. If more than a single piece of information is required, as in questions 4, 5, 6, and 10, then the students' responses should be given as many points as there are correct pieces of information in their response.

Scoring as levels of language ability

When we want to test our students' ability to use the language in speaking or writing, we generally need to elicit more language than we can obtain from limited production responses. Thus, we will use tasks that include prompts aimed at eliciting extended production responses. Typical tasks that elicit extended production responses are those that are included in essay/composition exams or oral interviews. For scoring extended production responses, the criteria for evaluating the quality of students' responses are defined as several levels on one or more rating scales of language ability.

➤ A **rating scale** (sometimes called a "scoring rubric") specifies different levels on the ability to be assessed and provides descriptors for each of these levels.

There are two different kinds of rating scales: global rating scales and analytic rating scales.

Global rating scales

➤ A **global rating scale** (sometimes called a "holistic" scale) is a rating scale in which the students' performance is rated in terms of its general quality or level of ability. A global scale provides a single rating or score for a student's assessment performance.

An example of a global rating scale is provided in Table 12.3. This example is from the Common European Frame of Reference (Council of Europe, 2001, p. 58). Global rating scales are widely used in large-scale, high-stakes assessments primarily because raters can use them to rate test takers' responses very quickly. However, global scales are not likely to be very useful for classroom-based assessments for two reasons. First, in most classroom-based assessments we are interested in assessing specific aspects of language ability or specific learning objectives that we have focused on in our instruction. Second, because global scales provide only a single score, they are not very useful for providing feedback to our students. For these reasons we do not recommend the use of global rating scales for classroom-based assessments.

	Overall oral production
C2	Can produce clear, smoothly flowing well-structured speech with an effective logical structure which helps the recipient to notice and remember significant points.
C1	Can give clear, detailed descriptions and presentations on complex subjects, integrating sub-themes, developing particular points and rounding off with an appropriate conclusion.
B2	Can give clear, systematically developed descriptions and presentations, with appropriate highlighting of significant points, and relevant supporting detail.
B1	Can give clear, detailed descriptions and presentations on a wide range of subjects related to his/her field of interest, expanding and supporting ideas with subsidiary points and relevant examples.
	Can reasonably fluently sustain a straightforward description of one of a variety of subjects within his/her field of interest, presenting it as a linear sequence of points.
A2	Can give a simple description or presentation of people, living or working conditions, daily routines, likes/dislikes, etc. as a short series of simple phrases and sentences linked into a list.
A1	Can produce simple mainly isolated phrases about people and places.

Table 12.3 Example global rating scale

Analytic rating scales

➤ An **analytic rating scale** is a rating scale in which the students' performance is rated in terms of multiple components, each of which is rated on a separate scale. An analytic scale provides a "profile" of several different ratings or scores for a student's assessment performance.

An example of an analytic rating scale for a writing test is provided in Table 12.4. For this writing test, students choose a vehicle from the list provided and write a descriptive paragraph about it in 100–130 words.

Analytic rating scales are useful for classroom-based assessment because they make it possible for us to include specific learning objectives in our definition of the ability to be assessed. In addition, because they provide separate ratings or scores for each aspect of the ability, they have more potential for providing feedback to our students.

For extended production responses, the criteria for evaluating students' responses are specified in a rating scale. The procedure for arriving at a score is for the teacher to assign points according to the rating scale.

Points	Grammar	Vocabulary	Cohesion
4	Wide range of grammar structures with very few inaccuracies	Wide range of vocabulary with very few inaccuracies	Wide range of cohesive devices with very few inaccuracies
3	Good range of grammar structures with occasional inaccuracies	Good range of vocabulary with occasional inaccuracies	Good range of cohesive devices with occasional inaccuracies
2	Limited range of grammar structures with frequent inaccuracies	Limited range of vocabulary with frequent inaccuracies	Limited range of cohesive devices with frequent inaccuracies
1	Very limited range of grammar structures with very frequent inaccuracies	Very limited range of vocabulary with very frequent inaccuracies	Very limited range of cohesive devices with very frequent inaccuracies

Table 12.4 Example analytic rating scale

Combining scores and reporting the results

For any test, you will need to arrive at a total score that is based on the scores or ratings of your students' responses to individual test tasks or items. If the test includes several parts, each measuring a different aspect of language ability, you may want to arrive at a total score that is based on the scores for the different parts. This total score can show you if there is a need to make changes in your instruction and can provide feedback to your students on their overall achievement. You can also use this score to inform various stakeholders, for example, parents/guardians or school officials, about your students' overall achievement. For this reason, the score you report needs to be meaningful and useful to different groups of stakeholders. Thus, in addition to specifying how you will score or rate your students' responses to individual assessment tasks, you will also need to specify the kind of total score—a number or a grade or mark—you will use to report their performance on the entire test and how you will arrive at that score.

In many situations, you may also need to combine the scores from several different tests given at different times, to arrive at a total score or a grade or mark for a school term or an entire school year. This score, grade, or mark will typically be used to make summative decisions about your students.

In all three situations—arriving at a total score for a single test, combining scores from multiple parts of a test, or combining scores from different tests—you need to decide on the kind of score you will report and specify how you will arrive at this. In deciding how to arrive at a score to be reported, you need to consider:

- the purposes for which the score will be used
- the intended audience (stakeholders) to whom the score will be reported
- the kind of score that will be most meaningful and useful for the intended purposes and audience.

Total score for a single test

To arrive at a total score for a single test, you will combine the scores for the individual items.

Purposes

Many of the classroom-based tests you give your students will cover a fairly limited amount of instructional content, such as a short quiz over a single lesson. The primary uses of these tests are typically to make low-stakes formative decisions:

- provide feedback to your students on their overall performance on the test
- help you make changes to your instruction if needed
- report your students' overall achievement to stakeholders.

Intended audiences

The audiences, or stakeholders, who will receive scores from individual classroom-based tests is generally limited to your students, yourself, parents/guardians, and possibly school officials.

Kind of score to be reported

Many different kinds of total scores can be reported for single tests, and the kind of total score you report depends mainly on who will receive it. The score that will be reported for a single test can be arrived at in several different ways.

1 For selected and limited production responses

- As the number of tasks or items correctly answered
- As number of correct answers out of the total possible
- As the percentage correct
- As a grade or mark

For individuals very close to the test itself, i.e. you and your students, the "raw" score, or the number of tasks correctly answered, will be meaningful because both you and your students know how many tasks there were in the test. However, for individuals further away from the test, for example, parents/guardians or school officials, these raw scores may not be meaningful, because these stakeholders are not likely to know how many tasks were in the test. Reporting a raw score of "14" to them, for example, will not be meaningful. This is because if there were 15 items on the test, then 14 would be a very good score, while if there were 50 items on the test, 14 could be a very low score. For this reason, it is generally more meaningful to report the score either as a number correct out of a total (for example, 14 out of 20) or as a percentage correct (for example, 70%). The percentage correct can be calculated by dividing the number of correct responses by the total number of items and multiplying this by 100 (for example, $14 \div 20 \times 100 = 70\%$).

2 For extended production responses

- As a profile of analytic ratings/scores
- As a total score for the ratings
- As a grade or mark

A profile of the analytic ratings you give will be meaningful for you and your students. For example, if you gave ratings of "3, 4, 2" for grammar, vocabulary, and cohesion, respectively, you and your students know the rating scales that were used – the areas of ability, the number of scale levels, and the descriptors of those different levels. However, in order for these ratings to be meaningful to other stakeholders, you will need to include the actual rating scales used along with the profile of ratings. You may also want to report a total, or composite score, based on the analytic ratings.

➢ A **composite score** is a total score that is arrived at by taking into account all the different analytic ratings, all the scores from different parts of a test, or all the scores from different tests given at different times.

There are two ways to arrive at a composite score for analytic ratings: compensatory and non-compensatory. The approach you use will depend on the purpose for which the score will be used.

Compensatory composite score

In some situations, you may believe that high ratings on some scales can compensate for low ratings on other scales. For example, for the Rating Scale in Table 12.4 (on page 155), with ratings for grammar, vocabulary, and cohesion, you may feel that high ability in either or any one of these three areas can compensate for relatively low ability in the other two. Then you will want to use a compensatory composite score to report your students' achievement.

➢ A **compensatory composite score** is the total or average of all the analytic ratings, all the scores from different parts of a test, or all the scores from different tests given at different times.

There are two possible ways to arrive at a compensatory composite score: treating the different ratings as equally important, or treating them as of unequal importance.

Ratings of equal importance

In some cases, you may believe that all the ratings are equally important. Then you can arrive at a compensatory composite score by either adding the ratings together to arrive at a total score or by calculating the average of the scores. For the Rating Scale in Table 12.4, for example, if the teacher believed that all of the components were of equal importance, he could arrive at a total score simply by adding the scores for these ratings together, as follows:

Total score = grammar rating + vocabulary rating + cohesion rating

In the example in Table 12.4, with analytic ratings of 3, 4, and 2, the total score would be 9: (3 + 4 + 2 = 9).

Alternatively, the teacher could arrive at an average score for all the analytic ratings as follows:

$$\text{Average score} = \frac{(\text{total score})}{(\text{number of ratings})} \quad (3)$$

For the example above, the average score would be 3: (3 + 4 + 2 = 9, 9 ÷ 3 = 3).

Ratings of unequal importance

In other cases, you may believe that some ratings are more important than others. You can give these ratings more "weight" in the composite total score by multiplying these by a number that represents their relative importance. In the previous example, suppose that the teacher believed that cohesion was the most important component, that grammar was the next most important, with vocabulary being the least important. In this case, the teacher might assign weights to the ratings of these components to reflect their relative importance, as follows:

Weighted total score = (cohesion rating x 3) + (grammar rating x 2) + (vocabulary rating x 1)

In the example above, with analytic ratings of 3, 4, and 2, the weighted total score would be 19: ((3 x 3) + (4 x 2) + (2 x 1) = 19).

Alternatively, he could arrive at a weighted average score for the weighted components by dividing the total score by the total number of weights, as illustrated in Table 12.5.

Part	Rating	Weight	Weighted rating
Cohesion	3	3	9
Grammar	4	2	8
Vocabulary	2	1	2
	Total	6	19

$$\text{Weighted average score} = \frac{\text{(total score)}}{\text{(number of weights)}}$$

In this example, the weighted average score would be 3.2: (19/6 = 3.16; rounded to the nearest decimal, 3.2).

Table 12.5 *Weighted average score for example ratings*

Non-compensatory composite score

If the composite score for the ratings will be used for making high-stakes summative decisions, such as pass/not pass to the next grade, or certifying students' levels of ability, then you may want to consider using a non-compensatory composite score.

➤ A **non-compensatory composite score** (sometimes referred to as a "conjunctive composite score") is equal to the *lowest* rating received on any of the analytic ratings, any of the scores for different parts of a test, or any score from different tests given at different times.

This approach assumes that high levels in one or more areas of ability *cannot* compensate for low levels in other areas. To use this score for making decisions about students, you will specify a rating for each scale that you consider to be the minimum acceptable for passing or certification. Then, in order to pass or be certified, a student must achieve that level on every scale. In the example in Table 12.5 with three analytic ratings, if we decided that a rating of 3 is the minimum acceptable for passing, then a student with a profile of ratings of 3, 4, 2 would receive a non-compensatory score of 2 and thus would not pass. The criteria for passing in this approach are more demanding than in the compensatory approach. The advantage, however, is that this approach assures the relevant stakeholders that your students have achieved the criterion level in every area of the ability.

Grade or mark

Another way of reporting students' achievement on a test is as a grade (e.g. A, B, C) or a mark (e.g. 1, 2, 3). (These are defined and discussed on page 162.)

Score based on multiple tests

When you need to use scores from classroom-based tests to make medium- to high-stakes summative decisions, you will want to base these decisions on more information than can be provided by a single test. In general, the higher the stakes of the decision, the more information about your students' achievement you will need. Thus, for making summative decisions about your students, you will need to obtain a total score that is based on multiple tests.

There are two situations in which you need to arrive at a total score based on multiple tests: a test that consists of several different parts, and different tests given at different times.

Tests with multiple parts

To arrive at a total score for a test with multiple parts, you will combine the scores for the different parts to arrive at a composite score.

Purposes

You will sometimes want to develop classroom-based tests that cover more material, or different areas of language ability than can be covered in a single test. Tests like these will typically include different parts for the different areas of language ability to be tested. Since they generally cover larger amounts of material, or longer periods of instruction, these tests may be used to make both low-stakes formative and medium- to high-stakes summative decisions, for example:

- providing feedback to your students on their overall performance on the test
- helping you make changes to your instruction, if needed
- reporting your students' overall achievement to stakeholders
- in combination with other tests given during the year, deciding which students will pass to the next grade, or which students will be certified at a particular level of ability.

Intended audiences

The audiences or stakeholders who will receive scores from classroom-based tests with multiple parts may include your students, yourself, parents/guardians, teachers in the next grade, and school officials.

Different tests given at different times

To arrive at a total score based on scores from different tests given at different times, you will combine the scores for the different tests to arrive at a composite score.

Purposes

When you need to arrive at a score that will reflect your students' overall achievement over a substantial period of instruction, such as a school term or an entire year, your primary purpose will be to use this score to make high-stakes decisions about which students will pass to the next grade, or which ones will be certified at a given level of language ability.

Intended audiences

The audiences or stakeholders who will receive scores that reflect your students' overall achievement over an extended period of time include potentially all of the stakeholder groups you have identified in Claim 1 for your assessment.

Arriving at a way to report students' achievement

In both situations—a test with different parts or different tests given at different times—the procedures you can follow for arriving at a way to report your students' achievement are essentially the same. There are three ways you can report their achievement:

- a compensatory composite score
- a non-compensatory composite score
- a grade or mark.

Compensatory composite score

A compensatory composite score can be arrived at following the same procedures as discussed on page 157, using the scores of the parts of the test as components. As with ratings, these compensatory composite scores can be arrived at in two ways: treating the scores from the different parts as equally important, or treating them as of unequal importance.

Non-compensatory composite score

A non-compensatory composite score can be arrived at following the same procedures as discussed on page 159, using the scores of the parts of the test as components.

Grade or mark

In many situations where you need to use information about students' test performance for making summative decisions, you will need to give them a grade or a mark.

> A **grade** expresses the students' levels of achievement in terms of a letter, e.g. A, B, C, with "A" being the highest.

> A **mark** expresses the students' level of achievement in terms of a number, e.g. 3, 2, 1, with "3" being the highest.

A grade or a mark is simply a different way of reporting your students' achievement from reporting a score. However, the grade or mark you give will be based on a total score. Thus, in order to arrive at a grade or mark, you need to specify a procedure for converting a total score to a grade or mark. There are two different approaches for doing this: norm-referenced and criterion-referenced.

> A **norm-referenced (NR)** grade or mark reports a student's achievement relative to the achievement of other students in a group, e.g. a class, a grade, a school.

> A **criterion-referenced (CR)** grade or mark reports how well a student has achieved the learning objectives of a course of instruction.

To arrive at NR grades or marks, sometimes called "grading on the curve", students' scores are converted to grades or marks according to their relative standing in the group. For example, you might decide to give grades as illustrated in Table 12.6.

Percentages of students	Grade	Mark
Top 5%	A	1
Next 15%	B	2
Next 60%	C	3
Next 15%	D	4
Lowest 5%	F	5

Table 12.6 Example of NR grades or marks

According to Table 12.6, 5% of the students with the highest scores will receive an A or 1; 15% with the next highest scores will receive a B or 2, and so on. If there are 100 students in the class, the five students with the highest scores will receive As or 1s, while the 15 students with the next highest scores will receive Bs or 2s, and so on.

There are some problems with using NR grading for classroom-based assessments. One problem is that only a certain percentage of the students can receive high grades or marks. Thus, even if the majority of the students in the class master the learning objectives, only a small percentage of the students will receive high grades or marks. A second problem is that a certain percentage of students will always receive the lowest grade, no matter how well they perform in the class. For example, if the lowest 5% of the students actually received scores equal to, say, 70% correct, they will still receive a failing grade, even though their score indicates that they have mastered most of the course objectives.

NR grading can also have a negative impact on learning. First, it tends to promote competition, rather than cooperation, among students. Second, it penalizes students who are achieving well but are not in the top percentage of students, and thus can cause these students to lose their motivation and interest in learning. Finally, because NR grading is based on the rank-order of the students, NR scores do not reflect the actual achievement of students in terms of their mastery of learning objectives. For these reasons, we would strongly urge classroom teachers to avoid this approach for awarding grades or making pass/not pass decisions about their students.

To arrive at CR grades or marks, students' scores are converted to grades or marks according to their mastery of the course content. If teaching and learning have been successful and the majority of the students have mastered the course content, then they will receive high grades or marks, irrespective of how many students this might be. Thus, CR grading reflects how well students have mastered the learning objectives of the course, which can be useful for both formative and summative purposes. It can be useful for providing general feedback to students on their overall level of achievement and for helping the teacher evaluate the overall success of his or her instruction. CR grading can also be useful to stakeholders such as teachers in subsequent grades, university admissions officers, or employers because it is tied directly to the content of the course, and can thus be interpreted as the degree of mastery of this content. Finally, we would note that research suggests that CR grading promotes cooperation among students and appropriately rewards students who achieve the course objectives. For these reasons, we would strongly urge classroom teachers to adopt this approach for making decisions about their students.

Reference

Council of Europe. (2001). *Common European Framework of Reference for Languages: learning, teaching, assessment.* Cambridge: Cambridge University Press.

PART IV: EXAMPLES OF CLASSROOM-BASED LANGUAGE ASSESSMENTS

In Part IV, we provide 9 fully specified examples that illustrate the process of developing classroom-based language assessments that has been described in Parts II and III. Extracts of these examples are included in the chapters as illustrations and examples of specific parts of the assessment development process. Further examples can be found on the companion website at www.oup.com/elt/teacher/lact

EXAMPLE ASSESSMENTS

To illustrate our approach to developing classroom-based assessments, we provide 15 examples. Nine examples are given in this book, and another six examples are available on the companion website at: www.oup.com/elt/teacher/lact. Each example includes the following:

- a brief overview of the assessment, which includes:
  - the intended test takers (age group, level of language ability)
  - the language to be assessed
  - the language use activity
  - the intended uses of the assessment
- the "setting" which describes the type of classroom in which the assessment will be used, the intended uses of the assessment, the decisions to be made, and a short description of the assessment task
- the claims in the AUA for the assessment, including some possible backing for these claims
- the following steps in developing the assessment task:
  - step 1: the TLU task selected for development of the assessment task
  - step 2: description of the TLU task
  - step 3: the modified task/assessment task template
  - step 4: a model assessment task.

We have included examples of four language use activities (listening, speaking, reading, and writing), for different age groups, and for different levels of ability, as follows:

- age groups:
  - young learners (approximately 5–12 years old)
  - teens (approximately 13–19 years old)
  - adults (approximately 20 years old and over)
- general levels of language ability:
  - beginning
  - intermediate
  - advanced

We would note that we have used "age group" as a general way to designate stages or levels of cognitive, emotional, and social development. We recognize that these levels are broad and general, and that the exact ages at which a "young learner" develops into a "teen" and a "teen" into an "adult" will vary from individual to individual and across cultures and settings. When we say that a particular task is aimed at a particular age group, this is our best guess, and should be taken only as a suggestion. Thus, you should not feel obliged to try out these examples only with the age groups we have suggested. You may find, for example, that an assessment we have suggested for teens would be suitable for your young adult students, or that some we have suggested for adults would be suitable for your older teen students. We would also note that some of our examples are for secondary school or university. Depending on your particular situation, these examples may also be appropriate for students in adult education programs.

We would make similar comments about the ability levels we have used. We have specifically avoided reference to widely used standards for language ability levels, such as the CEFR (Council of Europe, 2001) or American Council on the Teaching of Foreign Languages Proficiency Guidelines (2012). This is because we have no evidence to support claims that these example assessments are at the levels described in such standards. In addition, because of the diversity in educational systems and language programs around the world, it was not possible for us to define levels of language in terms of any specific course or syllabus. Therefore, we have decided to use the terms, "beginning", "intermediate", and "advanced" to indicate the general level of language ability for which an example assessment is intended. As with age groups, we realize that these levels are broad and general, and that there are no universal dividing lines between these ability levels. Thus, you may find that an assessment that we have targeted for intermediate level might be appropriate for your upper-beginning level students, or one that we have targeted as advanced level might be appropriate for your upper-intermediate students.

In summary, we want you to feel free to try these assessments out with your students. The age groups and general language ability levels we have indicated for these assessments should be taken only as very general guidance, and not as absolute. Therefore, you should feel free to try out assessment tasks from these examples that you feel would be appropriate for your own students, irrespective of the age or ability levels we have indicated. We suggest that you look at the actual assessment tasks in these examples, and then decide whether or not you feel they would be appropriate for your own students.

Brief descriptions of the examples are provided in Table E0.1. Table E0.2 provides a quick reference guide to help you find examples according to level of ability, age group, and skill.

Example*	Skill	Topic, task	Age	Level	Decisions	Page
1	Speaking	Describing animals	Young learners	Beginning	Formative, summative	169
2	Reading	Greenwich Village, filling gapped sentences	Teens or adults	Advanced	Summative	181
3	Speaking	Describing my favorite place	Teens	Intermediate	Formative, summative	190
4	Listening	Answering questions about free-time activities	Teens	Intermediate	Summative	200
5	Listening	Answering questions about best moment of life	Teens	Beginning	Summative	210
6	Writing	Describing a musical instrument	Teens	Intermediate	Formative, summative	222
7	Speaking	Discussing an environmental issue	Teens or adults	Advanced	Summative	232
8	Writing	Letter of application for a job	Teens or adults	Advanced	Formative, summative	242
9	Reading	Street art, matching headings	Teens	Intermediate	Summative	253
(10)	Reading	Poem about food, matching and coloring pictures	Young learners	Beginning	Summative	–
(11)	Writing	Letter of complaint	Teens or adults	Advanced	Formative, summative	–
(12)	Writing	Report on shopping habits	Adults	Advanced	Formative, summative	–
(13)	Listening, writing	Lecture on the history of the English language, writing a summary	Adults	Advanced	Summative	–
(14)	Speaking	Discussing prompts about current topics	Teens or adults	Advanced	Summative	–
(15)	Listening	Listening to directions, drawing colored geometric forms	Young learners	Beginning	Summative	–

Table E0.1 Brief description of Examples

*Examples in parentheses "( )" can be found on the companion website at: www.oup.com/elt/teacher/lact

Level of Ability	Beginning		Intermediate		Advanced	
Age	Young learners	Teens	Teens	Adults	Teens	Adults
Listening	(15)*	5	4			(13)
Speaking	1		3		7, (14)	7, (14)
Reading	(10)		9		2	2
Writing			6		8, (11)	8, (11), (12), (13)

Table E0.2 Quick reference guide to examples

*Examples in parentheses "( )" can be found on the companion website at: www.oup.com/elt/teacher/lact

Example 1: Speaking, describing animals (young learners, beginning level)

Brief overview of the assessment

Test takers	Students
Age group	Young learners
Level of language ability	Beginning
Language	ESL/EFL
Language use activity	Speaking, describing animals
Intended uses	Formative feedback for teacher and students; summative decisions

Setting

A teacher in an ESL/EFL classroom in a primary/elementary school needs to develop a classroom assessment for his beginning level students. This assessment will be used for two different purposes. One purpose is to make sure that the students who pass the grade are prepared for instruction at the next grade. In order to do this, the teacher will use the results of this assessment, along with other assessments given during the course of the school year, to make summative decisions about which students will pass to the next grade. The second purpose is to help his students improve their speaking and to improve his teaching. In order to do this, the teacher will also use the results of this assessment to make formative decisions about his teaching and to provide feedback to his students. The assessment will be based on a unit of instruction in the course, and this is one task from the assessment, in which students describe animals from pictures by speaking.

Assessment use argument

Claim 1: Intended consequences

The consequences of using the classroom speaking assessment will be beneficial to stakeholders as indicated in Tables E1.1 and E1.2.

Intended consequences	Intended stakeholders
1a Students who have mastered the learning objectives of the entire term will benefit by receiving appropriate instruction at the next level.	Students ESL/EFL teachers in the next level
1b Students who have not mastered the learning objectives of the entire term will benefit by receiving appropriate instruction at the same level.	Students ESL/EFL teachers in the current level
2 Students will improve their speaking.	Students Teacher
3 The teacher will improve his teaching.	Students Teacher

Table E1.1 Intended consequences and intended stakeholders

Other possible consequences and stakeholders who might be affected are included in Table E1.2.

Other possible consequences	Stakeholders who might be affected
Teachers will be able to teach students who are prepared for their level.	ESL/EFL teachers in the current level ESL/EFL teachers in the next level
There will be fewer complaints from teachers, students, and parents/guardians.	School administrators
The reputation of the school will improve.	The school
Parents/Guardians will be satisfied with their children's speaking and help their children continue to improve.	Parents/Guardians, students, teachers

Table E1.2 Other possible consequences and stakeholders who might be affected

Some possible backing for intended consequences in Claim 1

- Students receiving instruction at the appropriate level:
  - teacher talks with ESL/EFL teachers in the next course/grade about how well students who moved on to the next course/grade are performing in speaking

- o teacher talks with ESL/EFL teachers in the same course/grade about how well students who did not move to the next grade are performing in speaking.
- Students' improvement in speaking:
  - o teacher observes students' speaking performance in class
  - o teacher talks with students about their use of feedback from the assessment to improve their speaking
  - o teacher asks the students to answer a questionnaire on how they have improved their speaking
  - o teacher compares students' performance on the next speaking assessment with their performance on this one.
- Teacher's improvement in teaching:
  - o teacher makes notes on how he changed his instruction for speaking activities
  - o teacher gets feedback from students through a survey or questionnaire
  - o teacher asks one or two fellow ESL/EFL teachers to observe his classroom teaching.

Claim 2: Intended decisions

The high-stakes summative decisions are made by the teacher at the end of the school year. The low-stakes formative decisions are made by the teacher and the students before the next unit of instruction. These decisions affect the stakeholders as indicated in Table E1.3. The decisions take into consideration the educational values of the school and the societal values of the community, and follow the rules and regulations of the school. They are equitable for the stakeholders listed in Table E1.3.

Decision(s) to be made	Individual(s) who will make the decision(s)	When the decision(s) will be made	Stakeholders who will (or might be) affected by the decision(s)
Summative, high stakes			
Decide which students pass to the next grade (scores from this assessment will count as part of students' total grade for the term)	Teacher	At the end of the school term	Students Teachers (Future teachers) (School administrators) (The school) (Parents/Guardians)

Formative, low stakes			
Provide students with feedback on their speaking performance	Teacher	Immediately after the assessment	Students Teachers (Parents/Guardians)
Make appropriate changes to teaching	Teacher	Before the next unit of instruction	Students Teachers (Parents/Guardians)
Continue with planned teaching; review, or give additional support tasks	Teacher	Before the next unit of instruction	Students Teachers (Parents/Guardians)
Review and/or practice learning objectives on which students need to improve	Students	After they receive the teacher's feedback	Teachers Students (Parents/Guardians)

Table E1.3 Intended decisions

Some possible backing for intended decisions in Claim 2

Values-sensitivity

- High-stakes summative decisions:
  - teacher meets with students, fellow teachers, school administrators, and parents/guardians to discuss the relevant values that need to be considered in the decisions to be made
  - teacher reviews school rules and regulations regarding the use of assessments for decisions about which students will pass to the next grade.
- Low-stakes formative decisions:
  - teacher considers how consistent the decisions to be made are with his own values and beliefs about effective instructional practice.

Equitability

- High-stakes summative decisions:
  - teacher documents procedures for 1) setting standards and cut scores based on all of the assessments given during the course of the school year; 2) monitoring how these are implemented in practice; and 3) informing students and other stakeholders about these.
- Low-stakes formative decisions:
  - equitability is not a concern in low-stakes formative decisions because these are not made for the purpose of classifying students into groups.

Claim 3: Intended interpretations

The interpretations about three aspects of students' speaking ability—accurate grammar, vocabulary, and pronunciation—are relevant to the formative and summative decisions to be made. The interpretations are sufficient for the low-stakes formative decisions to be made, but not sufficient for the high-stakes summative decisions. These summative decisions will be made on the basis of this assessment and other classroom assessments that will be given during the course of instruction. The interpretations are meaningful with respect to the content of the course and of the current lesson, generalizable to the current language class, and are impartial to all students.

Some possible backing for intended interpretations in Claim 3

Relevance and sufficiency:

- teacher meets with ESL/EFL teachers in the current and next grade during the development of the assessment to discuss the interpretations of speaking ability that will be relevant for making the decisions about which students will pass the course

- teacher conducts follow-up meetings with these ESL/EFL teachers on how useful the interpretations actually were in making these decisions.

Meaningfulness:

- teacher provides documentation of relevant instructional materials, e.g. course syllabus, textbook, teaching notes, instructional activities, and lists of the learning objectives of the course, with the specific assessment tasks that are linked to these

- teacher collects feedback from students and other relevant stakeholders about their understanding of the areas of speaking ability to be assessed.

Generalizability:

- teacher provides an analysis of the administrative procedures and task characteristics (TCs) of the instructional tasks in the current classroom

- teacher compares the administrative procedures and TCs of these instructional tasks with those of the assessment tasks

- teacher collects feedback from students and fellow teachers about the degree of correspondence between target language use (TLU) tasks and assessment tasks.

Impartiality:

- teacher carefully reviews the assessment tasks for possible sources of bias

- teacher asks fellow teachers to review the assessment tasks for possible sources of bias

- teacher collects feedback from students about assessment tasks that they felt were possibly biased.

Claim 4: Assessment records

The scores from the speaking assessment are consistent across different times and days of administration, and across different administrations to different pairs and classes of students. Students' scores are consistent across the pictures of different animals and different pairs of students. Students' performances are scored consistently by the teacher, according to a consistent application of the Rating

Scale. The possible sources of inconsistency for this assessment are listed in Table E1.4.

Possible sources of inconsistency in scores

1 Inconsistencies in the administration of the assessment
   • different times or days of administration
   • different administrations to different pairs of students
   • different administrations to different classes of students

2 Inconsistencies across different assessment tasks
   • different animals in the pictures
   • differing amounts of detail in the pictures
   • differences between the students who make up the pair

3 Inconsistencies in how students' performances are scored
   • different applications of the Rating Scale from one student to the next
   • different applications of the Rating Scale from one pair to the next

Table E1.4 Possible sources of inconsistency in scores

Some possible backing for intended assessment records in Claim 4

The possible sources of inconsistency and possible backing to assure that these sources will be minimized are given in Table E1.5.

Possible sources of inconsistency	Possible backing to assure consistency

1 Inconsistencies in the administration of the assessment
   • different times or days of administration
   • different administrations to different pairs of students
   • different administrations to different classes of students
	• Documentation: administrative procedures to be followed
	• Teacher's notes from administering the assessment at different times during the class period, on different days, with different pairs of students, and with different classes of students

2 Inconsistencies across different assessment tasks
   • different animals in the pictures
   • differing amounts of detail in the pictures
   • differences between the students who make up the pair
	• Documentation: task specifications for the pictures to be used in the assessment
	• Teacher's notes on any differences that were observed in how different pictures may have affected students' performances
	• Teacher's notes on how the attributes of students who were paired may have affected their performances

3 Inconsistencies in how students' performances are scored
  • different applications of the Rating Scale from one student to the next
  • different applications of the Rating Scale from one pair to the next
	• Documentation: Rating Scale, Recording Form, and instructions for scoring
	• Teacher's notes on how the Rating Scale may have been applied differently from one student to the next or across pairs of students

Table E1.5 Possible backing for possible sources of inconsistency

Assessment task development

Step 1 TLU task selected for development of assessment task

1 Short descriptive label for TLU task: describing animals orally in groups in the language classroom.

2 Areas of language ability the TLU task engages: using accurate grammar, vocabulary, and pronunciation in speaking.

Step 2 Description of the TLU task

1 Activities and procedures to be followed:

  a The teacher explains the speaking activity to the class.

    i Each group gets a picture of an animal to describe.

    ii Group members describe their animal orally to the class.

    iii The other students in the class try to guess which animal the group has.

  b Students are arranged in groups of three to four.

  c The teacher gives each group a picture of an animal and tells the students not to show their picture to the other groups.

  d Students work on a description of their animal in their groups, taking notes as needed.

  e The teacher moves around and helps groups.

  f Each student in each group has about half a minute to present a part of their group's description orally to the class.

  g The other students in the class may ask questions after each presentation and guess the animal.

  h Teacher provides verbal feedback on the quality of the descriptions.

2 Task characteristics of TLU task:

TLU task: speaking, describing animals in groups	
Areas of language ability the TLU task engages: using accurate grammar, vocabulary, and pronunciation in speaking	
Task characteristics	
Setting	<u>Physical circumstances</u>: teacher in front of classroom; students in groups of 3–4 *Equipment/Materials*: pictures of animals; paper and pencil <u>Participants</u>: teacher and students (young learners, beginning level) <u>Time of the task</u>: during the class period; two class periods required

Input	<u>Form</u>:
	Aural:
	    Teacher: description of the task, questions, and comments
	    Students: descriptions of animals and questions
	Visual: a picture of an animal for each group; words and phrases that the students may write on paper
	<u>Language</u>: English
	Teacher: short utterances describing and explaining; questions; simple grammar and vocabulary
	Other students: fairly short utterances describing their pictures; questions and answers; simple grammar and vocabulary
	Length: aural: short utterances; *visual:* short (single picture)
	<u>Topical content</u>: physical characteristics of animals

Expected response	<u>Form</u>: *Oral:* students' descriptions of the animals; students' questions; students' responses to teacher's and other students' questions *Visual:* words, phrases, and sentences that students write on paper to support their speaking <u>Language</u>: English; short descriptive utterances, adjectives, and questions *Length*: about half a minute per student <u>Topical content</u>: physical characteristics of animals

Step 3 The modified task/assessment task template

Description of the modified task: speaking individually, describing an animal from a picture, in pairs

Areas of language ability to be assessed: using accurate grammar, vocabulary, and pronunciation in speaking.

1 Activities and procedures to be followed

  a On the day before the assessment the teacher tells the students:

    i They will have an assessment of their speaking the next day.

    ii The purposes of the assessment are:

      a) to give each student a grade or mark that will count as part of his or her grade or mark for the school year

      b) to provide feedback to individual students about their speaking ability.

    iii The teacher will assign the students to pairs for the assessment.

    iv The test will be given individually to each student in the pair.

      a) One student in the pair will be given a picture of an animal that will be different from the ones they described in class. The other student cannot see this student's picture.

      b) The first student will be given half a minute to prepare his or her description.

      c) The first student will then have one minute to describe the animal in the picture to his or her partner. The other student will be asked to guess the animal. This will not be scored.

      d) Then the test will be given to the second student in the pair, following the same procedure as with the first student.

  b On the day of the assessment, the teacher assesses each student in each pair individually.

    i The teacher briefly explains the assessment task again.

    ii The teacher makes sure the students understand the procedure.

    iii The teacher calls the names of the students in the first pair.

    iv The teacher and these two students go to the Speaking Corner of the classroom.

    v The teacher shows the first student a picture of an animal.

    vi The first student takes half a minute to think about his or her description.

    vii Then the first student takes about one minute to describe the animal orally to his or her partner. The other student guesses the animal.

    viii The teacher scores the first student's performance using the Rating Scale on the Recording Form and also makes notes for feedback on the student's speaking using the Recording Form.

    ix The teacher then administers the assessment to the second student, following the same procedure as with the first student.

    x The teacher lets the two students go back to the class and calls the next pair of students for the assessment.

c During the next lesson after the assessment:

    i The teacher gives the students their Recording Forms, with their scores and written feedback.

    ii The teacher gives the class general feedback on their areas of strength and the areas in which they need to improve.

    iii The teacher also provides suggestions for ways in which students can improve their speaking.

d Administrative procedures: The assessment takes place during a class period. It is given as a paired speaking activity between two students, with the teacher observing and listening, in a Speaking Corner of the classroom. The teacher calls the first pair of students to be assessed and explains the assessment task to make sure that the students understand the procedure. The teacher gives the first student a picture of an animal and allows him or her to take half a minute to think about how he or she will describe it. Then the student has one minute to describe the animal to his or her partner. After the first student has finished, the teacher follows the same assessment procedure with the second student. While each student is speaking, the teacher scores his or her performance using the Rating Scale and enters these scores on the Recording Form. The teacher also enters notes for feedback on the student's speaking on the Recording Form. At the end of the assessment, the two students return to the class. The teacher then calls the next pair for the assessment.

2 Task characteristics of the modified task/assessment task template

Assessment task: speaking individually, describing an animal from a picture, in pairs
Areas of language ability to be assessed: using accurate grammar, vocabulary, and pronunciation in speaking

Task characteristics	
Setting	<u>Physical circumstances</u>: the teacher with a pair of students seated at a table in the Speaking Corner of the classroom *Equipment/Materials*: pictures of animals; Recording Form, pen/pencil (for the teacher); table and three chairs for the teacher and students <u>Participants</u>: teacher and a pair of students (young learners, beginning level) <u>Time of the task</u>: during the class period; more than one class period required depending on the number of students
Input	<u>Form</u>: *Aural*: the teacher's spoken description of the task *Visual*: one picture per student of an animal that is different from the ones used in the TLU task <u>Language</u>: English *Teacher: aural*: short spoken description and explanation; simple grammar and vocabulary *Length: aural*: short utterances; *visual*: short (single picture) <u>Topical content</u>: physical characteristics of animals

Expected response	Form: Oral: student's description of the animal in the picture Visual: (none) Language: English; short descriptive utterances, adjectives Length: about one minute per student; two minutes per pair of students Topical content: physical characteristics of animals

3 Modified task/assessment task template recording method

Recording method for assessment task	Types of assessment record: score and written feedback Aspects of ability: three aspects of speaking: use of accurate grammar, vocabulary (adjectives), and pronunciation Scoring method Criteria: (See Rating Scale below) For each aspect: needs improvement – 1; meets expectations – 2; exceeds expectations – 3 Score reported: total score = accurate grammar + accurate vocabulary + accurate pronunciation Procedures: the teacher listens to individual students' responses and enters a score for each aspect of speaking in the Rating Scale for each student. The teacher then adds up the scores to arrive at a total score and enters this on the Recording Form. The teacher also enters written feedback on the student's speaking on the Recording Form. This is given back to the students in the next lesson.

Step 4 Model assessment task

"Here's a picture of an animal. You are going to describe it to your partner the way we did it in class. You have half a minute to look at it and think about how you want to describe it." (Teacher waits half a minute.) "Now describe the animal to your partner. You have one minute." (Teacher repeats this with the second student.)

Recording Form

Assessment task: Speaking, describing the physical characteristics of an animal

Student name: _____ Date: _____

Student paired with: _____

Animal picture: _____

Rating Scale: Aspect of speaking	Needs improvement 1	Meets expectations 2	Exceeds expectations 3	Feedback on student's speaking
Accurate grammar				
Accurate vocabulary (especially adjectives)				
Accurate Pronunciation				

Total score: _____

Example 2: Reading, Greenwich Village, filling gapped sentences (teens or adults, advanced level)

Brief overview of the assessment

Test takers	Students
Age group	Teens or adults
Level of language ability	Advanced
Language	ESL/EFL
Language use activity	Reading for cohesion and coherence
Intended uses	Summative decisions

Setting

A teacher in an ESL/EFL classroom in a secondary school or university needs to develop a classroom assessment for her advanced level students. This assessment will be used for one purpose. She wants to make sure that the students who pass the grade are prepared for instruction at the next level. In order to do this, the teacher will use the results of this assessment, along with other assessments given during the course of the school year, to make summative decisions about which students will pass to the next grade. The assessment will be based on a unit of instruction in the course, and this is one task from the assessment, in which students read a written text with gapped sentences and then choose the sentences from a list that best fit in the gaps.

Assessment use argument

Claim 1: Intended consequences

The consequences of using the classroom reading assessment will be beneficial to stakeholders as indicated in Tables E2.1 and E2.2.

Intended consequences	Intended stakeholders
1a Students who have mastered the learning objectives of the entire term will benefit by receiving appropriate instruction at the next level.	Students ESL/EFL teachers in the next level
1b Students who have not mastered the learning objectives of the entire term will benefit by receiving appropriate instruction at the same level.	Students ESL/EFL teachers in the current level

Table E2.1 Intended consequences and intended stakeholders

Other possible consequences and stakeholders who might be affected are included in Table E2.2.

Other possible consequences	Stakeholders who might be affected
Teachers will be able to teach students who are prepared for their level.	ESL/EFL teachers in the current level ESL/EFL teachers in the next level

Table E2.2 Other possible consequences and stakeholders who might be affected

Some possible backing for intended consequences in Claim 1

- Students receiving instruction at the appropriate level:
  - teacher talks with ESL/EFL teachers in the next course/grade about how well students who moved on to the next course/grade are performing in reading
  - teacher talks with ESL/EFL teachers in the same course/grade about how well students who did not move to the next course/grade are performing in reading.

Claim 2: Intended decisions

The high-stakes summative decisions are made by the teacher at the end of the school year. These decisions affect the stakeholders as indicated in Table E2.3. The decisions take into consideration the educational values of the school and the societal values of the community, and follow the rules and regulations of the school. They are equitable for the stakeholders listed in Table E2.3.

Decision(s) to be made	Individual(s) who will make the decision	When the decision(s) will be made	Stakeholders who will (or might be) affected by the decision(s)
Summative, high stakes			
Decide which students pass to the next grade (scores from this assessment will count as part of students' total grade for the term)	Teacher	At the end of the school term	Students Teachers (Future teachers) (School administrators) (The school) (Parents/ Guardians)

Table E2.3 Intended decisions

Some possible backing for intended decisions in Claim 2

Values-sensitivity

- High-stakes summative decisions:
  - teacher meets with students, fellow teachers, school administrators, and parents/guardians to discuss the relevant values that need to be considered in the decisions to be made
  - teacher reviews school rules and regulations regarding the use of assessments for decisions about which students will pass to the next grade.

Equitability:

- High-stakes summative decisions:
  - teacher documents procedures for 1) setting standards and cut scores based on all of the assessments given during the course of the school year, 2) monitoring how these are implemented in practice, and 3) informing students and other stakeholders about these.

Claim 3: Intended interpretations

The interpretations about students' comprehension of cohesion and coherence in reading are relevant to the high-stakes summative decisions to be made, but are not sufficient for these decisions. These decisions will be made on the basis of this assessment and other classroom assessments that will be given during the course of instruction. The interpretations are meaningful with respect to the content of the course and of the current lesson, generalizable to the current language class, and are impartial to all students.

Some possible backing for intended interpretations in Claim 3

Relevance and sufficiency:

- teacher meets with ESL/EFL teachers in the current and next grades during the development of the assessment to discuss the interpretations of reading ability that will be relevant for making the decisions about which students will pass the course
- teacher conducts follow-up meetings with these ESL/EFL teachers on how useful the interpretations actually were in making these decisions.

Meaningfulness:

- teacher provides documentation of relevant instructional materials, e.g. course syllabus, textbook, teaching notes, instructional activities, and lists of the learning objectives of the course, with the specific assessment tasks that are linked to these
- teacher collects feedback from students and other relevant stakeholders about their understanding of the areas of reading ability to be assessed.

Generalizability:

- teacher provides an analysis of the administrative procedures and TCs of the instructional tasks in the current classroom
- teacher compares the administrative procedures and TCs of these instructional tasks with those of the assessment task
- teacher collects feedback from students and fellow teachers about the degree of correspondence between TLU tasks and assessment tasks.

Impartiality:

- teacher carefully reviews the assessment tasks for possible sources of bias
- teacher asks fellow teachers to review the assessment tasks for possible sources of bias
- teacher collects feedbacks from students about assessment tasks that they felt were possibly biased.

Claim 4: Assessment records

The scores from the reading assessment are consistent across different times and days of administration, and across different administrations to different groups of students. Students' performances are scored consistently by the teacher, according to the Scoring Key. The possible sources of inconsistency for this assessment are listed in Table E2.4.

Possible sources of inconsistency in scores
1 Inconsistencies in the administration of the assessment • different times or days of administration • different administrations to different groups of students
2 Inconsistencies in how students' performances are scored • different applications of the Scoring Key from one student to the next

Table E2.4 Possible sources of inconsistency in scores

Some possible backing for intended assessment records in Claim 4

The possible sources of inconsistency and possible backing to assure that these sources will be minimized are given in Table E2.5.

Possible sources of inconsistency	Possible backing to assure consistency
1 Inconsistencies in the administration of the assessment • different times or days of administration • different administrations to different groups of students	• Documentation of administrative procedures to be followed • Teacher's notes from administering the assessment at different times during the class period, on different days, with different groups of students

2 Inconsistencies in how students' performances are scored • different applications of the Scoring Key from one student to the next	• Documentation: Scoring Key and instructions for scoring • Teacher's notes on how the Scoring Key may have been applied differently from one student to the next

Table E2.5 Possible backing for possible sources of inconsistency

Assessment task development

Step 1   TLU task selected for development of assessment task

1   Short descriptive label for TLU task: reading a text and filling in gapped sentences

2   Areas of language ability the TLU task engages: comprehension of cohesion and coherence in reading

Step 2   Description of the TLU task:

1   Activities and procedures to be followed:

a   The teacher explains the reading activity to the class.

b   Students work individually.

c   Students are given a text with five sentence gaps (sentences have been removed), and a list of seven numbered sentences from which they choose five sentences that best fit in the gaps in the paragraph.

d   Students then read the text and write the numbers of the sentences that best fit the gaps in the text.

e   The teacher and students discuss the answers in class.

f   Students revise their answers as needed.

2   Task characteristics of TLU task:

TLU task: reading and filling in gapped sentences	
Areas of language ability the TLU task engages: comprehension of cohesion and coherence in reading	
Task characteristics	
Setting	Physical circumstances: teacher in front of classroom; students seated individually *Equipment/Materials*: reading text with gaps; pen/pencil Participants: teacher and students (teens or adults, advanced level) Time of the task: during the class period; one class period required

Input	Form:
	Aural: teacher's description of the task, questions, comments
	Visual: reading text with five gaps; seven sentences
	Language: English:
	Teacher: short utterances explaining and describing; simple grammar and vocabulary
	Length: aural: short sentences and phrases; *visual:* medium – reading text with one paragraph; fairly complex grammar and vocabulary with cohesion and coherence and list of seven sentences
	Topical content: Marilyn Monroe
Expected response	Form:
	Visual: students write the numbers of sentences from the list that match the gaps in the paragraph
	Language: non-language
	Length: 20 minutes
	Topical content: Marilyn Monroe

3   Reading text and answer sheet:

Marilyn Monroe

It is over 40 years since Marilyn Monroe died, but theories concerning her death still fascinate the world. A) _____ Marilyn had a reputation as a dumb blonde who had such a problem with drink, drugs, and depression that she could never remember her lines. B) _____ She dated Frank Sinatra, even though he had connections with the Mafia, and she also had affairs with President John Kennedy and his brother Bobby. When Marilyn was found dead in bed at her home in Los Angeles in the early hours of Sunday, August 5, 1962, police assumed it was suicide, as there was an empty bottle of sleeping pills on the table beside her. However, witnesses, including her psychiatrist and some of her friends, insisted she was not suicidal at the time. C) _____ There were other suspicious events. Marilyn's housekeeper disappeared immediately after she was found, only to reappear a year later as an employee of the Kennedys. D) _____ Marilyn's diaries also disappeared. Were they so revealing that they had to be destroyed? E) _____ He never spoke about it while he was alive, in case he also met an untimely death, but he did in his memoirs, which were published as soon as he died.

1   Other witnesses said they saw Bobby Kennedy visit her house that night, even though he claimed to be in San Francisco.

2   Marilyn's ex-husband Joe DiMaggio was convinced the Kennedys had her killed.

3 Howver, her beauty and fame brought her into contact with some of the biggest names of the day.

4 Neighbors claim they saw Marilyn leave the house dressed up in fancy clothes.

5 Why would they employ her unless they wanted her to keep silent?

6 Whenever her name is mentioned, people recall the mystery of her final hours and although the official verdict was suicide, many believe that she was murdered by the Mafia or the FBI.

7 Marilyn Monroe was one of the most sought-after movie stars of her time and will forever stay in people's memories.

Answer Key:

A 6   B 3   C 1   D 5   E 2

Step 3 The modified task/assessment task template:

1 Activities and procedures to be followed:

  a A week before the assessment the teacher tells the students:

    i They will have an assessment of their reading ability the following week.

    ii The purpose of the assessment is to give each student a mark that will count as part of his or her grade for the school term.

    iii They will have to read a text with gapped sentences and will have a list of sentences from which they can choose the sentences that best fill the gaps. They will write the numbers of the correct sentences in the gaps in the text.

  b On the day of the assessment:

    i The teacher explains the reading assessment to the class.

    ii Students will be given a reading text from which six sentences have been removed and replaced with gaps.

    iii Students will be given a list of eight numbered sentences that include the ones that have been removed from the text, plus two additional ones.

    iv Students will have to fill the gaps in the reading passage by writing the numbers of the appropriate sentences in the gaps in the text.

  c Administrative procedures: The assessment takes place during one class period. The teacher explains the assessment at the beginning of the class period. The assessment is administered to the class as a group, with students working individually. They read a gapped text and fill in the gaps by writing the number of the sentence in the gap.

2 Task characteristics of the modified task/assessment task template

Assessment task: reading and filling in gapped sentences	
Areas of language ability to be assessed: comprehension of cohesion and coherence in reading	
Task characteristics	
Setting	<u>Physical circumstances</u>: teacher in front of classroom; students seated individually *Equipment/Materials*: reading text with gaps, pen/pencil <u>Participants</u>: teacher and students (teens or adults, advanced level) <u>Time of the task</u>: during the class period; 20 minutes required

Input	<u>Form</u>:
	  Aural: teacher's description of the task
	  Visual: reading text with six gaps; eight sentences
	<u>Language</u>: English:
	  Teacher: short utterances explaining and describing; simple grammar and vocabulary
	  Length: *aural*: short sentences and phrases; *visual*: medium: reading text with one paragraph; list of eight sentences
	<u>Topical content</u>: Greenwich Village

Expected response	<u>Form</u>:
	  Visual: students write the numbers of sentences from the list that match the gaps in the paragraphs
	<u>Language</u>: non-language
	  Length: short (only numbers)
	<u>Topical content</u>: Greenwich Village

3 Modified task/assessment task template recording method

Recording method for assessment task	<u>Type of assessment record</u>: score <u>Aspects of ability</u>: comprehension of cohesion and coherence in reading <u>Scoring method</u> <u>Criteria</u>: (See the Scoring Key below.) *For each correct gap completion*: I point <u>Score reported</u>: number of correct choices for gaps (six maximum) <u>Procedures</u>: the teacher reads each student's answers and assigns the points according to the Scoring Key, adds these up to get a total score, and enters this on the student's paper. The papers with the scores are given back to the students in the next lesson.

Step 4 Model assessment task

Instructions for the assessment task:

Students are given an answer sheet with a reading text and a list of sentences.

Teacher's description of the task:

"Here's your reading text and answer sheet. Choose the correct sentence from the ones below that best fits in each gap. Write the number of that sentence in the gap. There are two sentences that you do not need .You will have 20 minutes for this task. Are there any questions?" (Teacher answers any clarification questions the students may have.) "You may begin now."

Reading text and answer sheet:

I'm a Greenwich Villager and proud of it

I live in Greenwich Village, New York, which is in the 'downtown' (southern) part of Manhattan and includes Washington Square Park, New York University, and a maze of picturesque little streets. A) ___ So why do I like it so much? It's an artistic and intellectual neighborhood with people playing chess in the park, artists selling paintings on the sidewalk, and students discussing life in coffee shops. B) ___ There's a surprise around every corner – maybe a brand new restaurant that wasn't there last week, a snoring down-and-out sleeping in the doorway, or a celebrity being pursued by paparazzi and fans. A sense of history pervades Greenwich Village. It was first inhabited by Native Americans, then Dutch Settlers, and then the British, who in 1713 named it 'Greenwich' after a town in England. The Village really was a small, rural village until the 1800s, when people escaping outbreaks of disease began moving there. C) ___ Many famous people have lived in Greenwich Village, including the writer Jack Kerouac, the singer Bob Dylan, and the actress Uma Thurman. D) ___ The heart of the Village is an area of pretty, twisting streets west of Sixth Avenue, where there are endless theatres, used bookstores, coffee shops, trendy boutiques, and of course restaurants. E) ___ The Village is packed with food shops and restaurants from every region of the world. Mouth-watering aromas are everywhere from first thing in the morning until late at night. The Village is a genuine 24/7 part of the town. F) ___ They flock from every corner of the world to sit on the benches or beside the fountain, talking, playing musical instruments, and celebrating the freedom of friendship and youth. My mother, who grew up in New York City, used to say that Times Square is for tourists, but the Village is the real New York.

1 A large part of the Village experience has to do with food.

2 Washington Square Park is like a magnet for young people.

3 I still remember the corner stores everywhere around here from when I was a child.

---

4 Ever since, the Village has been a haven for artists, writers, poets, and musicians.

5 Life in the Village is never dull.

6 Tourists always visit Times Square.

7 It's my favorite part of town.

8 The popular sitcom *Friends* was set here, and busloads of tourists looking for places mentioned in the show come here every weekend.

Total score: _____

Scoring Key:

A 7   B 5   C 4   D 8   E 1   F 2

Example 3: Speaking, describing my favorite place (teens, intermediate level)
Brief overview of the assessment

Test takers	Students
Age group	Teens
Level of language ability	Intermediate
Language	ESL/EFL
Language use activity	Speaking, describing your favorite place
Intended uses	Formative feedback for teacher and students; summative decisions

Setting

A teacher in an ESL/EFL classroom in a secondary school needs to develop a classroom assessment for his beginning level students. This assessment will be used for two different purposes. One purpose is to make sure that the students who pass the grade are prepared for instruction at the next level. In order to do this, the teacher will use the results of this assessment, along with other assessments given during the course of the school year, to make summative decisions about which students will pass to the next grade. The second purpose is to help his students improve their speaking and to improve his teaching. In order to do this, the teacher will also use the results of this assessment to make formative decisions about his teaching and to provide feedback to his students. The assessment will be based on a unit of instruction in the course, and this is one task from the assessment in which the students describe their favorite place by speaking.

Assessment use argument

Claim 1: Intended consequences

The consequences of using the classroom speaking assessment will be beneficial to stakeholders as indicated in Tables E3.1 and E3.2.

Intended consequences	Intended stakeholders
1a Students who have mastered the learning objectives of the entire term will benefit by receiving appropriate instruction at the next level.	Students ESL/EFL teachers in the next level
1b Students who have not mastered the learning objectives of the entire term will benefit by receiving appropriate instruction at the same level.	Students ESL/EFL teachers in the current level
2 Students will improve their speaking.	Students Teacher
3 The teacher will improve his teaching.	Students Teacher

Table E3.1 Intended consequences and intended stakeholders

Other possible consequences and stakeholders who might be affected are included in Table E3.2.

Other possible consequences	Stakeholders who might be affected
Teachers will be able to teach students who are prepared for their level.	ESL/EFL teachers in the current level ESL/EFL teachers in the next level
There will be fewer complaints from teachers, students, and parents/guardians.	School administrators
The reputation of the school will improve.	The school
Parents/Guardians will be satisfied with their children's speaking and help their children continue to improve.	Parents/Guardians, students, teachers

Table E3.2 Other possible consequences and stakeholders who might be affected

Some possible backing for intended consequences in Claim 1

See Example 1 on page 170 for detailed backing.

Claim 2: Intended decisions

The high-stakes summative decisions are made by the teacher at the end of the school year. The low-stakes formative decisions are made by the teacher and the students before the next unit of instruction. These decisions affect the stakeholders as indicated in Table E3.3. The decisions take into consideration the educational values of the school and the societal values of the community, and follow the rules and regulations of the school. They are equitable for the stakeholders listed in Table E3.3.

Decision(s) to be made	Individual(s) who will make the decision(s)	When the decision(s) will be made	Stakeholders who will (or might be) affected by the decision(s)
Summative, high stakes			
Decide which students pass to the next grade (scores from this assessment will count as part of students' total grade for the term)	Teacher	At the end of the school term	Students Teachers (Future teachers) (School administrators) (The school) (Parents/ Guardians)
Formative, low stakes			
Provide students with feedback on their speaking performance	Teacher	Immediately after the assessment	Students Teachers (Parents/ Guardians)
Make appropriate changes to teaching	Teacher	Before the next unit of instruction	Students Teachers (Parents/ Guardians)
Continue with planned teaching; review, or give additional support tasks	Teacher	Before the next unit of instruction	Students Teachers (Parents/ Guardians)
Review and/or practice learning objectives covered	Teacher Students	After they receive the teacher's feedback	Teachers Students (Parents/ Guardians)

Table E3.3 Intended decisions

Some possible backing for intended decisions in Claim 2

See Example 1 on page 172 for detailed backing.

Claim 3: Intended interpretations

The interpretations about three aspects of students' speaking ability—accurate grammar, vocabulary, and pronunciation—are relevant to the formative and summative decisions to be made. The interpretations are sufficient for the low-stakes formative decisions, but not sufficient for the high-stakes summative decisions to be made. These summative decisions will be made on the basis of this assessment and other classroom assessments that will be given during the course of instruction. The interpretations are meaningful with respect to the content of the course and of the current lesson, generalizable to the current language class, and are impartial to all students.

Some possible backing for intended interpretations in Claim 3

See Example 1 on page 173 for detailed backing.

Claim 4: Assessment records

The scores from the speaking assessment are consistent across different times and days of administration, and across different administrations to different groups of students. Students' scores are consistent across the different places they describe. Students' performances are scored consistently by the teacher, according to the Rating Scale. The possible sources of inconsistency for this assessment are listed in Table E3.4.

Possible sources of inconsistency in scores
1 Inconsistencies in the administration of the assessment • different times or days of administration • different administrations to different groups of students
2 Inconsistencies across different assessment tasks • different places the students describe
3 Inconsistencies in how students' performances are scored • different applications of the Rating Scale from one student to the next

Table E3.4 Possible sources of inconsistency in scores

Some possible backing for intended assessment records in Claim 4

The possible sources of inconsistency and possible backing to assure that these sources will be minimized are given in Table E3.5.

Possible sources of inconsistency	Possible backing to assure consistency
1 Inconsistencies in the administration of the assessment • different times or days of administration • different administrations to different students • different administrations to different groups of students	• Documentation of administrative procedures to be followed • Teacher's notes from administering the assessment at different times during the class period, on different days, with different students, and with different groups of students
2 Inconsistencies across different assessment tasks • different places that the students describe	• Documentation: task specifications for the possible places to be used in the assessment • Teacher's notes on any differences that were observed in how different places may have affected students' performances
3 Inconsistencies in how students' performances are scored • Different applications of the Rating Scale from one student to the next	• Documentation: Rating Scale, Recording Form, and instructions for scoring • Teacher's notes on how the Rating Scale may have been applied differently from one student to the next

Table E3.5 Possible backing for possible sources of inconsistency

Assessment task development

Step 1 TLU task selected for development of assessment task

1 Short descriptive label for TLU task: describing a favorite building orally to a partner in the language classroom

2 Areas of language ability the TLU task engages: using accurate grammar, vocabulary, and pronunciation in speaking

Step 2 Description of the TLU task

1 Activities and procedures to be followed:

  a The teacher explains the speaking activity to the class.

  b Students work in pairs.

  c Each pair decides on a favorite building and takes notes for their description.

d Students work on descriptions of their building in their pairs.

e The teacher moves around and helps pairs as needed.

f Each student presents a part of their description to the class.

g The other students in the class discuss the quality of the descriptions and give feedback on the pair's performance, in terms of the amount of information provided.

2 Task characteristics of TLU task:

TLU task: speaking, describing a favorite building to a partner in the language classroom
Areas of language ability the TLU task engages: using accurate grammar, vocabulary, and pronunciation in spoken language
Task characteristics

Setting	Physical circumstances: teacher in front of classroom; students in pairs *Equipment/Materials*: paper and pencil for note taking for students Participants: teacher and students (teens, intermediate) Time of the task: during the class period; one class period required

Input	Form:
	  Aural:
	    Teacher: description of the task; questions and comments
	    Students: descriptions; discussion of the quality of the descriptions
	  Visual: words and phrases that students write on paper
	Language: English
	  Teacher: short spoken description and explanation
	  Students: descriptive sentences; short comment sentences
	  Length: fairly long (description of building)
	Topical content: favorite building

Expected response	Form:
	  Oral: students' descriptions of their favorite building; students' responses to teacher's and students' comments
	  Visual: students write words and phrases on paper to support speaking
	Language: English; descriptive sentences (adjectives); comments on students' performances; responses to teacher's and students' comments
	  Length: about one minute per student
	Topical content: favorite building

Step 3 The modified task/assessment task template

Description of the modified task: speaking individually, describing a favorite place

Areas of language ability to be assessed: using accurate grammar, vocabulary, and pronunciation in speaking

1 Activities and procedures to be followed:

  a On the day before the assessment the teacher tells the students:

    i They will have an assessment of their oral performance the next day.

    ii The purposes of the assessment are:

      a) to give each student a grade or mark that will count as part of his or her grade for the school year.

      b) to provide feedback to individual students about their speaking ability.

    iii They will have to describe something similar to the task in class.

    iv They will have to describe individually and not in pairs.

  b On the day of the assessment, the students are assessed individually:

    i The teacher briefly explains the assessment task again.

    ii The teacher makes sure the students understand the procedure.

    iii The teacher says the task is to describe their favorite place.

    iv Each student picks his or her favorite place and takes five minutes to write down some notes to guide his or her description.

    v The teacher calls each student individually to the Speaking Corner. Other students work on an assignment.

    vi Each student has two minutes to describe his or her favorite place orally to the teacher.

    vii The teacher scores each student's performance using the Rating Scale on the Recording Form and also makes notes for feedback on the student's speaking using the Recording Form.

    viii The teacher shows the student his or her score and gives verbal feedback.

    ix The teacher then administers the assessment to another student, following the same procedure as with the first student.

c Administrative procedures: The assessment takes place during a class period. All students take notes on the topic, "their favorite place". While one student is called by the teacher to take the assessment, the other students work on another assignment individually. Students return to their seats after their assessments are completed. The assessment is given as an individual activity between the teacher and a student in a Speaking Corner of the classroom. Each student has two minutes to describe his or her favorite place. The teacher scores each student in the Rating Scale while the student is speaking. At the end of the assessment, the teacher shows the student his or her scores and gives the student some verbal feedback on his or her performance. The student then returns to the class.

2 Task characteristics of the modified task/assessment task template

Assessment task: speaking individually, describing a favorite place	
Areas of language ability to be assessed: using accurate grammar, vocabulary, and pronunciation in spoken language	
Task characteristics	
Setting	Physical circumstances: the teacher with a student in the Speaking Corner of the classroom *Equipment/Materials*: paper and pencil for student to take notes Participants: teacher and a student (teens, intermediate) Time of the task: during the class period; more than one class period required depending on the number of students
Input	Form: *Aural*: teacher's description of the task *Visual*: words and phrases that the students may write on paper Language: English *Teacher: aural*: short spoken description and explanation *Length: aural*: fairly long (description of favorite place) Topical content: a favorite place
Expected response	Form: *Oral*: student's description of his or her favorite place *Visual*: the words and phrases that the student writes on paper to support speaking Language: English: descriptive sentences, adjectives *Length*: about two minutes per student Topical content: a favorite place

3 Modified task/assessment task template recording method

Recording method for assessment task	Types of assessment record: score and written feedback Aspects of ability: three aspects of speaking – grammatical accuracy, use of accurate vocabulary, pronunciation Scoring method 　Criteria: (See the Rating Scale below.) 　*For each aspect: 3 – Exceeds expectations; 2 – Meets expectations, 1 – Needs improvement* 　Score reported: total score = accurate grammar + accurate vocabulary + pronunciation 　Procedures: the teacher listens to individual students' responses and enters a score for each aspect of speaking in the Rating Scale for each student, and then adds up the scores to arrive at a total score and enters this on the Recording Form. The teacher also enters written feedback on the student's speaking on the Recording Form. This is given back to the students during the next lesson.

Step 4 Model assessment task

Speaking prompt:

"Use the notes you have made about your favorite place to guide your speaking. You have two minutes to describe your favorite place. You may start now."

Recording Form

Assessment task: Speaking, describing the physical characteristics of a favorite place

Student name: _____ Date: _____

Student paired with: _____

Favorite place: _____

Rating Scale: Aspect of speaking	Needs improvement 1	Meets expectations 2	Exceeds expectations 3	Feedback on student's speaking
Accurate grammar				
Accurate vocabulary (especially adjectives)				
Accurate Pronunciation				

Total score: _____

Photocopiable © Oxford University Press

Example 4: Listening, answering questions about free-time activities (teens, intermediate level)

Brief overview of the assessment

Test takers	Students
Age group	Teens
Level of language ability	Intermediate
Language	ESL/EFL
Language use activity	Comprehension of specific details in listening
Intended uses	Summative decisions

Setting

A teacher in an ESL/EFL classroom in a secondary school needs to develop a classroom assessment for his intermediate-level students. This assessment will be used for one purpose. He wants to make sure that the students who pass the grade are prepared for instruction at the next level. In order to do this, the teacher will use the results of this assessment, along with other assessments given during the course of the school year, to make summative decisions about which students will pass to the next grade. The assessment will be based on a unit of instruction in the course, and this is one task from the assessment in which students listen to a conversation about free-time activities and answer questions.

Assessment use argument

Claim 1: Intended consequences

The consequences of using the classroom listening assessment will be beneficial to stakeholders as indicated in Tables E4.1 and E4.2.

Intended consequences	Intended stakeholders
1a Students who have mastered the learning objectives of the entire term will benefit by receiving appropriate instruction at the next level.	Students ESL/EFL teachers in the next level
1b Students who have not mastered the learning objectives of the entire term will benefit by receiving appropriate instruction at the same level.	Students ESL/EFL teachers in the current level

Table E4.1 Intended consequences and intended stakeholders

Other possible consequences and stakeholders who might be affected are included in Table E4.2.

Other possible consequences	Stakeholders who might be affected
Teachers will be able to teach students who are prepared for their level.	ESL/EFL teachers in the current level ESL/EFL teachers in the next level

Table E4.2 Other possible consequences and stakeholders who might be affected

Some possible backing for intended consequences in Claim 1

See Example 2 on page 182 for detailed backing.

Claim 2: Intended decisions

The high-stakes summative decisions are made by the teacher at the end of the school year. These decisions affect the stakeholders as indicated in Table E4.3. The decisions take into consideration the educational values of the school and the societal values of the community, and follow the rules and regulations of the school. They are equitable for the stakeholders listed in Table E4.3.

Decision(s) to be made	Individual(s) who will make the decision(s)	When the decision(s) will be made	Stakeholders who will (or might be) affected by the decision(s)
Summative, high stakes			
Decide which students pass to the next grade (scores from this assessment will count as part of students' total grade for the term)	Teacher	At the end of the school term	Students Teachers (Future teachers) (School administrators) (The school) (Parents/Guardians)

Table E4.3 Intended decisions

Some possible backing for intended decisions in Claim 2

See Example 2 on page 183 for detailed backing.

Claim 3: Intended interpretations

The interpretations about students' ability to comprehend specific details in listening are relevant to the high-stakes summative decisions to be made, but are not sufficient for these decisions. These decisions will be made on the basis of this assessment and other classroom assessments that will be given during the course of instruction. The interpretations are meaningful with respect to the content of the course and of the current lesson, generalizable to the current language class, and are impartial to all students.

Some possible backing for intended interpretations in Claim 3

See Example 2 on page 183 for detailed backing.

Claim 4: Assessment records

The scores from the listening assessment are consistent across different times and days of administration, and across different administrations to different groups of students. Students' performances are scored consistently by the teacher, according to the Scoring Key. The possible sources of inconsistency for this assessment are listed in Table E4.4.

Possible sources of inconsistency in scores

1 Inconsistencies in the administration of the assessment
  • different times or days of administration
  • different administrations to different groups of students

2 Inconsistencies across different questions
3 Inconsistencies in how students' performances are scored   • different applications of the Scoring Key from one student to the next

Table E4.4 Possible sources of inconsistency in scores

Some possible backing for intended assessment records in Claim 4

The possible sources of inconsistency and possible backing to assure that these sources will be minimized are given in Table E4.5.

Possible sources of inconsistency	Possible backing to assure consistency

1 Inconsistencies in the administration of the assessment
  • different times or days of administration
  • different administrations to different groups of student
	• Documentation of administrative procedures to be followed
	• Teacher's notes from administering the assessment at different times during the class period, on different days, and with different groups of students

2 Inconsistencies across different questions • different lengths • different levels of complexity	• Documentation: task specifications for the questions to be used in the assessment • Teacher's notes on any differences that were observed in how different lengths and complexity of questions may have affected students' performances
3 Inconsistencies in how students' performances are scored • different applications of the Scoring Key from one student to the next	• Documentation: Scoring Key and instructions for scoring • Teacher's notes on how the Scoring Key may have been applied differently from one student to the next

Table E4.5 Possible backing for possible sources of inconsistency

Assessment task development

Step 1 TLU task selected for development of assessment task

1 Short descriptive label for TLU task: listening to a conversation about free-time activities and answering questions

2 Areas of language ability the TLU task engages: comprehension of specific details in listening

Step 2 Description of the TLU task:

1 Activities and procedures to be followed:

   a The teacher explains the listening activity to the class.

   b Students are given an answer sheet with ten questions about a conversation they will listen to.

   c Students listen to a short conversation about life experiences and write their answers to the questions on the answer sheet.

   d They discuss their answers with a partner, and correct these accordingly.

   e The teacher discusses the answers with the students.

2 Task characteristics of TLU task:

TLU task: listening and answering questions
Areas of language ability the TLU task engages: comprehension of specific details in listening

Task characteristics	
Setting	<u>Physical circumstances</u>: teacher in front of classroom; students seated individually *Equipment/Materials*: questions on paper, pen/pencil, audio playback equipment (e.g. computer, digital player, CD player) <u>Participants</u>: teacher and students (teens, intermediate) <u>Time of the task</u>: during the class period; one class period required
Input	<u>Form</u>: 　*Aural*: 　　*Teacher*: description of the task; pre-recorded conversation 　　*Students*: discussion with other students about their answers 　*Visual*: questions on paper <u>Language</u>: English 　*Teacher*: utterances from teacher: spoken text, fairly simple grammar and vocabulary 　*Students*: short utterances discussing their answers with each other; simple grammar and vocabulary; short: written answers 　*Length*: *aural*: pre-recorded short conversation; *visual*: fairly short (questions to answer) <u>Topical content</u>: life experiences
Expected response	<u>Form</u>: 　*Oral*: discussion about answers 　*Visual*: students' written answers to questions <u>Language</u>: English 　*Length*: short answers <u>Topical content</u>: life experiences

3 Listening TLU task:

Life experiences Ruben: Hey, Camilla, how are you? Camilla: Fine, thanks. I had a great weekend. Ruben: Really? What did you do? Camilla: I went on a blind date! It was great fun. Ruben: A blind date? Wow. I've never done that. What did you do?

Camilla: Well, the guy – Philip – is my cousin's friend. Four of us met at a restaurant, but I was the first to arrive. I saw this guy alone, and I thought it was Philip, so I started talking to him.

Ruben: Let me guess – you were talking to the wrong person.

Camilla: Yes! It was so embarrassing!

Ruben: I've done that. It is very embarrassing.

Camilla: Anyway, Philip finally arrived, and he was really nice. Even when I spilled a drink on him.

Ruben: You spilled a drink on your blind date? Was he angry?

Camilla: No. Not at all.

Ruben: Wow. I've done some silly things, but I've never spilled a drink on anyone.

Camilla: So, what's the most embarrassing thing you've ever done?

Ruben: There are too many to say.

Camilla: Oh, come on.

Ruben: Let's see... I've laughed at the wrong time in class. I've bumped into a glass door in the store...

Camilla: I haven't done either of those things. But you forgot to mention one thing: you've worn your shirt inside out!

Ruben: No, I haven't!

Camilla: Look! You're wearing it inside out right now! I've definitely never done that!

Answer sheet:

Questions and answers **(Write your answers in the box after each question.)**
1 What did Camilla do on the weekend?
2 What was the name of Camilla's blind date?
3 Where did Camilla and Philip plan to meet?
4 Who did Camilla see when she arrived at the restaurant?
5 Who did Camilla think the person was?

6	Why did Camilla feel embarrassed?
7	How did Philip react when Camilla spilled her drink on him?
8	What has Ruben never done?
9	What are two embarrassing things Ruben has done?
10	What embarrassing thing is Ruben doing now?

Answers:

1 She went on a blind date.

2 Philip

3 at a restaurant

4 a guy alone

5 Philip, her blind date

6 the guy was not Philip, her blind date

7 he was nice/he wasn't angry

8 spilled a drink on anyone

9 laughed at the wrong time in class; bumped into a glass door in the store

10 wearing his shirt inside out

Step 3 The modified task/Assessment Task template:

1 Activities and procedures to be followed:

a A week before the assessment the teacher tells the students:

  i They will have an assessment of their listening ability the following week.

  ii The purpose of the assessment is to give each student a mark that will count as part of his or her grade to pass the course.

  iii Students will listen to a conversation between two speakers.

  iv Students will then answer listening comprehension questions.

b On the day of the assessment:

  i The teacher briefly explains the listening activity to the class.

  ii Students are given an answer sheet with questions on a conversation they will listen to.

  iii Students listen to a short conversation about free-time activities and write their answer to questions about the conversation on the answer sheet.

c Administrative procedures: The assessment takes place during one class period. The teacher explains the assessment at the beginning of the class period. The assessment is administered to the class as a group, with students working individually. They listen to the conversation and answer questions.

2 Task characteristics of the modified task/assessment task template

Assessment task: listening and answering questions
Areas of language ability to be assessed: comprehension of specific details in listening

Task characteristics	
Setting	<u>Physical circumstances</u>: teacher in front of classroom; students seated individually *Equipment/Materials*: questions on answer sheet, pen/pencil, audio playback equipment (e.g. computer, digital player, CD player) <u>Participants</u>: teacher and students (teens, intermediate) <u>Time of the task</u>: during the class period; 20 min. required
Input	<u>Form</u>: *Aural*: teacher's: description of the task, a pre-recorded conversation *Visual*: questions on answer sheet about the conversation <u>Language</u>: English *Teacher:* spoken text, simple grammar and vocabulary *Students:* short: written answers *Length:* *aural*: pre-recorded conversation of two min.; *visual*: short answers to questions <u>Topical content</u>: free-time activities
Expected response	<u>Form</u>: *Visual*: students' written answers to questions <u>Language</u>: English *Length*: short words and phrases <u>Topical content</u>: free-time activities

3 Modified task/assessment task template recording method

Recording method for assessment task	<u>Types of assessment record</u>: score <u>Aspects of ability</u>: comprehension of specific details in listening <u>Scoring method</u> <u>Criteria</u>: (See the Scoring Key below.) <u>Score reported</u>: one point for each correct response according to the Scoring Key (15 maximum) <u>Procedures</u>: the teacher reads each student's answers, assigns the points according to the Scoring Key, adds these up to get a total score, and enters this on the student's answer sheet. The answer sheets with the scores are given back to the students in the next lesson.

Step 4 Model assessment task

Instructions for the assessment task:

Students are given an answer sheet with questions and space for their short answers.

Teacher's description of the task:

"First, you will listen to a conversation between two people. While listening to the conversation, you will write your answers to the questions on the answer sheet provided. You will have 10 minutes to complete your answers. Then you will listen to the conversation again and will have three minutes to correct your answers if necessary. Your score will be the number of correct answers. Are there any questions?" (Teacher answers students' questions.) "OK, let's begin."

Audio Script:

Bev: Hi, Austin

Austin: Hi, Bev. I'm going to the café. Would you like to come?

Bev: I'd love to … but I'm not allowed to eat anything unhealthy right now. Well, I can have water or juice, I guess. And we can talk.

Austin: Are you on a …? I can't think of the word. It's when you eat only special food.

Bev: A diet?

Austin: That's it. Are you on a diet?

Bev: Sort of. I'm doing some training. I'm on the baseball team and we have a big game tomorrow. The coach is making us eat special food at certain times.

Austin: Wow. So when are you allowed to eat?

Bev: The coach lets us eat at normal mealtimes—breakfast, lunch, dinner—but not snacks. And he won't let us drink soda, only water, juice, or milk.

Austin: So are you doing exercise, too?

Bev: Not today. He doesn't make us exercise the day before a game. We always take a break. He lets us rest because we've exercised and done training every day this week.

Austin: What time is the game?

Bev: It's at 4 o'clock. Can you come?

Austin: No, I can't. I'm not allowed to go out on Thursday afternoons. My mom makes me stay at home and practice the violin!

Answer sheet:

Questions and answers (Write your answers in the box after each question.)		Score/ possible points
1	Where is Austin going?	__ / 1
2	Why does Bev hesitate when Austin asks her to go with him to the café?	__ / 1
3	What kind of team is Bev on?	__ / 1
4	When is Bev allowed to eat, according to her coach?	__ / 2
5	What does the coach allow Bev to drink?	__ / 3
6	What does Bev do on the day before the game?	__ / 2
7	When did Bev train for the big game?	__ / 1
8	What time does Bev's game start?	__ /1
9	On what day of the week is Bev's game?	__ / 1
10	Why can't Austin go to Bev's game?	__ / 2
	Total score	__ / 15

Scoring Key:

Question	Answer	Point(s)
1	café	1 point
2	She can't eat unhealthy (food).	1 point
3	(a) baseball	1 point
4	(at) normal mealtimes / breakfast, lunch, and dinner	1 point each (2 points total)
5	water / juice / milk	1 point each (3 points total)
6	(take) a break from exercise; rest	1 point each (2 points total)
7	every day this week, except today	1 point
8	4 o'clock	1 point
9	Thursday	1 point
10	stay home / practice violin	1 point each (2 points total)
	Total possible points	15

Example 5: Listening, answering questions about best moment of life (teens, beginning level)

Brief overview of the assessment

Test takers	Students
Age group	Teens
Level of language ability	Beginning
Language	ESL/EFL
Language use activity	Listening for major ideas
Intended uses	Summative decisions

Setting

A teacher in an ESL/EFL classroom in a secondary school needs to develop a classroom assessment for his beginning level students. This assessment will be used for one purpose. He wants to make sure that the students who pass the grade are prepared for instruction at the next level. In order to do this, the teacher will use the results of this assessment, along with other assessments of other skills, to make summative decisions about which students will pass to the next grade. The assessment will be based on a unit of instruction in the course, and this is one task from the assessment in which the students listen to four different speakers talking about the best moment of their lives.

In this example, we illustrate two different options for students' expected responses and a different scoring method for each. One expected response option is for students to choose the correct answers from among several choices given. The other expected response option is for them to write their answers in the blanks provided. There are also two different scoring methods, one for each expected response option.

Assessment use argument

Claim 1: Intended consequences

The consequences of using the classroom listening assessment will be beneficial to stakeholders as indicated in Tables E5.1 and E5.2.

Intended consequences	Intended stakeholders
1a Students who have mastered the learning objectives of the entire term will benefit by receiving appropriate instruction at the next level.	Students ESL/EFL teachers in the next level
1b Students who have not mastered the learning objectives of the entire term will benefit by receiving appropriate instruction at the same level.	Students ESL/EFL teachers in the current level

Table E5.1 Intended consequences and intended stakeholders

Other possible consequences and stakeholders who might be affected are included in Table E5.2.

Other possible consequences	Stakeholders who might be affected
Teachers will be able to teach students who are prepared for their level	ESL/EFL teachers in the current level ESL/EFL teachers in the next level

Table E5.2 Other possible consequences and stakeholders who might be affected

Some possible backing for intended consequences in Claim 1

See Example 2 on page 182 for detailed backing.

Claim 2: Intended decisions

The high-stakes summative decisions are made by the teacher at the end of the school year. These decisions affect the stakeholders as indicated in Table E5.3. The decisions take into consideration the educational values of the school and the societal values of the community, and follow the rules and regulations of the school. They are equitable for the stakeholders listed in Table E5.3.

Decision(s) to be made	Individual(s) who will make the decision(s)	When the decision(s) will be made	Stakeholders who will (or might be) affected by the decision(s)
Summative, high stakes			
Decide which students pass to the next grade (scores from this assessment will count as part of students' total grade for the term)	Teacher	At the end of the school term	Students Teachers (Future teachers) (School administrators) (The school) (Parents/ Guardians)

Table E5.3 Intended decisions

Some possible backing for intended decisions in Claim 2

See Example 2 on page 183 for detailed backing.

Claim 3: Intended interpretations

The interpretations about students' ability to comprehend major ideas in listening are relevant to the high-stakes summative decisions to be made, but are not sufficient for these decisions. These decisions will be made on the basis of this assessment and other classroom assessments that will be given during the course of instruction. The interpretations are meaningful with respect to the content of the course and of the current lesson, generalizable to the current language class, and are impartial to all students.

Some possible backing for intended interpretations in Claim 3

See Example 2 on page 183 for detailed backing.

Claim 4: Assessment records

The scores from the reading assessment are consistent across different times and days of administration, and across different administrations to different groups of students. Students' performances are scored consistently by the teacher, according to the Scoring Key. The possible sources of inconsistency for this assessment are listed in Table E5.4.

Possible sources of inconsistency in scores
1 Inconsistencies in the administration of the assessment • different times or days of administration • different administrations to different groups of students
2 Inconsistencies across different speakers • different speeds of speaking • differences in clearness of speaking • differences between male and female speakers
3 Inconsistencies in how students' performances are scored • different applications of the Scoring Key from one student to the next

Table E5.4 Possible sources of inconsistency in scores

Some possible backing for intended assessment records in Claim 4

The possible sources of inconsistency and possible backing to assure that these sources will be minimized are given in Table E5.5.

Possible sources of inconsistency	Possible backing to assure consistency
1 Inconsistencies in the administration of the assessment • different times or days of administration • different administrations to different groups of student	• Documentation of administrative procedures to be followed • Teacher's notes from administering the assessment at different times during the class period, on different days, with different groups of students
2. Inconsistencies across different speakers • different speeds of speaking • differences in clearness of speaking • differences between male and female speakers	• Documentation: task specifications for the different speakers in the assessment • Teacher's notes on differences across the speakers that may have affected students' performances
3. Inconsistencies in how students' performances are scored • different applications of the Scoring Key from one student to the next	• Documentation: Scoring Key and instructions for scoring • Teacher's notes on how the Scoring Key may have been applied differently from one student to the next

Table E5.5 Possible backing to assure the consistency of scores

Assessment task development

Step 1 TLU task selected for development of assessment task

1 Short descriptive label for TLU task: listening to four speakers and answering questions about the best moment in their lives

2 Areas of language ability the TLU task engages: comprehension of major ideas in listening

Step 2 Description of the TLU task:

1 Activities and procedures to be followed:

   a The teacher explains the listening activity to the class.

   b Students listen to four different speakers talking about the same topic.

   c Students are given a table with the speakers' names given and blanks for information about these.

   d Students write short answers in the table according to what each person said.

   e They discuss their answers with a partner, and correct these accordingly.

   f The teacher gives the students the correct answers and discusses these with the students.

2 Characteristics of the TLU task:

TLU task: listening, writing short answers
Areas of language ability the TLU task engages: comprehension of major ideas in listening
Task characteristics

Setting	<u>Physical circumstances</u>: teacher in front of classroom; students seated individually
	Equipment/Materials: answer sheet with table for answers, pen/pencil, audio playback equipment (e.g. computer, digital player, CD player)
	<u>Participants</u>: teacher and students (teens, beginning level)
	<u>Time of the task</u>: during the class period; 15–20 min. required

Input	Form:
	Aural:
	Teacher: description of the task, pre-recorded interviews
	Students: discussion with other students about their answers
	Visual: questions in a table
	Language: English
	Teacher: utterances from teacher: spoken text, fairly simple grammar and vocabulary
	Students: short utterances discussing their answers with each other; simple grammar and vocabulary; short, written answers
	Length: aural: pre-recorded short interviews, long (4 spoken interviews), visual: fairly short (questions to answer)
	Topical content: clothes
Expected response	Form:
	Oral: discussion about answers
	Visual: students' short answers in the blanks in the table
	Language: English
	Length: short, words and phrases
	Topical content: clothes

3 Listening TLU task:

Clothes

Speaker 1: I've got some new trainers and I love them! They're black with orange and white stripes down the side, and I think they're really cool. I wear them everywhere: when I go to school, when I'm out with my friends and when I do things with my family. But I don't wear them when I do sport – I've got an old pair for that. My new ones cost a lot of money, so I need to look after them.

Speaker 2: My sister buys a lot of clothes because she has her own money – she's a nurse at the local hospital. She often gives me things when she doesn't want them anymore, but they're usually a bit big for me. But now I've got one of her tops and I love it! It was too small for her, so it's perfect for me. It's black and white and looks great with my new shorts. I wear it all the time.

Speaker 3: My mum isn't very happy with the clothes I wear. She says I look a mess. And she doesn't really like my favorite pair of jeans. They're quite new, actually, but they don't look it. They're quite loose and they're really comfortable, so I wear them a lot. Most of my friends wear the same kind of clothes as me, and they don't have any problems with their parents!

Speaker 4: I'm really excited because it's my birthday next week and I've got the perfect dress for my party. I'm a bit bored of wearing the same clothes every day and this dress is a bit different – I'm sure none of my friends has anything the same. It's short and it's quite colorful: half of it is black and the other half is pink. I've got some high black shoes and some black tights to wear with it.

Answer sheet:

	What item of clothing is each speaker talking about?	**Why do they like the item of clothing they got?**
Speaker 1		
Speaker 2		
Speaker 3		
Speaker 4		

Answers:

	What item of clothing is each speaker talking about?	**Why do they like the item of clothing they got?**
Speaker 1	new trainers	She thinks they're cool.
Speaker 2	black and white top	It fits well and looks good with her new shorts.
Speaker 3	favorite pair of jeans	They're loose and comfortable.
Speaker 4	short colorful dress	It's different from what she usually wears.

Step 3 The modified task/assessment task template:

1 Activities and procedures to be followed:

  a A week before the assessment the teacher tells the students:

    i They will have an assessment of their listening ability the following week.

    ii The purpose of the assessment is to give each student a mark that will count as part of his or her grade to pass the course.

    iii Students listen to the one minute interview and choose the correct information according to what each person in the interview stated.

  b On the day of the assessment:

    i Students listen to four different speakers talking about the same topic.

    ii Students are given a table with the speakers' names given and blanks for information about these.

    iii Students write short answers in the list according to what each person stated.

  c Administrative procedures

    i The assessment takes place during one class period. The teacher explains the assessment at the beginning of the class period. The assessment is administered to the class as a group, with students working individually. Students are given an answer sheet, which is a table with the speakers' names and blanks for information that each speaker mentions in his or her talk. Students then listen to an audio recording with four short interviews with four different speakers. Then the students are given three minutes to write short answers in the blanks for each speaker. The students listen to the interviews again and are given three minutes to correct their answers.

2 Modified task TCs with TCs for recording method

Assessment task: listening and choosing the correct information	
Areas of language ability to be assessed: comprehension of major ideas in listening	
Task characteristics	
Setting	<u>Physical circumstances</u>: teacher in front of classroom; students are seated individually *Equipment/Materials*: answer sheet with table for answers; pen/pencil, audio playback equipment (e.g. computer, digital player, CD player) <u>Participants</u>: teacher and students (teens, beginning level) <u>Time of the task</u>: during the class period; 15–20 min. required
Input	<u>Form</u>: *Aural*: teacher's description of the task, pre-recorded interviews *Visual*: table with questions <u>Language</u>: English *Teacher*: short utterances describing and explaining, simple grammar and vocabulary *Length*: *aural*: long (4 spoken interviews) <u>Topical content</u>: talking about the best moment of people's lives
Expected response Option 1; selected response	<u>Form</u>: *Visual*: students mark the correct answer for each of the 4 speakers in the table <u>Language</u>: none *Length*: short <u>Topical content</u>: talking about the best moment of people's lives
Expected response Option 2; limited production response	<u>Form</u>: *Visual*: students write short answers to the questions in the table <u>Language</u>: English *Length*: short, words and phrases <u>Topical content</u>: talking about the best moment of people's lives

3 Modified task/assessment task template recording method

Recording method for assessment task	Option 1	<u>Types of assessment record</u>: score <u>Aspects of ability</u>: comprehension of major ideas in listening <u>Scoring method</u> <u>Criteria</u>: (See the Scoring Key below.) <u>Score reported</u>: 1 point for each correct choice according to the Scoring Key <u>Procedures</u>: the teacher checks each student's answers, assigns the points according to the Scoring Key, adds these up to get a total score, and enters these on the student's answer sheet. The answer sheets with the scores are given back to the students in the next lesson.
	Option 2	<u>Types of assessment record</u>: score <u>Aspects of ability</u>: comprehension of major ideas in listening <u>Scoring method</u> <u>Criteria</u>: (See the Scoring Key below.) <u>Score reported</u>: 1 point for each correct written answer according to the Scoring Key <u>Procedures</u>: the teacher checks each student's answers, assigns the points according to the Scoring Key, adds these up to get a total score, and enters these on the student's answer sheet. The answer sheets with the scores are given back to the students in the next lesson.

Step 4 Model assessment task

Instructions for the assessment task:

Students are given an answer sheet with a table to write their answers.

Teacher's description of the task:

"Listen to the interviews of four people. Then look at the information about each person on the answer sheet. Choose the correct information according to the interviews and mark the box with the matching information for each person. Listen to the interviews again. Correct your answers if necessary."

Audio Script:

The best moment of your life

Interviewer: What's the best moment of your life so far?

Mark: The best moment of my life? That's easy! It was when my daughter was born three years ago. Those little fingers and toes – she was the most beautiful thing in the world! I took about a thousand photos of her in that first week.

Now my wife and I take turns to stay at home and take care of her during the day. She's growing up fast and she's more fun now. But those first moments with her were amazing.

Interviewer: What's the best moment of your life so far?

Jenny: It was when I passed my driving test last summer. When I took the test the first time, I didn't pass. I was really sad. But the second time, I passed! It was a fantastic feeling. Finally, I could drive without my mum in the car. I was free!

Interviewer: What's the best moment of your life so far?

Peter: Well, one of the best was when I got my job. When I left university, there weren't many jobs. I went to a lot of interviews, but everyone said no. It was really difficult. Then I heard from a TV company, and they wanted me to join them as a journalist! Yay! I was so excited! I started work the next week, and it's a brilliant job.

Interviewer: What's the best moment of your life so far?

Isabel: Probably the best moment was when I retired from my job last year. I didn't hate my job. In fact I really liked it. But now I've got a lot of free time, and I can take a break when I want. I can go on long holidays to interesting places. Life really is fun when you get older!

Option 1

Answer Sheet:

What was the best moment of his or her life?	Jenny	Isabel	Mark	Peter
1 retired from job				
2 birth of baby girl				
3 got a job				
4 passed driving test				
5 birth of baby boy				
Why was this the best moment of his or her life?				
6 felt free				
7 having fun				
8 felt excited				
9 was thrilled				
10 first moments amazing				
Total score: _____				

Scoring Key:

What was the best moment of his or her life?	Jenny	Isabel	Mark	Peter
1 retired from job		✓		
2 birth of baby girl			✓	
3 got a job				✓
4 passed driving test	✓			
5 birth of baby boy				
Why was this the best moment of his or her life?				
6 felt free	✓			
7 having fun		✓		
8 felt excited				✓
9 was thrilled				
10 first moments amazing			✓	
Total score: _____				

Option 2

Instructions for the Assessment task:

(Students are given an answer sheet with a table to write their answers.)

Teacher's description of the task:

> "Listen to the interviews of four people. Take notes and then write short answers in the box for each person answering the questions. Listen to the interviews again. Correct your answers if necessary."

Audio Script

(See audio script for Option 1)

Answer Sheet:

What was the best moment of his or her life?		Possible points
Mark		2
Jenny		I
Peter		I
Isabel		I
Why was this the best moment of his or her life?		
Mark		2
Jenny		I
Peter		I
Isabel		I
	Total score	__ / 10

Scoring Key:

What was the best moment of his or her life?		Points
Mark	birth, daughter	I point each (2 points total)
Jenny	pass(ed) driving test	I point
Peter	got job	I point
Isabel	retire(d)	I point
Why was this the best moment of his or her life?		
Mark	first moments, amazing	I point each (2 points total)
Jenny	felt/was free	I point
Peter	brilliant job	I point
Isabel	having fun	I point
	Total points	10

Example 6: Writing, describing a musical instrument (teens, intermediate level)

Brief overview of the assessment

Test takers	Students
Age group	Teens
Level of language ability	Intermediate
Language	ESL/EFL
Language use activity	Writing a descriptive paragraph
Intended uses	Formative feedback for teacher and students; summative decisions

Setting

A group of ESL/EFL teachers in the same grade in a secondary school need to develop a classroom assessment for their intermediate-level students. This assessment will be used for two different purposes. One purpose is to make sure that the students who pass the grade are prepared for instruction at the next level. In order to do this, the teachers will use the results of this assessment, along with other assessments given during the course of the term, to make summative decisions about which students will pass to the next grade. The second purpose is to help their students improve their writing and to improve their teaching. In order to do this, the teachers will use the results of this assessment to make formative decisions about their teaching and to provide feedback to their students. The assessment will be based on a unit of instruction in the course, and this is one task from the assessment, in which the students write a descriptive paragraph about a musical instrument.

Assessment use argument

Claim 1: Intended consequences

The consequences of using the classroom writing assessment will be beneficial to stakeholders as indicated in Tables E6.1 and E6.2.

Intended consequences	Intended stakeholders
1a Students who have mastered the learning objectives of the entire term will benefit by receiving appropriate instruction at the next level.	Students ESL/EFL teachers in the next level
1b Students who have not mastered the learning objectives of the entire term will benefit by receiving appropriate instruction at the same level.	Students ESL/EFL teachers in the current level
2 Students will improve their writing.	Students Teacher
3 The teacher will improve his teaching.	Students Teacher

Table E6.1 Intended consequences and intended stakeholders

Other possible consequences and stakeholders who might be affected are included in Table E6.2.

Other possible consequences	Stakeholders who might be affected
Teachers will be able to teach students who are prepared for their level.	ESL/EFL teachers in the current level ESL/EFL teachers in the next level
There will be fewer complaints from teachers, students, and parents/guardians.	School administrators
The reputation of the school will improve.	The school
Parents/Guardians will be satisfied with their children's writing and help their children continue to improve.	Parents/Guardians, students, teachers

Table E6.2 Other possible consequences and stakeholders who might be affected

Some possible backing for intended consequences in Claim 1

See Example 1 on page 170 for detailed backing.

Claim 2: Intended decisions

The high-stakes summative decisions are made by the teacher at the end of the school year. The low-stakes formative decisions are made by the teacher and the students before the next unit of instruction. These decisions affect the stakeholders as indicated in Table E6.3. The decisions take into consideration the educational values of the school and the societal values of the community, and follow the rules and regulations of the school. They are equitable for the stakeholders listed in Table E6.3.

Decision(s) to be made	Individual(s) who will make the decision(s)	When the decision(s) will be made	Stakeholders who will (or might be) affected by the decision(s)
Summative, high stakes			
Decide which students pass to the next grade (scores from this assessment will count as part of students' total grade for the term)	Teacher	At the end of the school term	Students Teachers (Future teachers) (School administrators) (The school) (Parents/Guardians)
Formative, low stakes			
Provide students with feedback on their written performance	Teacher	During the next lesson	Students Teachers (Parents/Guardians)
Make appropriate changes to teaching	Teacher	Before the next unit of instruction	Students Teachers (Parents/Guardians)
Continue with planned teaching; review, or give additional support tasks	Teacher	Before the next unit of instruction	Students Teachers (Parents/Guardians)
Review and/or practice learning on which students need to improve	Students	After they receive the teacher's feedback	Teachers Students (Parents/Guardians)

Table E6.3 Intended decisions

Some possible backing for intended decisions in Claim 2

See Example 1 on page 172 for detailed backing.

Claim 3: Intended interpretations

The interpretations about four aspects of the students' writing ability—task achievement, grammar, vocabulary, and mechanics—are relevant to the formative and summative decisions to be made. The interpretations are sufficient for the low-stakes formative decisions, but not sufficient for the high-stakes summative decisions to be made. These summative decisions will be made on the basis of this assessment and other classroom assessments that will be given during the course of instruction. The interpretations are meaningful with respect to the content of the course and of the current lesson, generalizable to the current language class, and are impartial to all students.

Some possible backing for intended interpretations in Claim 3

See Example 1 on page 173 for detailed backing.

Claim 4: Assessment records

The scores from the writing assessment are consistent across different times and days of administration, and across different administrations to different groups of students. Students' performances are scored consistently by the teacher, according to the Rating Scale. Possible sources of inconsistency for this assessment are listed in Table E6.4.

Possible sources of inconsistency in scores
1 Inconsistencies in the administration of the assessment • different times or days of administration • different administrations to different groups of students
2 Inconsistencies across different assessment tasks • different musical instruments • differing amounts of detail for musical instrument chosen
3 Inconsistencies in how students' performances are scored • different applications of the Rating Scale from one student to the next

Table E6.4 Possible sources of inconsistency in scores

Some possible backing for intended assessment records in Claim 4

The possible sources of inconsistency and possible backing to assure that these sources will be minimized are given in Table E6.5.

Possible sources of inconsistency	Possible backing to assure consistency
1 Inconsistencies in the administration of the assessment • different times or days of administration • different administrations to different groups of students	• Documentation of administrative procedures to be followed • Teacher's notes from administering the assessment at different times during the class period, on different days, and with different groups of students
2 Inconsistencies across different assessment tasks • different musical instruments • differing amounts of detail for musical instrument chosen	• Documentation: task specifications for the musical instruments to be used in the assessment • Teacher's notes on any differences that were observed in how different musical instruments may have affected students' performances
3 Inconsistencies in how students' performances are scored • different applications of the Rating Scale from one student to the next	• Documentation: Rating Scale, Recording Form, and instructions for scoring • Teacher's notes on how the Rating Scale may have been applied differently from one student to the next

Table E6.5 Possible backing for possible sources of inconsistency

Assessment task development

Step 1 TLU task selected for development of assessment task

1 Short descriptive label for TLU task: writing a descriptive paragraph about a musical instrument

2 Areas of language ability the TLU task engages: task achievement in descriptive writing, using appropriate range of grammar, vocabulary, and correct mechanics

Step 2 Description of the TLU task

1 Activities and procedures to be followed:

  a The teacher explains the writing activity to the class.

  b Students and the teacher read an example of a descriptive paragraph and discuss what the main features of a descriptive paragraph are.

  c The teacher gives the class a list of musical instruments.

  d Students then choose an instrument and write their paragraph individually.

  e The students read their paragraphs in groups of four and receive feedback from other students for revision.

   f The students then revise their descriptive paragraphs individually.

   g The teacher reads each descriptive paragraph and gives written feedback to each student.

   h Students revise their descriptive paragraphs if needed.

2 Characteristics of the TLU task:

TLU task: writing a descriptive paragraph about a musical instrument
Areas of language ability the TLU task engages: task achievement in descriptive writing, using appropriate range of grammar, vocabulary, and correct mechanics

Task characteristics	
Setting	<u>Physical circumstances</u>: teacher in front of classroom; students in groups of four *Equipment/Materials*: pen/pencil, paper (or computer), pictures of musical instruments <u>Participants</u>: teacher and students in groups of four (teens, intermediate) <u>Time of the task</u>: during the class period; one class period required

Input	<u>Form</u>:
	Aural:
	   Teacher: description of the task; discussion of the features of a descriptive paragraph
	   Students: discussion of the task, reading paragraphs out loud; feedback
	Visual: features and characteristics of a descriptive paragraph in textbook or on the board; teacher's written feedback, pictures of musical instruments
	<u>Language</u>: English
	Length: *aural*: short utterances; *visual*: long (several pictures), example of a descriptive paragraph in the textbook; written text, fairly simple grammar and vocabulary; list of musical instruments
	<u>Topical content</u>: musical instrument

Expected response	<u>Form</u>: *Visual*: students write a descriptive paragraph about a musical instrument <u>Language</u>: English; written text; fairly simple grammar and vocabulary *Length*: one paragraph (100–130 words) <u>Topical content</u>: musical instrument

Step 3 The modified task/assessment task template

1 Activities and procedures to be followed:

  a A week before the assessment the teacher tells the students:

    i They will have an assessment of their writing ability the following week.

    ii The purposes of the assessment are:

      a) to give each student a mark that will count as part of his or her grade for the school term

      b) to provide feedback to individual students about their writing ability.

    iii They will have to write a descriptive paragraph on a topic they will be given on the day of the assessment.

    iv The students will have the entire class period to write their descriptive paragraph.

    v The teacher explains that he will score their descriptive paragraphs according to the Rating Scale which he gives them and describes to them. This scale includes features of writing that have been covered in the class. He explains that he will also give them written feedback.

  b On the day of the assessment:

    i The teacher explains the writing assessment to the class.

    ii Students will have the whole class period to complete their descriptive paragraph.

    iii The teacher reviews the Rating Scale with the students, reminding them to pay attention to the features of writing that are included in the Rating Scale.

    iv Students are given a list of musical instruments that are different from those used in the TLU task and the writing prompt (see below).

  c During the next class after the assessment:

    i The teacher returns students' descriptive paragraphs to them, along with their Recording Forms with their scores and written feedback.

    ii The teacher gives general feedback to the class, discussing general positive features and weaknesses in their paragraphs.

  d Administrative procedures:

    i The assessment takes place during one class period. The teacher explains the assessment at the beginning of the class period. The assessment is administered to the class as a group, with students working individually. They write a descriptive paragraph about a musical instrument.

2 Task characteristics of the modified task/assessment task template

Assessment task: writing a descriptive paragraph about a musical instrument	
Areas of language ability to be assessed: task achievement in descriptive writing, using appropriate range of grammar, vocabulary, and correct mechanics	
Task characteristics	
Setting	<u>Physical circumstances</u>: teacher in front of classroom; students are seated individually *Equipment/Materials*: pen/pencil, paper (or computer), pictures of musical instruments <u>Participants</u>: teacher and students (teens, intermediate level) <u>Time of the task</u>: during the class period; one class period required
Input	<u>Form</u>: *Aural*: teacher's spoken description of the task *Visual*: a list with pictures of musical instruments <u>Language</u>: English *Teacher*: short utterances describing and explaining, simple grammar and vocabulary *Length*: *aural*: short utterances; *visual*: long (several pictures) <u>Topical content</u>: musical instrument
Expected response	<u>Form</u>: *Visual*: a written descriptive paragraph about a musical instrument <u>Language</u>: English: organized with fairly simple grammar and vocabulary *Length*: one paragraph (100–130 words) <u>Topical content</u>: musical instrument

3 Modified task/assessment task template recording method

Recording method for assessment task	<u>Type of assessment record</u>: score and written feedback <u>Aspects of ability</u>: four aspects of writing: task achievement, grammar, vocabulary, and mechanics <u>Scoring method</u>: <u>Criteria</u>: (See the Rating Scale below) *For each aspect*: 1–4, according to the Rating Scale <u>Score reported</u>: total score = task achievement + grammar + vocabulary + mechanics <u>Procedures</u>: the teacher reads the students' paragraphs and arrives at scores according to the Rating Scale, enters their scores on the Recording Form, then adds up the scores to arrive at a total score and enters this on the Recording Form. The teacher provides written feedback on the Recording Form. This is given back to the students during the next lesson.

Step 4 Model assessment task

Teacher's description of the task:

"Here's the prompt for your writing test." (The teacher gives students the writing prompt.) "Read it through and let me know if you have any questions." (Teacher allows time for students to read the prompt.) "Are there any questions?" (The teacher answers any clarification questions the students may have.) "You'll have 45 minutes to complete your paragraph. You may begin now."

Writing prompt:

Choose a musical instrument from the list and write a descriptive paragraph about it in **100–130 words**. Use the same structure for your paragraph that we have been using in class. You will receive a score on the structure of your paragraph, according to the Rating Scale we discussed in class. You have **45 minutes** to complete your descriptive paragraph.

Rating Scale:

Points	Task achievement	Grammar	Vocabulary	Mechanics
4	• Includes all content points • Meets all descriptive paragraph requirements	• Wide range of grammatical structures with very few inaccuracies	• Wide range of vocabulary with very few inaccuracies	• Very few errors in English writing conventions • Very few errors in punctuation and spelling
3	• Includes most content points • Meets most descriptive paragraph requirements	• Good range of grammar structures with occasional inaccuracies	• Good range of vocabulary with occasional inaccuracies	• Few errors in English writing conventions • Few errors in punctuation and spelling
2	• Includes some content points • Meets some descriptive paragraph requirements	• Limited range of grammar structures with frequent inaccuracies	• Limited range of vocabulary with frequent inaccuracies	• Frequent errors in English writing conventions • Frequent errors in punctuation and spelling
1	• Includes few content points • Meets few descriptive paragraph requirements	• Very limited range of grammar structures with very frequent inaccuracies	• Very limited range of vocabulary with very frequent inaccuracies	• Very frequent errors in English writing conventions • Very frequent errors in punctuation and spelling

Recording Form

Assessment task: Writing a descriptive paragraph

Student name: _____ Date: _____

Rating Scale: Aspect of writing	Score	Feedback on student's writing
Task achievement		
Grammar		
Vocabulary		
Mechanics		

Total score: _____

Example 7: Speaking, discussing an environmental issue (teens or adults, advanced level)

Brief overview of the assessment

Test takers	Students
Age group	Teens or adults
Level of language ability	Advanced
Language	ESL/EFL
Language use activity	Speaking, dialogue; discussion about an environmental issue
Intended uses	Summative decisions

Setting

A teacher in a content-based ESL/EFL classroom in a secondary school or university needs to develop a classroom assessment for his advanced-level students. This assessment will be used for one purpose. He wants to make sure that the students who pass the grade are prepared for instruction at the next level. In order to do this, the teacher will use the results of this assessment, along with other assessments given during the course of the school year, to make summative decisions about which students will pass to the next grade. The assessment will be based on the content of students' science class and the corresponding unit of instruction in their ESL/EFL class. This is one task from the assessment, in which the students discuss an environmental issue.

Assessment use argument

Claim 1: Intended consequences

The consequences of using the classroom speaking assessment will be beneficial to stakeholders as indicated in Tables E7.1 and E7.2.

Intended consequences	Intended stakeholders
1a Students who have mastered the learning objectives of the entire term will benefit by receiving appropriate instruction at the next level.	Students ESL/EFL teachers in the next level
1b Students who have not mastered the learning objectives of the entire term will benefit by receiving appropriate instruction at the same level.	Students ESL/EFL teachers in the current level

Table E7.1 Intended consequences and intended stakeholders

Other possible consequences and stakeholders who might be affected are included in Table E7.2.

Other possible consequences	Stakeholders who might be affected
Teachers will be able to teach students who are prepared for their level	ESL/EFL teachers in the next level

Table E7.2 Other possible consequences and stakeholders who might be affected

Some possible backing for intended consequences in Claim 1:

See Example 2 on page 182 for detailed backing.

Claim 2: Intended decisions

The high-stakes summative decisions are made by the teacher at the end of the school year. These decisions affect the stakeholders as indicated in Table E7.3. The decisions take into consideration the educational values of the school and the societal values of the community, and follow the rules and regulations of the school. They are equitable for the stakeholders listed in Table E7.3.

Decision(s) to be made	Individual(s) who will make the decision(s)	When the decision(s) will be made	Stakeholders who will (or might be) affected by the decision(s)
Summative, high stakes			
Decide which students pass to the next grade (scores from this assessment will count as part of students' total grade for the term)	Teacher	At the end of the school term	Students Teachers (Future teachers) (School administrators) (The school) (Parents/Guardians)

Table E7.3 Intended decisions

Some possible backing for intended decisions in Claim 2

See Example 2 on page 183 for detailed backing.

Claim 3: Intended interpretations

The interpretations about five aspects of students' speaking ability—task achievement, knowledge of topical content, use of accurate grammar, vocabulary and pronunciation—are relevant to the summative decisions to be made. The interpretations are not sufficient for the high-stakes summative decisions to be made. These summative decisions will be made on the basis of this assessment and other classroom assessments that will be given during the course of instruction. The interpretations are meaningful with respect to the content of the course and of the current lesson, generalizable to the current language class, and are impartial to all students.

Some possible backing for intended interpretations in Claim 3

See Example 2 on page 183 for detailed backing.

Claim 4: Assessment records

The scores from the speaking assessment are consistent across different times and days of administration, and across different administrations to different groups of students. Students' scores are consistent across the different topics and different pairs of students. Students' performances are scored consistently by the teacher, according to the Rating Scale. The possible sources of inconsistency for this assessment are listed in Table E7.4.

Possible sources of inconsistency in scores
1 Inconsistencies in the administration of the assessment   • different times or days of administration   • different administrations to different pairs of students   • different administrations to different groups of students
2 Inconsistencies across different topics   • different topics for discussion   • differences in the pairings of the students
3 Inconsistencies how students' performances are scored   • different applications of the Rating Scale from one student to the next   • different applications of the Rating Scale from one pair to the next

Table E7.4 Possible sources of inconsistency in scores

Some possible backing for intended assessment records in Claim 4

The possible sources of inconsistency and possible backing to assure that these sources will be minimized are given in Table E7.5.

Possible sources of inconsistency	**Possible backing to assure consistency**
1 Inconsistencies in the administration of the assessment • different times or days of administration • different administrations to different pairs of students • different administrations to different groups of students	• Documentation of administrative procedures to be followed • Teacher's notes from administering the assessment at different times during the class period, on different days, with different pairs of students, and with different groups of students

2 Inconsistencies across different topics • different topics for discussion • differences in the pairings of the students	• Documentation: task specifications for the topics to be used in the assessment • Teacher's notes on any differences that were observed in how different topics may have affected students' performances • Teacher's notes on how the attributes of students who were paired may have affected their performances
3 Inconsistencies in how students' performances are scored • different applications of the Rating Scale from one student to the next • different applications of the Rating Scale from one pair to the next	• Documentation: Rating Scale and instructions for scoring • Teacher's notes on how the Rating Scale may have been applied differently from one student to the next or across pairs of students

Table E7.5 Possible backing to assure the consistency of scores

Assessment task development

Step 1 TLU task selected for development of assessment task

1 Short descriptive label for TLU task: discussing an environmental issue orally in the language classroom

2 Areas of language ability the TLU task engages: speaking, dialogue; discussing an environmental issue in pairs

Step 2 Description of the TLU task:

1 Activities and procedures to be followed:

a The teacher explains the speaking activity to the class.

   i Each group will discuss one of the environmental issues that have just been covered in their science and English classes.

b The teacher and students discuss the features of a discussion.

c Students are given a statement about the environment to discuss.

d Students work individually on their own points of view and opinions for the discussion, taking notes as needed.

e Students then form groups of three to four.

f Students work collaboratively in their groups discussing their points of view and opinions about the issue.

g The teacher moves around, listens to the groups, and facilitates the discussion as needed.

h Each group presents the main points of their discussion to the class.

i The other students in the class may ask questions after each presentation.

j The teacher provides general verbal feedback on the quality of the discussions.

2 Task characteristics of TLU task:

TLU task: speaking, group discussion of an environmental issue in the language classroom
Areas of language ability the TLU task engages: task achievement, knowledge of topical content, use of accurate grammar, vocabulary, and pronunciation in speaking

Task characteristics	
Setting	<u>Physical circumstances</u>: teacher in front of classroom; students in groups of 3–4 *Equipment/Materials*: paper and pencils for taking notes <u>Participants</u>: teacher and students (teens or adults, advanced level) <u>Time of the task</u>: during the class period; two class periods required
Input	<u>Form</u>: *Aural*: *Teacher*: description of the task, questions and comments *Students*: discussions of environmental issue and questions *Visual*: words and phrases that the students may write on paper <u>Language</u>: English *Teacher*: simple grammar and vocabulary, statements *Students*: medium to long utterances; advanced grammar and vocabulary, questions and answers *Length*: *aural*: long utterances; *visual*: short (words and phrases) <u>Topical content</u>: an environmental issue
Expected response	<u>Form</u>: *Visual*: words, phrases, and sentences that students write on paper to support their speaking *Oral*: students' discussions of an environmental issue, students' questions, students' responses to teacher's and other students' questions <u>Language</u>: English; medium to long utterances; advanced grammar and vocabulary, questions and answers *Length*: *visual*: about two minutes; *oral*: about ten minutes for groups' discussions and about five minutes per group for presentations <u>Topical content</u>: an environmental issue

Step 3 The modified task/assessment task template:

1 Activities and procedures to be followed:

  a On the day before the assessment the teacher tells the students:

    i They will have an assessment of their speaking the next day.

      a) The purpose of the assessment is to give each student a mark that will count as part of his or her grade for the school term.

    ii The teacher will assign the students to pairs for the assessment.

    iii The test will be given individually to each pair.

      a) The students are given a question on an environmental issue that is different from the one they did in class.

      b) The students will be given two minutes to prepare their discussion.

      c) The students are given five minutes to discuss the topic.

  b On the day of the assessment, the teacher assesses pairs of students individually.

    i The teacher briefly explains the assessment task again.

    ii The teacher makes sure students understand the procedure.

    iii The teacher calls the names of the students in the first pair.

    iv The teacher shows the pair a question about an environmental issue.

    v The students take one minute to read the topic and think about their discussion points.

    vi The students discuss the environmental issue.

    vii The teacher scores the students' performance using the Rating Scale.

    viii The teacher lets the two students go back to the class and calls the next pair of students for the assessment.

  c During the next lesson:

    i The teacher gives the students their Recording Forms.

    ii The teacher gives the class general feedback on their areas of strength and the areas in which they need to improve.

  d Administrative procedures:

    i The assessment takes place during a regular classroom period. It is given as a paired speaking activity between two students, with the teacher observing and listening, in a Speaking Corner of the classroom. The teacher calls the first pair of students to be assessed. The teacher explains the assessment task and makes sure that the students understand the procedure. The teacher gives the students a question about an environmental issue and allows them to take one minute to think about how they will discuss the question with each other. Then the students have five minutes to discuss the topic. While the students are speaking, the teacher scores each student using the rating scale. The teacher then calls the next pair for the assessment.

2 Task characteristics of the modified task/assessment task template

Assessment task: speaking, paired discussion of an environmental issue	
Areas of language ability to be assessed: task achievement, knowledge of topical content, use of accurate grammar, vocabulary, and pronunciation in speaking	
Task characteristics	
Setting	<u>Physical circumstances</u>: teacher with a pair of students seated at a table in the Speaking Corner of the classroom *Equipment/Materials*: paper and pencils for taking notes (for the students); Recording Form, Rating Scale, pen/pencil (for the teacher) <u>Participants</u>: teacher and a pair of students (teens or adults, advanced level) <u>Time of task</u>: during the class period; task requires more than one class period depending on number of students

Input	<u>Form</u>:
	  Aural: teacher's spoken description of the task
	  Visual: words and phrases that the students may write on paper
	<u>Language</u>: English
	  Teacher: aural: short spoken description and explanation; simple grammar and vocabulary
	  Length: aural: short utterances; *visual*: short (words and phrases)
	<u>Topical content</u>: an environmental issue

Expected response	<u>Form</u>:
	  Visual: students' notes for their discussion
	  Oral: students' discussion of an environmental issue
	<u>Language</u>: English; medium to long utterances; advanced grammar and vocabulary, questions and answers
	  Length: visual: one minute to read and think about their discussion; *oral*: about five minutes for each pair to discuss the issue.
	<u>Topical content</u>: an environmental issue

3 Modified task/assessment task template recording method

Recording method for assessment task	<u>Type of assessment record</u>: score
	<u>Aspects of ability</u> : five aspects of speaking: task achievement, knowledge of topical content, grammar, vocabulary, pronunciation
	<u>Scoring method</u>
	   <u>Criteria</u>: (See the Rating Scale below.)
	   For each aspect: 4 – All/wide; 3 – Most/Good; 2 – Some/Moderate;
	    1 – Few/Limited
	   <u>Score reported</u>: total score = task achievement + knowledge of topical content + grammar + vocabulary + pronunciation
	   <u>Procedures</u>: the teacher listens to students' discussions and enters a score for each aspect of speaking in the Rating Scale for each student; the teacher then adds up the scores to arrive at a total score and enters this on the Recording Form. This is given back to the students during the next lesson.

Step 4 Model assessment task

Teacher's description of the task: "Here is a question about an environmental issue that I want you to discuss between the two of you." (Teacher chooses one of the prompts from the list below and gives it to the students.) "Now, take a minute to make notes to guide your discussion." (Teacher waits for one minute.) "OK. You'll now have five minutes to discuss this issue together. You may begin now."

Prompts:

1 What do you think can be done to reduce fossil fuel emissions? Who do you think is responsible for reducing fossil fuel emissions? Why?

2 What do you think can be done to reduce the amount of waste material that is produced? Who do you think is responsible for reducing the amount of waste material that is produced? Why?

3 What do you think can be done to reduce the amount of air pollution? Who do you think is responsible for reducing the amount of air pollution? Why?

4 What do you think can be done to clean up the oceans? Who do you think is responsible for cleaning up the oceans? Why?

5 What do you think can be done to help preserve endangered species of plants and animals? Who do you think is responsible for helping to preserve endangered species of plants and animals? Why?

6 What do you think can be done to help preserve the tropical rainforests? Who do you think is responsible for helping to preserve the tropical rainforests? Why?

Points	Task achievement	Knowledge of topical content	Grammar	Vocabulary	Pronunciation
4	• Meets all discussion requirements	• Wide knowledge of the assigned topic	• Wide range of grammar structures with very few inaccuracies	• Wide range of vocabulary with very few inaccuracies	• High degree of control; very few errors
3	• Meets most discussion requirements	• Good knowledge of the assigned topic	• Good range of grammar structures with occasional inaccuracies	• Good range of vocabulary with occasional inaccuracies	• Good control; occasional errors
2	• Meets some discussion requirements	• Moderate knowledge of the assigned topic	• Moderate range of grammar structures with frequent inaccuracies	• Moderate range of vocabulary with frequent inaccuracies	• Moderate control; frequent errors
1	• Meets few discussion requirements	• Limited knowledge of the assigned topic	• Limited range of grammar structures with very frequent inaccuracies	• Limited range of vocabulary with very frequent inaccuracies	• Limited control; very frequent errors

Recording Form

Assessment task: Speaking, discussion of an environmental issue

Student name: _____   Date: _____

Student paired with: _____

Number of prompt chosen: _____

Rating Scale: Aspect of speaking	Few/Limited 1	Some/Moderate 2	Most/Good 3	All/Wide 4
Task achievement				
Knowledge of topical content				
Grammar				
Vocabulary				
Pronunciation				

Total score: _____

Example 8: Writing a letter of application for a job (teens or adults, advanced level)

Brief overview of the assessment

Test takers	Students
Age group	Teens or adults
Level of language ability	Advanced
Language	ESL/EFL
Language use activity	Writing a letter of application
Intended uses	Formative feedback for teacher and students; summative decisions

Setting

A teacher in an ESL/EFL classroom in a secondary school or university needs to develop a classroom assessment for her advanced-level students. This assessment will be used for two different purposes. One purpose is to make sure that the students who pass the grade are prepared for instruction at the next level. In order to do this, the teacher will use the results of this assessment, along with other assessments given during the course of the school year, to make summative decisions about which students will pass to the next grade. The second purpose of the assessment is to help her students improve their writing and to improve her teaching. In order to do this, the teacher will use the results of this assessment to make formative decisions about her teaching and to provide feedback to her students. The assessment will be based on a unit of instruction in the course, and this is one task from the assessment, in which the students write a letter of application for a job.

Assessment use argument

Claim 1: Intended consequences

The consequences of using the classroom writing assessment will be beneficial to stakeholders as indicated in Tables E8.1 and E8.2.

Intended consequences	Intended stakeholders
1a Students who have mastered the learning objectives of the entire term will benefit by receiving appropriate instruction at the next level.	Students ESL/EFL teachers in the next level
1b Students who have not mastered the learning objectives of the entire term will benefit by receiving appropriate instruction at the same level.	Students ESL/EFL teachers in the current level
2 Students will improve their writing.	Students Teacher
3 The teacher will improve her teaching.	Students Teacher

Table E8.1 Intended consequences and intended stakeholders

Other possible consequences and stakeholders who *might* be affected are included in Table E8.2.

Other possible consequences	Stakeholders who might be affected
Teachers will be able to teach students who are prepared for their level	ESL/EFL teachers in the current level ESL/EFL teachers in the next level
There will be fewer complaints from teachers, students, and parents/guardians	School administrators
The reputation of the school will improve.	The school
Parents/Guardians will be satisfied with their children's writing and help their children continue to improve.	Parents/Guardians, students, teachers

Table E8.2 Other possible consequences and stakeholders who might be affected

Some possible backing for intended consequences in Claim 1

See Example 1 on page 170 for detailed backing.

Claim 2: Intended decisions

The high-stakes summative decisions are made by the teacher at the end of the school year. The low-stakes formative decisions are made by the teacher and the students before the next unit of instruction. These decisions affect the stakeholders as indicated in Table E8.3. The decisions take into consideration the educational values of the school and the societal values of the community, and follow the rules and regulations of the school. They are equitable for the stakeholders listed in Table E8.3.

Decision(s) to be made	Individual(s) who will make the decision(s)	When the decision(s) will be made	Stakeholders who will (or might be) affected by the decision(s)
Summative, high stakes			
Decide which students pass to the next grade (scores from this assessment will count as part of students' total grade for the term)	Teacher	At the end of the school term	Students Teachers (Future teachers) (School administrators) (The school) (Parents/Guardians)
Formative, low stakes			
Provide students with feedback on their writing performance	Teacher	During the next lesson	Students Teachers (Parents/Guardians)
Make appropriate changes to teaching	Teacher	Before the next unit of instruction	Students Teachers (Parents/Guardians)
Continue with planned teaching; review, or give additional support tasks	Teacher	Before the next unit of instruction	Students Teachers (Parents/Guardians)
Review and/or practice learning on which students need to improve	Students	After they receive the teacher's feedback	Teachers Students (Parents/Guardians)

Table E8.3 Intended decisions

Some possible backing for intended decisions in Claim 2

See Example 1 on page 172 for detailed backing.

Claim 3: Intended interpretations

The interpretations about four aspects of students' writing ability—task achievement, grammar, vocabulary, and cohesion—are relevant to the formative and summative decisions to be made. The interpretations are sufficient for the low-stakes formative decisions, but not sufficient for the high-stakes summative decisions to be made. These summative decisions will be made on the basis of this assessment and other classroom assessments that will be given during the course of instruction. The interpretations are meaningful with respect to the content of the course and of the current lesson, generalizable to the current language class, and are impartial to all students.

Some possible backing for intended interpretations in Claim 3

See Example 1 on page 173 for detailed backing.

Claim 4: Assessment records

The scores from the writing assessment are consistent across different times and days of administration, and across different administrations to different groups of students. Students' performances are scored consistently by the teacher, according to the Rating Scale. Possible sources of inconsistency for this assessment are listed in Table E8.4.

Possible sources of inconsistency in scores
1 Inconsistencies in the administration of the assessment • different times or days of administration • different administrations to different groups of students
2 Inconsistencies in how students' performances are scored • different applications of the Rating Scale from one student to the next

Table E8.4 Possible sources of inconsistency in scores

Some possible backing for intended assessment records in Claim 4

The possible sources of inconsistency and possible backing to assure that these sources will be minimized are given in Table E8.5.

Possible sources of inconsistency	**Possible backing to assure consistency**
1 Inconsistencies in the administration of the assessment • different times or days of administration • different administrations to different groups of students	• Documentation of administrative procedures to be followed • Teacher's notes from administering the assessment at different times during the class period, on different days, with different groups of students
2 Inconsistencies in how students' performances are scored • different applications of the Rating Scale from one student to the next	• Documentation: Rating Scale, Recording Form, and instructions for scoring • Teacher's notes on how the Rating Scale may have been applied differently from one student to the next

Table E8.5 Possible backing for possible sources of inconsistency

Assessment task development

Step 1 TLU task selected for development of assessment task

1 Short descriptive label for TLU task: writing a letter of application for a job

2 Areas of language ability the TLU task engages: task achievement – following the format of a formal letter of application for a job, using appropriate range of grammar, vocabulary, and cohesion.

Step 2 Description of the TLU task

1 Activities and procedures to be followed:

  a The teacher explains the writing activity to the class.

    i Students are arranged in groups of three to four.

    ii Students in groups will write a letter of application for a job. This letter will follow the format of a formal letter of application that was discussed in class.

    iii Students are given a job description.

    iv Students decide on how to divide up the writing assignment in their groups.

  b Students work on the letter collaboratively in their groups, taking notes as needed.

  c The teacher moves around and helps the groups.

  d Each group presents its letter orally to the class.

  e The other students in the class give feedback on the writing in the letter.

  f The teacher provides verbal feedback on the writing in the letter.

  g Students discuss the feedback in their groups and rewrite their letters in the next lesson taking the feedback into consideration.

2 Task characteristics of TLU task:

TLU task: writing a letter of application for a job	
Areas of language ability the TLU task engages: task achievement – following the format of a formal letter of application for job, using appropriate range of grammar, vocabulary and cohesion	
Task characteristics	
Setting	<u>Physical circumstances</u>: teacher in front of classroom; students seated in groups *Equipment/Materials*: pen/pencil, paper (or computer) <u>Participants</u>: : teacher and students (adults; advanced) <u>Time of the task</u>: during the class period; one to two class periods required

Input	<u>Form</u>:
	Aural:
	    Teacher: description of the task; discussion of features and characteristics for a letter of application; verbal feedback
	    Students: discussion of the task, reading letters out loud; verbal feedback
	Visual: features and characteristics of a letter of application in textbook or on the board; example of a letter of application
	<u>Language</u>: English;
	    Teacher: short utterances describing and explaining, questions; simple grammar and vocabulary
	    Length: *aural*: short utterances; *visual*: words and short phrases on the board; longer sentences in the example
	<u>Topical content</u>: a formal job application letter

Expected response	<u>Form</u>:
	    Visual: students write a letter of application for a job
	<u>Language</u>: English: well organized; cohesion; fairly simple grammar and vocabulary; genre: formal letter
	    Length: 250–300 words
	<u>Topical content</u>: a formal job application letter

3 Prompt for TLU task:

"Read the following job description in your group and write a letter of application for the job in 250–300 words. Decide in your group who writes which part of the application or you can write it together."

Sandwich Subs team member in London, ON

If you are a friendly and outgoing person always with a smile on your face and looking for a part-time job, come join us at Sandwich Subs. Your energy and passion for guest service are what make you a top team member in this fast-paced environment, while your ability to multi-task and communicate with your fellow team members will contribute to your success. You will have flexible working hours and a good income.

Apply for this job if you:

* Enjoy working with a successful team in a safe environment

* Have a strong work ethic and are committed to your team

* Are reliable

* Have strong communication and interpersonal skills

We offer:

* Flexible schedules

* Competitive wages

* Purchase discounts

* Comprehensive training

* Health and dental benefits

* Advancement opportunities

* and much more. . .

Apply by email: sandwichsubs.com.ca or in writing to: Sandwich Subs, 416 Hill Street, London, Ontario, 4Y3 SYS

Step 3 The modified task/assessment task template

1 Activities and procedures to be followed:

  a A week before the assessment the teacher tells the students:

    i They will have an assessment of their writing ability the following week.

    ii The purposes of the assessment are:

      a) to give each student a mark that will count as part of his or her grade for the school term

      b) to provide feedback to individual students about their writing ability.

    iii They will have to write a letter of application for a job they will be given on the day of the assessment.

    iv The students will have an entire class period to write their letters of application.

v The teacher explains that she will score the letters according to the Rating Scale, which she shows them and describes to them. This scale includes features of writing that have been covered in class. She explains that she will also give them written feedback.

b On the day of the assessment:

i The teacher explains the writing assessment to the class.

ii Students will have the whole class period to complete their letter.

iii The teacher reviews the Rating Scale with the students, reminding them to pay attention to the features of writing that are included in the Rating Scale.

iv Students are given the writing prompt, and are allowed time to read this and ask clarification questions.

v Students work individually on their letters.

c During the next class after the assessment:

i The teacher returns students' letters of application to them, along with their Recording Forms with their scores and written feedback.

ii The teacher gives general feedback to the class, discussing general positive features and weaknesses in their letters.

d Administrative procedures:

i The assessment takes place during one class period. The teacher explains the assessment task and the Rating Scale at the beginning of the class period. The assessment is administered to the class as a group, with students working individually. They write a letter of application for a job they are given, which is different from the one they have been working on in class.

2 Task characteristics of the modified task/assessment task template

Assessment task: writing a formal letter of application for a job	
Areas of language ability to be assessed: task achievement – following the format of a formal letter of application for a job, using appropriate range of grammar, vocabulary, and cohesion	
Task characteristics	
Setting	Physical circumstances: teacher in front of classroom; students seated individually
	Equipment/Materials: pen/pencil, paper (or computer)
	Participants: teacher and students (adults; advanced)
	Time of the task: during the class period; one class period required

Input	Form:
	Aural: teacher's spoken description of the task
	Visual: writing prompt
	Language: English
	Teacher: aural: short spoken description and explanation; simple
	grammar and vocabulary
	Length: aural: short utterances; *visual*: long, job description
	Topical content: a letter of application for summer job as sales
	assistant
Expected response	Form:
	Visual: written text
	Language: English; written text, grammar and vocabulary
	appropriate to the writing task; well organized, with cohesion;
	genre: formal letter of application
	Length: 250–300 words
	Topical content: a letter of application for summer job as sales
	assistant

3 Modified task/assessment task template recording method

Recording method for assessment task	Types of assessment record: score and written feedback
	Aspects of ability: writing: task achievement, grammar, vocabulary,
	and cohesion
	Scoring method:
	Criteria: (See the Rating Scale below.)
	For each aspect: 1–4, according to the Rating Scale
	Score reported: total score = task achievement + grammar +
	vocabulary + cohesion
	Procedures: the teacher reads the students' letters and arrives
	at scores according to the Rating Scale, entering their scores
	on the Recording Form, then adds up the scores to arrive
	at a total score and enters this on the Recording Form. The
	teacher provides written feedback on the Recording Form.
	This is given back to the students during the next lesson.

Step 4 Model assessment task

Teacher's description of the task:

"Here's the prompt for your writing test." (The teacher gives students the writing prompt.) "Read it through and let me know if you have any questions." (Teacher allows time for students to read the prompt.) "Are there any questions?" (The teacher answers any clarification questions the students may have.) "You'll have 45 minutes to complete your letter. You may begin now."

Writing prompt:

"Suppose you have read the following job description in the newspaper:"

Summer job: Sales Assistant

If you are a motivated and outgoing person who is looking for a great summer job that offers flexible hours and good income, join our team at "The Market Place"! Working hours are Monday through Friday from 9.00 am–5.00 pm. You will receive benefits such as discounts on merchandise and food.

Your duties will be to assist the sales manager in the following:

• Answering customers' queries about merchandise needs

• Offering recommendations based on customers' needs and interests

• Restocking inventory

• Processing cash and card payments

• Dealing with customer refunds

• Dealing with customer complaints

Please apply in writing to the Human Resources Department at: The Market Place, 132 Baker Street, St Louis, MI, 63105

"You would like to apply for this job. Write a letter of application (150-200 words) to the human resources department of the store. Use the same structure for your letter that we have been using in class. Include all the necessary information. Your letter will be scored according to the Rating Scale we discussed in class. You have 45 minutes to complete your letter."

Rating Scale:

Points	Task achievement	Grammar	Vocabulary	Cohesion
4	• Includes all content points • Meets all application letter requirements	• Wide range of grammar structures with very few inaccuracies	• Wide range of vocabulary with very few inaccuracies	• Wide range of cohesive devices with very few inaccuracies
3	• Includes most content points • Meets most application letter requirements	• Good range of grammar structures with occasional inaccuracies	• Good range of vocabulary with occasional inaccuracies	• Good range of cohesive devices with occasional inaccuracies
2	• Includes some content points • Meets some application letter requirements	• Limited range of grammar structures with frequent inaccuracies	• Limited range of vocabulary with frequent inaccuracies	• Limited range of cohesive devices with frequent inaccuracies
1	• Includes few content points • Meets few application letter requirements	• Very limited range of grammar structures with very frequent inaccuracies	• Very limited range of vocabulary with very frequent inaccuracies	• Very limited range of cohesive devices with very frequent inaccuracies

Recording Form

Assessment task: Writing a letter of application for a job

Student name: _____   **Date:** _____

Rating Scale: **Aspect of writing**	**Score**	**Feedback on student's writing**
Task achievement		
Grammar		
Vocabulary		
Cohesion		

Total score: _____

Example 9: Reading, matching headings, street art (teens, intermediate level)

Brief overview of the assessment

Test takers	Students
Age group	Teens
Level of language ability	Intermediate
Language	ESL/EFL
Language use activity	Reading for major ideas
Intended uses	Summative decisions

Setting

A teacher in an ESL/EFL classroom in a secondary school needs to develop a classroom assessment for his intermediate students. This assessment will be used for one purpose. He wants to make sure that the students who pass the grade are prepared for instruction at the next level. In order to do this, the teacher will use the results of this assessment, along with other assessments given during the course of the school year, to make summative decisions about which students will pass to the next grade. The assessment will be based on a unit of instruction in the course, and this is one task from the assessment, in which students read a written text with six paragraphs about street art, and then choose, from a list, the headings that best describe each paragraph.

Assessment use argument

Claim 1: Intended consequences

The consequences of using the classroom reading assessment will be beneficial to stakeholders as indicated in Tables E9.1 and E9.2.

Intended consequences	Intended stakeholders
1a Students who have mastered the learning objectives of the entire term will benefit by receiving appropriate instruction at the next level.	Students ESL/EFL teachers in the next level
1b Students who have not mastered the learning objectives of the entire term will benefit by receiving appropriate instruction at the same level.	Students ESL/EFL teachers in the current level

Table E9.1 Intended consequences and intended stakeholders

Other possible consequences and stakeholders who might be affected are included in Table E9.2.

Other possible consequences	Stakeholders who might be affected
Teachers will be able to teach students who are prepared for their level.	ESL/EFL teachers in the current level ESL/EFL teachers in the next level

Table E9.2 Other possible consequences and stakeholders who might be affected

Some possible backing for intended consequences in Claim 1

See Example 2 on page 182 for detailed backing.

Claim 2: Intended decisions

The high-stakes summative decisions are made by the teacher at the end of the school year. These decisions affect the stakeholders as indicated in Table E9.3. The decisions take into consideration the educational values of the school and the societal values of the community, and follow the rules and regulations of the school. They are equitable for the stakeholders listed in Table E9.3.

Decision(s) to be made	Individual(s) who will make the decision(s)	When the decision(s) will be made	Stakeholders who will (or might be) affected by the decision(s)
Summative, high stakes			
Decide which students pass to the next grade (scores from this assessment will count as part of students' total grade for the term)	Teacher	At the end of the school term	Students Teachers (Future teachers) (School administrators) (The school) (Parents/Guardians)

Table E9.3 Intended decisions

Some possible backing for intended decisions in Claim 2

See Example 2 on page 183 for detailed backing.

Claim 3: Intended interpretations

The interpretations about students' comprehension of major ideas in reading are relevant to the high-stakes summative decisions to be made, but are not sufficient for these decisions. These decisions will be made on the basis of this assessment and other classroom assessments that will be given during the course of instruction. The interpretations are meaningful with respect to the content of the course and of the current lesson, generalizable to the current language class, and are impartial to all students.

Some possible backing for intended interpretations in Claim 3:

See Example 2 on page 183 for detailed backing.

Claim 4: Assessment records

The scores from the reading assessment are consistent across different times and days of administration, and across different administrations to different groups of students. Students' performances are scored consistently by the teacher, according to the Scoring Key. The possible sources of inconsistency for this assessment are listed in Table E9.4.

Possible sources of inconsistency in scores
1 Inconsistencies in the administration of the assessment • different times or days of administration • different administrations to different groups of students
2 Inconsistencies across different assessment tasks • different applications of the Scoring Key from one student to the next

Table E9.4 Possible sources of inconsistency in scores

Some possible backing for intended assessment records in Claim 4:

The possible sources of inconsistency and possible backing to assure that these sources will be minimized are given in Table E9.5.

Possible sources of inconsistency	Possible backing to assure consistency
1 Inconsistencies in the administration of the assessment • different times or days of administration • different administrations to different groups of student	• Documentation of administrative procedures to be followed. • Teacher's notes from administering the assessment at different times during the class period, on different days, with different groups of students
2 Inconsistencies across different assessment tasks • different applications of the Scoring Key from one student to the next	• Documentation: Scoring Key and instructions for scoring • Teacher's notes on how the Scoring Key may have been applied differently from one student to the next

Table E9.5 Possible backing for possible sources of inconsistency

Assessment task development

Step 1 TLU task selected for development of assessment task

1 Short descriptive label for TLU task: reading a text with five paragraphs and matching the headings for each paragraph

2 Areas of language ability the TLU task engages: reading for major ideas

Step 2 Description of the TLU task:

1 Activities and procedures to be followed:

  a The teacher explains the reading activity to the class.

  b Students work individually.

  c Students are given a text with five paragraphs. Each paragraph has a blank before it for a heading. Students are also given a list of seven headings which have to be matched with the paragraphs.

  d Students read the text and write the numbers of the headings that best fit the paragraphs in the blanks.

  e The teacher and students discuss the answers in class.

  f Students revise their answers if needed.

2 Task characteristics of TLU task:

TLU task: reading, matching paragraphs with headings	
Areas of language ability the TLU task engages: comprehension of major ideas in reading	
Task characteristics	
Setting	<u>Physical circumstances</u>: teacher in front of classroom; students seated individually *Equipment/Materials*: reading text, pen/pencil <u>Participants</u>: teacher and students (teens, intermediate level) <u>Time of the task</u>: during the class period; one class period required
Input	<u>Form</u>: *Aural*: teacher's description of the task, questions and comments *Visual*: reading text with five paragraphs and five blanks for the headings; seven headings <u>Language</u>: English *Teacher*: short utterances describing and explaining, simple grammar and vocabulary *Length*: *aural*: short utterances; *visual*: long (text with five paragraphs, seven headings, simple grammar; well organized, with cohesion and coherence) <u>Topical content</u>: the Earth's future

Expected response	Form: *Visual*: students write the numbers of matching headings in the blanks before each paragraph <u>Language</u>: non-language *Length*: 15 minutes <u>Topical content</u>: the Earth's future

3   Reading text and answer sheet:

The Earth's Future

Paragraph A: Heading: _____

We know that North America and South America are slowly moving closer to Asia. Some experts say that one day the Earth's continents will join together to make one big continent. If the continents join together, maybe we'll all learn to speak the same language!

Paragraph B: Heading: _____

Other people say that if we continue to litter, and we pollute the air and oceans, we'll have a big problem in the future. A lot of animals and fish will die. Some will become extinct. Others will learn to adapt to a new environment. For example, if we pollute the oceans and there is no food for the fish, some fish will learn to fly to catch food.

Paragraph C: Heading: _____

In the far distant future, some experts say the Sun will become hotter and hotter, a big "red giant". If the Sun becomes hotter, the Earth's temperature will go up. The snow and ice will melt, and the oceans will evaporate. Will this be the end of life on Earth?

Paragraph D: Heading: _____

Other people think the Earth will move away from the Sun and become colder. If the Earth becomes colder, the snow and ice won't melt. Children will ski to school.

Paragraph E: Heading: _____

Some experts are worried that we will use up all the fossil fuels on Earth. If there is no more fuel on Earth, people will probably have to go to live on other planets.

1 Some animals will adapt to the changes

2 Moving to other planets

3 The Earth as one continent

4 A colder Earth

5 An overpopulated Earth

6 A hotter Earth

7 The Earth is changing

Scoring Key:

A 3   B 1   C 6   D 4   E 2

Step 3 The modified task/assessment task template

1 Activities and procedures to be followed:

  a A week before the assessment the teacher tells the students:

    i They will have an assessment of their reading ability the following week.

    ii The purpose of the assessment is to give each student a mark that will count as part of his or her grade for the school term.

    iii They will have to read a text and match the paragraphs with headings.

  b On the day of the assessment:

    i The teacher explains the reading activity to the class.

    ii Students will be given a reading text with six paragraphs and a blank before each paragraph for a heading.

    iii Students will be given nine headings and they will have to choose the ones that best suit the paragraphs.

    iv Students will have to fill the blanks for the headings in the reading passage by writing the numbers of the appropriate blanks for the headings in the text.

  c Administrative procedures: The assessment takes place during one class period. The teacher explains the assessment at the beginning of the class period. The assessment is administered to the class as a group, with students working individually. They read a text with six paragraphs. Each paragraph should be matched with a heading that students chose from nine given headings.

2 Task characteristics of the modified task/assessment task template:

Assessment task: reading and matching headings with paragraphs	
Areas of language ability to be assessed: comprehension of major ideas in reading	
Task characteristics	
Setting	Physical circumstances: teacher in front of classroom; students seated individually Equipment/Materials: reading text with blanks for headings, pen/pencil Participants: teacher and students (teens, intermediate level) Time of the task: during the class period; 20 minutes required

Input	Form:
	    Aural: teacher's description of the task
	    Visual: reading text with six paragraphs and a list of nine
	       headings
	 Language: English
	    Teacher: short utterances describing and explaining, simple
	       grammar and vocabulary
	    Length: *aural*: short utterances; *visual*: long (written text with six
	       paragraphs and a list of nine headings), simple grammar; well
	       organized, with cohesion and coherence
	 Topical content: street art

Expected response	Form:
	    Visual: students write the numbers of matching headings in the
	       blanks before each paragraph
	 Language: non-language
	    Length: short (only numbers)
	 Topical content: street art

3 Modified task/assessment task template recording method

Recording method for assessment task	Types of assessment record: score
	 Aspects of ability: comprehension of major ideas in reading
	 Scoring method
	    Criteria: (See the Scoring Key below.)
	    For each correct blank heading completion: 1 point
	    Score reported: number of correct choices for headings (six
	       maximum)
	    Procedures: The teacher reads each student's answers and assigns
	       the points according to the Scoring Key, adds these up to get a
	       total score, and enters this on the student's paper. The papers
	       with the scores are given back to the students in the next lesson.

Step 4 Model assessment task

Instructions for the assessment task:

> Students are given an answer sheet with six paragraphs and a list of nine headings.

Teacher's description of the task:

> "Here's your reading text and answer sheet. Match the headings from the list of "Headings" with the paragraphs they describe the best. Write the number of the Heading in the space before the paragraph. There will be three headings that you do not need. Your score will be the number of correct matches between paragraphs and headings. You will have 20 minutes for this task. Are there any questions?" (Teacher answers any clarification questions the students may have.) "You may begin now."

Reading text and Scoring Key:

Street Art

Paragraph A: Heading _____

Explore the backstreets of any big town or city around the world, and you'll definitely see some street art. Street art describes the pictures that are found outside on public places, such as walls, doors, and the sides of buildings.

Paragraph B: Heading _____

One of the best places to see street art is in Melbourne, Australia's second largest city. Artists are given a permit to work in specific places around the city. Their pictures are so good that Melbourne's street art has become one of its most popular tourist attractions, especially on Hosier Lane.

Paragraph C: Heading _____

Street art lovers can discover Melbourne's backstreets alone, or they can go on an organized walking tour. With the artists as guides, the world of street art is explained to them.

Paragraph D: Heading _____

British street artist Banksy is one of the international artists who has street art in Melbourne. His pictures are recognized around the world. Banksy is not his real name. His real name and personal details are not known.

Paragraph E: Heading _____

The vibrant and colorful Melbourne street art is thought to be an important part of 21st-century popular culture. Sometimes street art is shown in art museums. Some street art is bought by celebrities, too.

Paragraph F: Heading _____

Art is always subjective, and for some people, street art is vandalism. It is done without permission on someone else's property, and it isn't attractive to look at. For other people, street art is beautiful, and it can improve an urban environment.

1 A great place to see street art

2 History of street art

3 Problems of street art

4 Defining street art

5 How street art has become famous

6 Opinions on street art

7 A well-known street artist

8 Street art as "art"

9 Fans of street art on guided tours

Total score: _____

Scoring Key:

A 4   B 1   C 9   D 7   E 8   F 6

References

American Council on the Teaching of Foreign Languages. (2012). *ACTFL Proficiency Guidelines 2012.* Alexandria, VA: American Council on the Teaching of Foreign Languages.

Council of Europe. (2001). *Common European Framework of Reference for Languages: learning, teaching, assessment.* Cambridge: Cambridge University Press.

APPENDIX 1 CHECKLIST OF THINGS TO THINK ABOUT BEFORE USING A LANGUAGE ASSESSMENT

1 Begin with consequences

Question: *Why* do I need to assess?

Answer: In order to bring about beneficial consequences.

What beneficial consequences do I want to bring about?

Who will be affected by these beneficial consequences?

Questions for examples of some specific beneficial consequences I might want to bring about:

- How will using an assessment help my students improve their learning?
- How will using an assessment help me improve my teaching?
- How can I assure my students and others who might be affected by the use of my assessment that the consequences of using my assessment are beneficial?
- How might using an assessment be *un*helpful to my students?

2 Consider decisions

Question: *When* and *how often* do I need to assess?

Answer: Whenever I need to make a decision.

What decisions do I need to make in order to help promote these beneficial consequences?

Questions for examples of some decisions I might need to make:

- What decisions do I need to make to help my students improve their learning?
- What decisions do I need to make to improve my teaching?
- How can I assure my students and others that my decisions are consistent with what I believe about good instructional practice, what my school and my community consider important, and with the rules and regulations of my school?
- How can I assure that the decisions I make are equitable for my students and others who might be affected by these decisions?

3 Identify the information you need

Question: *What* do I need to assess? What information about my students' language ability do I need in order to make the intended decisions?

How will I specify the ability to be assessed?

Answer: Base your ability definitions on the content of the course or unit of instruction that you are teaching or have taught, e.g. the learning objectives, the curriculum, the instructional materials, the instructional tasks in which you engage your students.

Questions for examples of different kinds of information I might need about test takers in order to make the intended decisions:

- Do I need to know if my students have mastered the learning objectives of the lesson or course?
- Do I need to know if my students are ready for the next grade or level in the program?
- Do I need to know if my students will be able to use the language in academic classes in school?
- Do I need to know if my students will be able to use the language at the university, or on a job?
- How can I assure that my interpretations about my students' language ability will be meaningful to my students and others?
- How can I assure my students and others that my assessment is not biased for or against any particular student or group of students?
- How can I assure my students and others that my interpretations about my students' language ability tell me something about their ability to use the language in settings outside the test itself?

4 Consider how you will get the information you need

Question: *How* can I assess my students? What performance from my students will give me this information, and how will I get this?

Answer: Develop assessment tasks that correspond as closely as possible to teaching/learning tasks used in the classroom.

Questions for examples of how I might get the information I need:

- Do I need to give my students an explicit assessment or test?
- What kinds of assessment tasks should I include in the assessment?
- How will I report the results of my observations or assessment? (e.g. scores, profile of strengths and areas for improvement, verbal descriptions as feedback on their work)
- How can I assure my students and others that my reports are consistent?

APPENDIX 2 PARTS OF AN ASSESSMENT TASK TEMPLATE

An assessment task template consists of three parts:

1 a set of activities and procedures to be followed in administering the assessment

2 a set of task characteristics (TCs) for the assessment task

3 a method for recording students' responses, including, if the assessment record is a score, a scoring method.

The parts of an assessment task template for an example speaking assessment task are illustrated below.

Activities and procedures

Activities and procedures for the assessment task template

Description of the modified task: Speaking individually, describing an animal from a picture, in pairs

Areas of language ability to be assessed: using accurate grammar, vocabulary, and pronunciation in speaking.

1 Activities and procedures to be followed

    a On the day before the assessment the teacher tells the students:

       i They will have an assessment of their speaking the next day.

       ii The purposes of the assessment are:

          a) to give each student a grade or mark that will count as part of his or her grade or mark for the school year.

          b) to provide feedback to individual students about their speaking ability.

       iii The teacher will assign the students to pairs for the assessment

       iv The test will be given individually to each student in the pair.

          a) One student in the pair will be given a picture of an animal that will be different from the ones they described in class. The other student cannot see this student's picture.

          b) The first student will be given half a minute to prepare his or her description.

          c) The first student will then have one minute to describe the animal in the picture to his or her partner. The other student will then be asked to guess the animal. This will not be scored.

          d) Then the test will be given to the second student in the pair, following the same procedure as with the first student.

b On the day of the assessment, the teacher assesses each student in each pair individually.

  i The teacher briefly explains the assessment task again.

  ii The teacher makes sure the students understand the procedure.

  iii The teacher calls the names of the students in the first pair

  iv The teacher and these two students go to the Speaking Corner of the classroom.

  v The teacher shows the first student a picture of an animal.

  vi The first student takes half a minute to think about his or her description.

  vii Then the first student takes about one minute to describe the animal orally to his or her partner. The other student guesses the animal.

  viii The teacher scores the first student's performance using the Rating Scale on the Recording Form and also makes notes for feedback on the student's speaking using the Recording Form.

  ix The teacher then administers the assessment to the second student, following the same procedure as with the first student.

  x The teacher lets the two students go back to the class and calls the next pair of students for the assessment.

c During the next lesson after the assessment:

  i The teacher gives the students' their Recording Forms, with their scores and written feedback.

  ii The teacher gives the class general feedback on their areas of strength and the areas in which they need to improve.

  iii The teacher also provides suggestions for ways in which students can improve their speaking

Task characteristics

TCs of the modified task/assessment task template

Task characteristics

Assessment task: speaking individually, describing an animal from a picture, in pairs	
Areas of language ability to be assessed: using accurate grammar, vocabulary, and pronunciation in speaking	
Task characteristics	
Setting	<u>Physical circumstances</u>: the teacher with a pair of students seated at a table in the Speaking Corner of the classroom 　*Equipment/materials*: pictures of animals; Recording Form, pen or pencil (for the teacher); table and three chairs for the teacher and students <u>Participants</u>: teacher and a pair of students (young learners, beginning level) <u>Time of task</u>: during the class period; task requires more than one class period depending on the number of students
Input	<u>Form</u>: 　*Aural*: teacher's description of the task 　*Visual*: one picture of an animal that is different from the ones used in the TLU task <u>Language</u>: English 　*Teacher*: short spoken description and explanation; simple grammar and vocabulary 　*Length: aural:* short utterances; *visual:* short (single picture) <u>Topical content</u>: physical characteristics of animals
Expected response	<u>Form</u>: 　*Oral*: student's description of the animal in the picture 　*Visual*: (none) <u>Language</u>: English; short descriptive utterances, adjectives 　*Length*: about one minute per student; two minutes per pair of students <u>Topical content</u>: physical characteristics of animals

Recording method

Recording Method for the assessment task template

Recording method for assessment task	<u>Types of assessment record</u>: score and written feedback <u>Aspects of ability</u>: three aspects of speaking: use of accurate grammar, vocabulary (adjectives), and pronunciation <u>Scoring method</u> <u>Criteria</u>: (See the Rating Scale below.) *For each aspect*: exceeds expectations – 3; meets expectations – 2; needs improvement – 1 <u>Score reported</u>: total score = accurate grammar + accurate vocabulary + pronunciation <u>Procedures</u>: the teacher listens to individual students' responses and enters a score for each aspect of speaking on the Rating Scale for each student; the teacher then adds up the scores to arrive at a total score and enters this on the Recording Form. The teacher also enters written feedback on the student's speaking on the Recording Form. This is given back to the students during the next lesson.

Recording Form

Assessment task: Speaking, describing the physical characteristics of an animal

Student name: _____ Date: _____

Student paired with: _____

Animal picture: _____

Rating Scale: Aspect of speaking	Needs improvement 1	Meets expectations 2	Exceeds expectations 3	Feedback on student's speaking
Accurate grammar				
Accurate vocabulary (especially adjectives)				
Accurate Pronunciation				

Total score: _____

APPENDIX 3 ANSWERS TO ACTIVITIES IN CHAPTERS 2 AND 3

Chapter 2

Activity 2.1

Decision	Formative	Summative	When made?
1 Changing teaching (e.g. materials, tasks)	✓		during or after
2 Making changes in approaches to, or strategies of, learning	✓		during or after
3 Placing learners into appropriate groups or levels in a language program	✓		before
4 Deciding which students pass to the next grade in school		✓	after
5 Deciding which students will move to the next level in a language course		✓	after
6 Deciding what areas to focus on in studying	✓		before
7 Deciding whether or not to move to the next unit of instruction	✓		after
8 Certifying students' levels of language ability		✓	after
9 Deciding what areas to focus on in teaching	✓		before, during or after
10 Deciding on supplemental materials for teaching	✓		before, during or after
11 Deciding which students will not pass the course		✓	after

Activity 2.2

Decision	Low-stakes	Medium-stakes	High-stakes
1 Changing teaching (e.g. materials, tasks)	✓		
2 Making changes in approaches to or strategies of learning	✓		
3 Placing learners into appropriate groups or levels in a language program		✓	
4 Deciding which students pass to the next grade in school			✓
5 Deciding which students will move to the next level in a language course		✓	
6 Deciding what areas to focus on in studying	✓		
7 Deciding which students to admit to a university			✓
8 Deciding whether or not to move to the next unit of instruction	✓		
9 Deciding which students need to take additional instruction focusing on specific learning objectives	✓	✓	
10 Deciding what qualifications students will have when they finish school			✓
11 Certifying students' level of language ability in order for them to get a job			✓
12 Deciding what areas to focus on in teaching	✓		
13 Deciding on supplemental materials for teaching	✓		
14 Deciding which students will not pass the course			✓

Activity 2.3

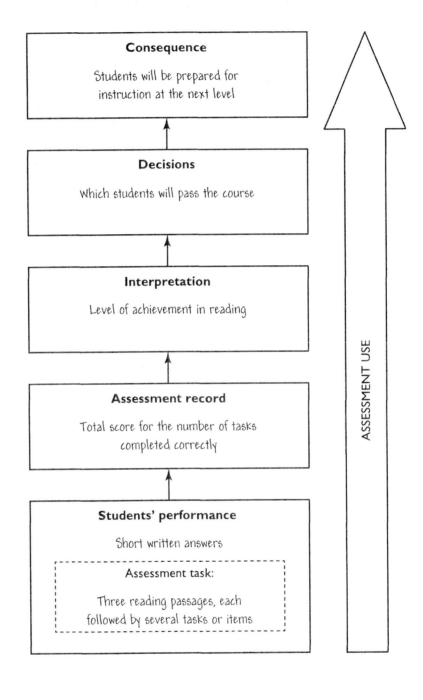

Chapter 3

Activity 3.1

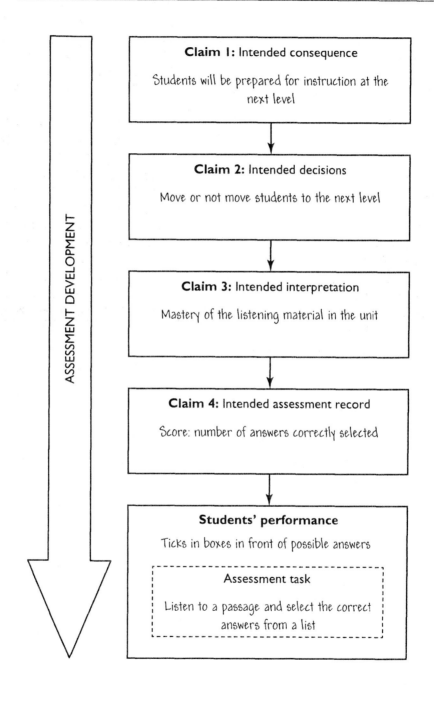

GLOSSARY

To make it easy to find the source definitions for these terms, the page numbers are given in brackets at the end of each entry.

accountability: Being able to convince stakeholders that the intended uses of an assessment are justified. (29)

analytic rating scale: A rating scale in which the students' performance is rated in terms of multiple components, each of which is rated on a separate scale. An analytic scale provides a "profile" of several different ratings or scores for a student's assessment performance. See also *rating scale* and *global rating scale*. (154)

assessment justification: The process that teachers, as test developers and test users, will follow to demonstrate the extent to which the intended uses of an assessment are justified. (29)

assessment performance: What students do in response to an assessment task. These responses might be actions, marks on an answer sheet, or samples of writing or speaking, or any combination of these. (74)

assessment record: A written or verbal description or a score that is assigned to a student's performance on an assessment task. (74)

assessment task template: This provides the basis for creating different assessment tasks that have many activities and procedures and task characteristics (TCs) in common. It consists of 1) a set of activities and procedures to be followed in administering the assessment; 2) a set of TCs; and 3) a recording method. See also *assessment task type*. (98)

assessment task type: This is defined by the activities and procedures, task characteristics (TCs), and a scoring method in an assessment task template. Multiple assessment tasks that are created by changing some of the TCs of the same assessment task template belong to the same assessment task type. (111)

assessment use argument (AUA): A series of claims or statements that define the links from a student's performance on an assessment to the intended consequences of using the assessment. (30)

backing: Evidence that the test developer and test user need to provide in order to support the claims in the AUA. (36)

beneficence: The degree to which the consequences of using an assessment and of the decisions that are made promote good and are not detrimental to stakeholders. (41)

blueprint: A detailed plan that specifies the content and format of an assessment, and the procedures and instructions for administering an assessment. (133)

claim: A statements that the test developer and/or test user make that specifies the intended use of the assessment, what it aims to assess, and how it intends to do this. (30)

classroom-based language assessment: A language assessment that is developed and/or used by one or more teachers in the classroom. (9)

compensatory composite score: A score that is equal to the total or average of all the analytic ratings, all the scores from different parts of a test, or all the scores from different tests given at different times. See also *composite score* and *non-compensatory composite score*. (157)

composite score: A score that is arrived at by taking into account all the different analytic ratings, all the scores from different parts of a test, or all the scores from different tests given at different times. See also *compensatory composite score* and *non-compensatory composite score*. (157)

consistency: The degree to which students' performances on different assessments (e.g. different administrations, tasks, and scorers/raters) of the same area of language ability yield essentially the same assessment records. (76)

criterion-referenced (CR): A grade or mark that reports how well a student has achieved the learning objectives of a course of instruction. See also *norm-referenced (NR) grade or mark*. (162)

cut score: The score, grade or mark on the assessment that is used as a basis for classifying students into different groups, such as "pass" and "not pass". See also *Score*. (51)

equitability: The degree to which different test takers who are at equivalent levels on the ability to be assessed have equivalent chances of being classified into the same group. (51)

explicit mode: A mode of classroom-based language assessment that is continuous and cyclical, a separate activity from classroom teaching, and used mostly for summative decisions. See also *implicit mode*. (16)

extended production response: A response to an assessment task in which students' responses are longer than a single sentence or utterance, and can vary from two sentences to longer stretches of discourse, such as a written paragraph or essay or a conversation or speech. See also *selected response* and *limited production response*. (150)

fairness: A quality of assessment use that depends on how well each link from students' performance on assessment tasks to assessment records, to decisions and to consequences can be supported or justified to stakeholders. If any link cannot be justified, then the assessment use is not likely to be fair. (28)

formative decision: A decision that leads to activities that are intended to improve instruction and learning. Formative decisions can be made before, during or after the processes of teaching and learning. See also *summative decision*. (11)

generalizability: The degree to which the assessment-based interpretations apply or extend to students' target language use domains. (66)

global rating scale: Sometimes known as a holistic scale; a rating scale in which the students' performance is rated in terms of its general quality or level of ability, and provides a single rating or score for a student's assessment performance. See also *analytic rating scale*. (153)

grade: A way of expressing students' levels of achievement in terms of a letter, e.g. A, B, C, with "A" being the highest. See also *mark*. (162)

high-stakes decision: A major, life-affecting decision in which the cost is very high for stakeholders if the wrong decision is made, and which the mistake is very difficult to correct. See also *low-stakes decision* and *medium-stakes decision*. (14)

impartiality: The degree to which the format and content of the assessment tasks and all aspects of the administration of the assessment are free from bias that may favor or disfavor some students. (67)

implicit mode: A mode of classroom-based language assessment that is instantaneous, continuous and cyclical, a part of classroom teaching, and used mostly for formative decisions. See also *explicit mode*. (16)

intended consequence: The effect on stakeholders that the test developer or test user wants to help bring about. (38)

intended decision: A specific action that the test developer or test user takes in order to help promote the beneficial consequences that are specified in Claim 1. (49)

intended interpretation: The understanding about our students' language ability, which we want to arrive at on the basis of their assessment records. (61)

intended stakeholders: The people, programs, or institutions that the test developer or test user wants to be affected by the use of the assessment. See also *stakeholders*. (40)

language assessment: In the singular ("a language assessment"), this term refers to a collection of many different individual language assessment tasks or items. As a general term ("language assessment"), it refers to the process of collecting samples of students' language performance. (9)

language assessment task: A language use task whose purpose is to collect samples of students' language performance. (9)

language assessment use: The process of interpreting students' assessment performance as information that tells us something about their language ability and enables teachers to use these interpretations to make decisions. (19)

language teaching: The process of engaging students in language use tasks for the purpose of improving their language ability. (9)

language teaching/learning task: A language use task in which teachers and students engage for the purpose of improving students' language ability. (9)

language use task: An activity that requires individuals to use language to achieve a particular goal or objective. (9)

limited production response: A response to an assessment task in which students' responses can vary from a single word or phrase (spoken or written), to a single sentence or utterance. See also *extended production response* and *selected response*. (150)

low-stakes decision: A minor decision in which the cost for stakeholders is very low if the wrong decision is made, and in which the mistake is easy to correct; see also *high-stakes decision* and *medium stakes decision*. (14)

mark: A way of expressing students' levels of achievement in terms of a number, e.g. 3, 2, 1, with "3" being the highest. See also *grade*. (162)

meaningfulness: The degree to which the intended interpretation: 1) provides stakeholders with information about the ability to be assessed; and 2) conveys this information in terms that they can understand and relate to. (64)

medium-stakes decisions: Neither very high-stakes decisions nor very low-stakes decisions. See also *high-stakes decision* and *low-stakes decision*. (14)

model assessment task: An assessment task that is created following the specifications in an assessment task template, and then serves as a basis for creating additional assessment tasks. (112)

negative washback: The effect of using an assessment that leads teachers and students to engage in teaching and learning activities that are *not* in accordance with their beliefs about teaching and learning and about what they believe is important for students to learn. See also *positive washback* and *washback*. (39)

non-compensatory composite score: Also known as a conjunctive score; a score that is equal to the *lowest* rating received on any of the analytic rating scales, any of the scores for different parts of a test, or any score from different tests given at different times. See also *composite score* and *compensatory composite score*. (159)

norm-referenced (NR): A grade or mark that reports a student's achievement relative to the achievement of other students in a group, e.g. a class, a grade, a school. See also *criterion-referenced (CR)*. (162)

positive washback: The effect of using an assessment that leads teachers and students to engage in teaching and learning activities that *are* in accordance with their beliefs about teaching and learning and about what they believe is important for students to learn. See also *negative washback* and *washback*. (39)

practicality: The relationship between the resources that are available and those that are needed in the development and use of the assessment. (25)

rating scale: Also known as a scoring rubric; this specifies different levels on the ability to be assessed, and provides descriptors for each of these levels. See also *analytic rating scale* and *global rating scale*. (153)

relevance: The degree to which the intended interpretations provide the information the test user needs to make the decision. (61)

score: An assessment record that is reported as a number or a letter. A score can be reported in different ways, for example, as the number of correct responses, a rating, a percentage, or a grade or a mark (e.g. A, B, C or 1, 2, 3). See also *cut score*. (74)

scoring key: This specifies the correct responses to assessment tasks and how many points each correct response counts. (151)

scoring method: The specification for how the teacher will arrive at a score on the basis of students' performances. It consists of the criteria for evaluating the correctness or quality of the students' responses, the score to be reported, and the procedures to be followed in arriving at a score. (149)

selected response: A response to an assessment task in which students select one or more responses from among several possible responses that are given. See also *extended production response* and *limited production response*. (150)

stakeholders: The people, language programs or courses, or institutions that may be affected by, or benefit from, the use of the assessment. See also *intended stakeholders*. (13)

sufficiency: The degree to which the intended interpretations provide enough information for the test user to make a decision. (62)

summative decisions: Decisions that are aimed at two purposes:

1 <u>advancement</u>: making sure that students who advance to the next level or course are prepared to benefit from instruction at the next level, and that students who do not advance will benefit from receiving additional instruction at the same level.

2 <u>certification</u>: making sure that students who are certified to be at a certain level of language ability have actually achieved the appropriate level of language ability specified in the certification.

Summative decisions involve classifying students into groups, and are made after the processes of teaching and learning. See also *formative decisions*. (11)

target language use (TLU) domain: A specific context outside the assessment itself in which students need to perform language use tasks. (65)

target language use (TLU) task: A language use task that students may need to perform in one or more of their TLU domains. (65)

task characteristics (TCs): Aspects or features of language use tasks that provide a way to describe the task with more precision than simply giving it a label. (92)

test developer: The person, persons, or institution responsible for developing, administering, and scoring the assessment. See also *test user*. (24)

test user: Also known as the decision maker; the person, persons, or institution that uses the information from the assessment to make decisions. See also *test developer*. (24)

values-sensitivity: The degree to which the use of an assessment and the decisions that are made take into consideration existing educational and societal values and relevant laws, rules, and regulations. (50)

washback: The effect or impact of using an assessment on instruction and learning. See also *negative washback* and *positive washback*. (39)

SUGGESTIONS FOR FURTHER READING

Developing language assessments

Bachman, L. F., & Palmer, A. S. (1996). *Language testing in practice: Designing and developing useful language tests.* Oxford: Oxford University Press.

Bachman, L. F., & Palmer, A. (2010). *Language assessment in practice: Developing language assessments and justifying their use in the real world.* Oxford: Oxford University Press.

Carr, N. T. (2011). *Designing and analyzing language tests.* Oxford: Oxford University Press.

Douglas, D. (2009). *Understanding language testing.* London: Routledge.

Fulcher, G. (2010). *Practical language testing.* London: Routledge.

Classroom language assessment

Brown, J. D. (1998). *New ways of classroom assessment.* Annapolis Junction, MD: TESOL Press.

Cheng, L. (2015). *Language classroom assessment.* Annapolis Junction, MD: TESOL Press.

Coombe, C. A., & Hubley, N. J. (2003). *Assessment practices.* Alexandria, VA: TESOL.

Jang, E. E. (2014). *Focus on assessment.* Oxford: Oxford University Press.

O'Malley, J. M., & Pierce, L. V. (1996). *Authentic assessment for English language learners.* New York: Addison-Wesley.

Teachers of English to Speakers of Other Languages. (2001). *Scenarios for ESL standards-based assessment.* Alexandria, VA: TESOL.

Assessing different aspects of language ability

Alderson, J. C. (2000). *Assessing reading.* Cambridge: Cambridge University Press.

Buck, G. (2001). *Assessing listening.* Cambridge: Cambridge University Press.

Fulcher, G. (2003). *Testing second language speaking.* London: Routledge.

Luoma, S. (2004). *Assessing speaking.* Cambridge: Cambridge University Press.

Purpura, J. E. (2004). *Assessing grammar.* Cambridge: Cambridge University Press.

Read, J. (2000). *Assessing vocabulary.* Cambridge: Cambridge University Press.

Weigle, S. C. (2002). *Assessing writing.* Cambridge, UK: Cambridge University Press.

Specific topics in language assessment

Bachman, L. F. (2004). *Statistical analyses for language assessment.* Cambridge: Cambridge University Press.

Chapelle, C. A., & Douglas, D. (2006). *Assessing Language ability through computer technology.* Cambridge: Cambridge University Press.

Douglas, D. (1999). *Assessing languages for specific purposes.* Cambridge: Cambridge University Press.

McKay, P. (2006). *Assessing young language learners.* Cambridge: Cambridge University Press.

INDEX

Page numbers annotated with 'g' refer to glossary entries.